# NEIGHBORS AT WAR!

# NEIGHBORS AT WAR!

## The Creepy Case Against
## Your Homeowners Association

# WARD LUCAS

*Television's Emmy award-winning investigative journalist*

Books may be purchased in bulk or otherwise by contacting the publisher and author at:

Hogback Publishing, Inc.
P.O. Box 27633
Denver CO 80227
Ward@NeighborsAtWar.com

Cover Design:  NZ Graphics, Inc. (Nick Zelinger)
Interior Design:  WESType Publishing Services, Inc. (Ronnie Moore)
Publisher:  Hogback Publishing, Inc.
Editor:  Editing By John (John Maling)
Consultant:  The Book Shepherd (Judith Briles)

Library of Congress Catalog Number: 2012912200
ISBN (paper): 978-0-9856978-0-8
ISBN (ebook): 978-0-9856978-1-5

1. Homeowners Associations   2. Government   3. Civil Rights
4. Political Science

First Edition Printed in the U.S.A.

*To all those homeowners who've suddenly discovered their loss of personal and property rights in the shadows of the "private neighborhoods" con game.*

# Contents

# Acknowledgments

This page is always difficult, simply because there are so many people involved in production of a book, and so many ways to inadvertently leave out a critical name. With that admission of my own weakness I now step off a ledge that has fatally injured so many others.

My proposals to agents and publishers first went out in 2008, just when the walls of the traditional New York publishing industry were collapsing. It would do no good to tally the number of rejection letters, but they could easily paper a good sized living room. And yes, I even ran into several enthusiastic "agents" who I soon discovered were high on the insiders' list of *Predators and Editors*.

Then I discovered Judith Briles and John Maling of The Book Shepherd. A longtime author, herself, Judith was gathering around her some of the best and brightest who'd been washed out of the traditional publishing machine, authors, editors, grammar teachers, format experts, digital conversion experts, publishing companies, social media gurus. Thus, it was my good fortune to stumble across Judith's "Author U" or "Author University." We met for almost weekly seminars, lectures, brainstorm sessions, and hands-on experience designed to help save the art of book creation. Judith calls herself, "The Book Shepherd," which is obviously what she has become to me.

And patient, patient Ronnie Moore of WESType Publishing Services in Boulder, Colorado; she's an all-nighter, like me, and she had standing permission to call me at any hour when she was confused by my bumbling. But she sorted through it all, designing the interior book layout for *Neighbors At War!* Her attention to detail is amazing.

Nick Zelinger, the genius who designed my book cover is as talented as they come. He made a zinger of a book cover, don't you agree? His company is NZ Graphics in Colorado.

Georgann Hall was the eagle-eye, finding missing punctuation and words that slipped by us all! Thanks, Georgann.

Ah, and that brings up the wild photo on the cover of **Neighbors At War!** It's the real deal! The owner of the home, Ashley Branden Spear, ran into a problem with his local Historical Preservation Commission. Despite allowing other nearby home-owners to use vinyl window frames, they refused to let him do so. To reconstruct the window frames cost him three quarters the amount of the entire house! Like other patriotic protestors before him, Branden decided to let the world know that he believes in such things as equal rights and due process and a Constitutional hands-off government. Since there were no paint color requirements by his Historical Preservation Commission, he carefully crafted the red, white and blue house that you see. That was three years ago, and his house in Cambridge, Maryland has been something of a tourist destination ever since.

There are others outside of our little group to whom I am personally indebted. Brian Delmar, in addition to being one of the most talented guitarists I've ever known, is a friend with real class, someone who took the time and patience to read my manuscript and tell me what worked and what didn't. And when we were just plain worn out, we'd pick up guitars and jam late into the evening.

And I owe much to Bob and Meri Haworth, Bob of Kingston Trio fame. Many a night we've spent at his house or mine, working out the stress through music. And yes, not only did Bob and Meri help read and edit, they also went through a Homeowner

Association nightmare of their own. Bob experienced firsthand the ugly underbelly of the HOA mess.

Then there was Becky Chapman, photographer extraordinaire. Her photographic talent is as good as anyone on the planet. When she takes a photo, it wins awards. That's how good she is.

Finally, I should thank the throng of people who helped debate when to use the following variations of the subject at hand: Homeowner Association? Home Owner Association? Homeowners Association? Homeowner's Association. Homeowners' Association? Since this argument will go on *ad nauseum*, I've decided to use the following policy: it's all correct. I will try to use words that are appropriate for a direct quote or when an HOA's self-chosen or incorporated name is used by the involved parties. Other times, I'll choose whichever phrase seems to roll off the tongue a little easier.

Live with it. Leave me alone.

Anyway, there were so many wonderful people along the way, fact checkers, photographers, people who are in for the HOA fight. I now join them. I, too, am in for the fight.

# 1
# Full Disclosure

*They who can give up essential liberty to obtain*
*a little temporary safety, deserve neither liberty nor safety.*
—Benjamin Franklin

**M**y friend, I hope this book will be an engaging read for you, sometimes amusing, sometimes a little scary. But let me tell you in advance what it is not. It is not an essay about bitchy neighbors, squabbling condo owners or land squatters. Although a number of interesting and colorful stories about such people are included here, the purpose of *Neighbors At War* is not the mere compilation of a menagerie of neighborhood nut cases.

While peeking at a typical neighborhood's lunatic fringe may provide some vicarious entertainment on a dull afternoon, my goal is hopefully more ambitious. Within *Neighbors At War*, my goal is to build a case for a national change in law that could someday end some of the growing madness surrounding Homeowners Associations.

One experiment, here, is in marrying the old media with the new. My research into the frustrations and wrangling over homeowners' rights is dynamic, ongoing and depends upon input from others. Thus, you're invited to dialogue and join me on my website:

*www.NeighborsAtWar.com*

On my site, you'll find instant access to all of this book's endnotes, extra photos, links to news videos and related updates. And you're invited to share your own stories, critiques and commentary. Your input may even become part of some future tome on life in one of America's HOAs.

Second, although this book addresses what many believe is a growing national crisis, parts of this story are deeply personal and adversarial. In the spirit of full disclosure, I am an unapologetic advocate of private property rights. Every human right stems from that little speck of freedom, the right to own a patch of ground. If we ever surrender that right, then speech is only chatter, religion is mindless self-delusion and due process is no more than a couple of archaic words in a dust encrusted law book.

Ah, and I should warn you that I'm not politically correct. No apologies, here. I'm just not. If you hold that candidness against me, then the hang-up is yours, not mine. People who use the PC movement to try to suppress the thoughts and speech of others miss out on the glorious texture of life.

Third, and most important, this is hopefully a "Paul Revere alarm" that American homeowners of all races, religions and persuasions are losing treasured Constitutional rights in some bizarre and unexpected ways. For some, it really is a battle for survival.

This, therefore, is not an objective journalist's account of the ins and outs of Homeowners Associations. Far more intelligent and better communicators and writers like Evan McKenzie, Lawrence Cheek, George Staropoli, Donie Vanitzian and Stephen Glassman have already covered that ground and each deserves his or her own plaudits. I believe I can only break new ground by weaving a small part of my own story into the tapestry of what's happening to millions of others who've stumbled or bumbled their way into HOA life. Besides, I've learned during my forty-year news magazine and TV journalism career that lessons in life have no value unless shared. History teaches that when advocacy is suppressed, despotism results. It has also taught us that bigotry thrives only where bigotry is not exposed. Yes, I occasionally dog-paddle against the current, but for those of you who appreciate advocacy, I thank you. And you'll find I'm not timid.

## One Against the Crowd

For quick background, I have been personally involved in five lawsuits involving two adjoining Homeowners Associations in Jefferson County, Colorado. Although at first glance my battle seems regional, it's actually a perfect Petri dish in which to examine what's happening to homeowners nationwide. Any battle-scarred homeowner in a rogue HOA can use my experiences to modify and polish his or her own legal strategies.

In my own case, two adjacent Homeowners Associations joined forces to wage a twenty year war to seize an historic old west property that I legally own, property that they never did. Sometimes they sue me, sometimes I sue them. In four out of five lawsuits I have won favorable judgments or settlements. In one case, I got an adverse decision reversed by the State Court of Appeals. In the fifth case, my big defeat, I failed to prove to a jury my claims of incessant and organized criminal harassment.

But during these five cases millions of dollars have been spent; millions of words have been generated. I paid dearly for those words; therefore I think I've earned the right to publish some of them. And every word is applicable to Homeowners Association excesses from New York to San Diego, from Washington State to the dumbest out-of-control HOA boards in Southern Florida. There is a fundamental principle being debated here:

> **Does a private real estate developer have the right to deprive eons of generations of future homeowners of basic Constitutional rights on some illusory promise of artificially inflated real estate values?**

From one standpoint, each and every lawsuit in which I was involved was unnecessary and wasteful. Most disputes can be settled long before legal action is taken. If sparring neighbors had just agreed to go out to lunch, leave the lawyers stewing at home, agreed to disagree in certain areas, but agreed to come to some kind of resolution outside of litigation, then peace would have prevailed, property values would have been preserved, and rancor and hatred would have never grown to the point that they tattooed the backside of an entire neighborhood forever. In my own case, I actually tried multiple times to initiate such a peace, but ended up getting sued for my efforts. It taught me that "being nice" is not an option offered in the American HOA Movement.

Not for a moment, though, do I consider myself a victim. Whining about one's status as a victim is as shallow as it is contemptible. Being a target, though, is different and I'll readily admit to intentionally stepping in front of the firing squad more than once. In fact, across this wonderful country there are countless numbers of people who've been targets of out-of-control Homeowners Associations. It's not a comfortable place to be, but then taking a stand against a mob never is.

All targets of HOA wrath inevitably learn these truths: when one property owner is trying to protect his ownership rights against others who are trying to protect their view, or when an elected but rank amateur board member is trying to exert the first bully power he's ever been delegated over others, the clash of egos can be explosive. Trial lawyers adore such disputes, of course, and despite claimed codes of ethics find many ways to incite them, encourage them, nourish them and profit from them. Shakespeare was right; Utopia can never exist while lawyers do. Another interpretation of the Great Bard: there are no lawyers in Heaven.

Some of the strategies used by HOA lawyers against individual homeowners are as nauseating as can be imagined. In one blatant land-grab case against me, they tried to establish under oath whether members of my family were Jewish. When that didn't fly, they tried to argue that a family member of mine was a homosexual (I told you this would be colorful). Finally, they claimed during trial to have somehow "lost" two years worth of subpoenaed board meeting records that were at the exact heart of my dispute.

They had no idea how it happened, they told the judge. Poof! The subpoenaed records just vanished. "Damn, we're so sorry, Judge. Gosh damn, we're so very sorry. But surely you wouldn't hold that against our HOA clients, would you?" I've since discovered this is actually a well-worn tactic of HOA lawyers in other cases across the country. So much for my former innocence.

My harassment lawsuit (a counter-suit, actually) against my Homeowners Association contained protests against such neighborhood niceties as dog poisoning, death threats by board officers, swastikas painted on my house, demands by elected board officers for under-the-table payments and even one incident of arson at my home. All of this happened within the two year period in question. Alas, those were the exact official records that vanished. HOA attorneys admitted so to the judge. Was there anything embarrassing in those two years worth of official records? Were certain board discussions a little too "organized" to pass the muster of oh-so-troubling federal and state laws? Without the records, of course, we can assume the worst case scenario, right?

My HOA dispute was essentially an argument over a century-old property line, no more, no less. Where did the allegations of my family's degree of Jewishness or alleged homosexuality fit in? If those seem like *non sequiturs*, then get ready for some whoppers. If an HOA lawyer infers, however subtly, "settle this lawsuit over our mutual property line in our favor, or we'll publicly humiliate your son," then are any ethical lines crossed?

Ah, probably not. We're speaking of HOA lawyers, here. But distill that further: "We think your son is a faggot. Give us money or we'll go public with that allegation." If such a threat was ever uttered on the streets of the Bronx, wouldn't that attract some sort of attention? It takes a Burton Turkus or a Rudy Giuliani to wage that kind of fight.

Such organized thuggery, though, produces three fascinating *unintended consequences* that could have interesting and instructive implications for any target of HOA excess. In my case, as a result of "vanishing board records," I am now, by default, the only possible community historian of my own HOA. What a great place to be! My adversaries cannot come forward now and comment unless they produce the records they mysteriously lost. To do so, they would have to admit lying to a District Court Judge.

The second unintended consequence involves the "give us your property or we'll expose your son" legal strategy. Because that pretty much was the threat used and carried out against me by HOA attorneys in a public forum, it now gives me the opportunity to spread the word about the consequences of bigotry and hate. Every time my story is repeated, the history of emotional and physical violence in the world of rogue HOAs is spread further and property values are suppressed even more. Prospective home buyers are increasingly reluctant to move into communities where hatred is *raison d'être*.

More than that, any Realtor or homeowner who markets or sells a property within a rogue subdivision is personally liable for damages if he or she doesn't provide full disclosure to prospective buyers. Real estate law requires the disclosure of any defect in a property. That includes neighborhood controversies. If, for example, an HOA has ever lost its liability insurance because of its past outrageous conduct, potential buyers have to be warned. It's the law. Realtors or owners trying to sell properties in my own subdivision, I suspect, will now have to provide each potential client with a copy of *Neighbors-At-War*. I'll consider discounts for bulk purchases, of course.

In a third unintended consequence, a tiny but growing band of revolutionaries in this country is at last beginning to say, "Enough!" They can no longer stomach the kind of meanness that can destroy the reputation of an entire neighborhood. The World Wide Web is giving them a forum they didn't have before. It is finally within their power to make a difference, to wake others up to the sneaky government grab which has cost countless numbers of Americans their homes, their retirement dreams, their peace of mind.

## The Private Government Movement

While my own case is creepy, it is far from unique. Across this country the most unconscionable kinds of intolerance, bigotry, racism and hatred are growing, fostered by HOA lawyers and paralleled by the growing phenomenon Evan McKenzie refers to as "the private government movement."

Stunningly, Americans everywhere are in the process of losing real access to our hallowed Bill of Rights, a set of constraints against government excesses carefully crafted by our country's founders to create unprecedented freedoms from government oppression. In an incredible way over the past thirty years, seventy million Americans have voluntarily, albeit unknowingly, surrendered those rights forever.

When I first began experiencing the organized assault by groups trying to take my property, I looked in vain for some kind of book, some kind of manual, to tell me what I was up against and how to fight back. Was I just one isolated miscreant? Had no one else experienced the same kinds of threats of loss of property, or the unbelievable upheaval in my personal life? My frustration was massive. There was nothing.

Hopefully, there's material in *Neighbors At War* that will encourage others to swim against the tide. In the opinion of many experts, the Homeowners Association Movement is a tide worth fighting. Advocacy has horrific costs for the advocate, of course, but it's the only element of a free society that keeps society free.

Don't just buy this book for yourself. Give it to a friend, a legislator, an abused HOA member, or to someone who just wonders why in recent years neighborhoods have become so angry, why the annual HOA meeting has become so confrontational, and why so few homeowners even bother to go.

Obviously, I have a mule in the race. But as I approach the finish line, I've earned the right to kick up some sand and keep one or two people awake at night with my braying. If I don't articulate the conflict adequately, the fault is mine. Perhaps you'll overlook my personal shortcomings. But here and there you might find a shred of material that could be of interest to those pondering life in an HOA.

To the Willowbrook Homeowners Association (my personal favorite)[1] and to 300,000 private governments across the country which have abolished the Bill of Rights and earned the title of "The Neighborhood Nazis," a few exact quotes from Lewis Carroll:

Let's go down the Rabbit Hole.[2]

It all gets curiouser and curiouser from here.[3]

Eat me.[4]

# 2
# On Waking Up

*They claim this mother of ours, the Earth, for their own use,*
*and fence their neighbors away from her and*
*deface her with their buildings and their refuse.*

—Sitting Bull

The wind was whistling past my open window this spring day as my car raced across the prairies of northeastern Colorado. The weather in May can be a little tricky in this part of the country, with puffy white thunderheads sometimes building quickly as weather systems move eastward over the Rocky Mountains into the central plains. I remember the drive, though, as starting out on the pleasant side. No weather problems ahead. The farms I passed were always interesting to watch with their neatly spaced onion fields and sugar beet rows. A silo of some sort sporadically popped into view and just as quickly vanished in the mirror.

Here and there was an occasional alfalfa field, with its rich, green foliage. Other than the visual stimulation, there were no exceptional sensations I particularly recall as this day began—just the hum of the car engine, the drone of tires against the miles of pavement and the hypnotic white dashes of road paint dipping under the hood as I sped down the highway.

The route was a familiar one. I had followed it many times over the years, going back and forth to various news assignments. In fact, it was this same stretch of road I had traveled on a job search three decades earlier when first interviewing for a reporter's position at a Denver television station. A lot of time, energy and life had been expended since that first trip. For all these years this highway, these fields, the quaint towns really hadn't changed much. It was always fun looking forward to the roadside landmarks, the tiny restaurants and the farmers' egg stands. In past years I had occasionally pulled over to buy a small bag of produce, a sandwich, or to chat with the proprietor.

Reporters are supposed to be observers of small details, a shortcoming that has often dogged me in my career. Small details are the killers. They can damage stories, friendships, careers, fortunes, relationships. The big picture is always easier for a writer to follow. The big picture creates clarity, boundaries, and psychic anchors for old memories. It lets the mind wander more freely, the heart feel more deeply.

Colorado, for me, has always been a state of big pictures. The mountains are huge, the canyons breathtaking. This route through the eastern flatlands is accompanied by an especially big sky, usually made larger by the deep blue tones that flow from one horizon to another. As long as I could remember, these fields stretched forever, mile after mile of multi-shaded green laid out like compass points north and south as far as the eye could see. Most motorists are probably like me, speeding through the landscape without paying much attention to what's here.

Over the years various assignments have taken me outside the city to explore more remote parts of the state. I've never been able to totally understand or explain why people stick to farming with all its sweat and disappointments. Farming has its rewards, it's said. It can't be financial. Too many farmers just barely eke out a living. Still, year after year, they pass the heritage on to sons and daughters. Perhaps part of the fun is the guessing game, wondering how the fields will take shape, how the weather will act, and how much the land will put forth.

One of the most majestic crops along this route is corn. The plants start out so tiny, but quickly rise higher than a man can reach. When a farmer first opens the gates on his irrigation dams, trickles of water move slowly down the ditches and furrows. Below the soil surface just out of sight, tiny white threadlike roots reach out to draw in the moisture. There's a real change in the air when parched plants get their first water of the week. I've never worked in a garden or field and know nothing about farming. But I have been up close, a time or two, when a field is watered. The fragrance is hard to describe. Country folk are well-accustomed to the damp smells of a field getting its first drink at the end of a dry spell.

Later in the summer there are different things to smell and watch. The corn ears begin bulging on each of the stalks, delicate at first, but long, fat and yellow as the days turn hotter. Fragrances change when the tassels come out, too. Maybe it's just imagination, but I really do think I could tell by smells alone when the corn ears are beginning to show. I've always thought of tassels on the light green husks as a sort of "thank you note" to whoever waters the field. Perhaps only a long-time farmer is impressed by the annual miracle of growth, but I like to imagine I can somehow relate.

I had actually met some of the farmers along this route. In fact, it was one of those farmers at a roadside stand who once told me what he claimed were the best two ways to cook corn, right in the husk. He said the ears should be soaked in saltwater for ten minutes, wrapped in foil, then tossed directly into the coals of a campfire. Ten minutes in the heat, and they'd be ready. Or, he said, forget the campfire thing, just toss an ear of corn, husk and all, directly into a microwave oven and set the timer for two minutes. Do it once, he told me. You'll never do it another way. I never tried the campfire method, but he was right about the microwave.

These fields always seemed like they had a sort of permanence here, some kind of God-given right to exist. Through occasional years of drought, a rare dust bowl and sporadic hail storms that can lay a crop out flat, they've survived and magically reappear each year. It's comforting to see them re-planted and tended. So it was with more than a little annoyance on this particular day that I noticed some changes in my pretty fields. The landscape didn't seem as endless as in past years. The colors weren't as intense. The big wooden hand-painted "produce for sale" signs were just sporadic. Worse than sporadic, on this day I saw only one familiar-looking yard sign and stopped to see who was there.

"How're things going?" I thought I recognized the fellow from some casual stop in a previous year.

"Goin' good," he said. "Goin' good."

"That's great." There were a few seconds of slightly awkward silence.

"I really just stopped in to say 'Hi'. I think I might have stopped by here a year or two ago. I think I bought a couple ears of corn from you then."

Some farm folks can seem a little reserved at first, probably because city folks invariably come off as pushy. But reporters who've been in the game for a while can generally get a conversation going without too much pumping. The rule is, "toss out a few words and then shut up." Like priming a water pump, it works.

"We're doing white corn this time around." He broke the silence. That meant I had won.

"All white?" I asked. "How about the other guys up here? White corn?"

"Yep. Every single one of 'em. All the farms in northern Colorado are planting white. Can't afford not to."

A few minutes and a few dozen words later I got back into my car, more than a little disappointed. The man with the familiar-looking face was just being a good businessman. He'd be making a lot more money this year, but he probably wouldn't be seeing many weekend motorists like me stopping by. White corn isn't really edible. It's for making ethanol.

## A Changing Land

Back on the highway, I picked up speed in the general direction of town, this time paying more attention to the scenery around me. Most of the crops were ankle high, about right for the time of year. But the fields seemed smaller than the ones in my memory, fewer. In places along the route, there was obvious construction activity going on. Big yellow earth moving vehicles had scraped up great patches of dirt, often peeling open hundreds of acres of land. It was the weekend, and the equipment was all parked and motionless, but there would be lots of action early Monday morning. What they were doing was pretty clear.

## Vanishing Fragrances

On the left side of the road, on the right, and the left again were new housing developments going up on this once lush farmland. In the middle of my fields were scores of meticulously mapped out neighborhoods of two and three story houses where just a few years ago solitary one-story red or white farmhouses had stood. A hundred houses here, a couple of hundred there, each house surrounded by dirt or newly placed sod.

The houses were shoulder-to-shoulder in their tightly organized regiments, seemingly no more than fifteen or twenty feet separating one from another. Left, right, left, they began to mark this rural highway like the cadence of an Army drill sergeant. So close to one another they stood, that one could easily imagine the Sunday morning sounds of a banging lawnmower, a slamming car door, or an argument in an open window echoing up and down the concrete streets. The incongruence of these sardine-tight houses under such a huge sky was a little difficult to process. Inevitable progress, I supposed.

In the dust floating around these close neighborhoods, I couldn't recognize the old fragrances, either. Country smells are pretty distinct, even to someone who spends most of his days in the city. But their absence now that I was finally paying attention was disturbing. Missing too, I was sure, was the clack of red-winged blackbirds that used to nest in tawny cattails at the ends of irrigation ditches, occasionally rousing into flight when an intruder approached. And surely lost in the din was the almost noiseless swish of breezes through prairie grass, and the quiet thump of deer hooves as they sailed over the wire fences on their nightly corn raids.

No self-respecting farmer would live in such housing developments, I decided. These couldn't be the homes of country people. The owners of these homes had to be townies, commuters who traveled to and from jobs in the city. They would be lawyers, accountants, sales managers who at the end of each day stirred martinis on granite counter tops. These were a different sort of people, folks not yet accustomed to the occasionally hard-scrabble life on the prairie. My mind tried, but couldn't yet take it all in.

The most startling discovery on this day was the colors, or rather the lack of them. No red barns, white silos or blue trimmed farmhouse windows. Each housing development I passed was beige. Light beige, medium beige, dark beige. Here and there a touch of gray marked a doorway or porch rail. But mile after maddening mile, the houses were beige. There were no red striped kiddies' swing sets, no tree houses, no backyard laundry lines. Each successive house on each perfectly staked-out street was a near carbon copy of its neighbor. Beige doors matched beige walls which complemented beige window frames which matched beige eaves. "Earth tones," they're called. The earth is such a colorful place with its brilliant reds, blues, pinks, purples, violets, greens. Whoever thought of "earth tones" as a way to describe the colors of Creation, I figured, was probably not very close to its Creator. But earth tones, theoretically, offend nobody. They're the ultimate in political correctness.

It was late spring. Colorado's April showers always summon the flowers of May, and there should have been flower boxes at every window, wild profusions of geranium-filled pots on each porch, a maroon tricycle on the sidewalk, a blue and white beach towel on a lawn chair. But the old colors were gone. The new ones looked stunningly like the barracks of a military post where I'd spent a few excruciating months in a former life. I didn't like my brief experience in the Army, living in beige barracks, wearing colorless uniforms. It was a strange mix of memories but in my mind, at least, the metaphors all worked.

I tried to put faces on the owners of these brand new homes. Nice people, I was sure. Like me, they'd all come to fulfill dreams, buy a piece of land, claim ownership of a slit of Colorado sky. No question they each had good intentions. They had children, went to church and dreamt of rural solitude. But something was just uncomfortably out of place all these miles out into the country, beige people living right on top of one another in beige boxes. These communities are the Forrest Gump of suburbia with their chocolate boxes of tasteless beige.

The open fields and rows of crops weren't completely gone. The green landscape still surrounded each of these island neighborhoods. But the housing areas just looked other-worldly popping out of what was once uninterrupted country, a weird imposition on the land. It's a mirage, I thought. They all think they're living in the country. I wondered how many of these transplanted homeowners had discovered their pristine new country housing projects were surrounded by fields of corn.

White corn.

Inedible.

# 3
# Never Marry "Brown"

*Christian virtues unite men. Racism separates them.*
—Sargent Shriver

One of my early childhood memories was growing up in the little Seattle suburb of Mercer Island. It's a seven mile long gem of an island at the end of a floating pontoon bridge in the middle of freshwater Lake Washington. On stormy days, the waters are roiled and gray with waves beating against the concrete sides of the bridge. But when the sun burns away the drizzle and clouds, the lake can reflect an almost perfect sky-blue.

Today, the number of bridges across the lake has grown and a quaint business center has been modernized to accommodate a community of Microsoft zillionaires. The world-famed Bill Gates' wealth and largess showed up about thirty years too late to have any impact on my family.

Mercer Island of the early 1960s was a suburb where one could be rich, or one could be poor. My father was from the latter group, having just retired from the military. With his last Army savings my dad bought a house and fulfilled my mother's lifelong dream of purchasing a tiny wooden sailboat. We spent hundreds of happy hours sailing around the lake in that crate. The leaky, homemade boat was cheap, stubby and ugly. With its massive moveable slate centerboard, it was never intended for racing. It was great for mooring, though. All we had to do to sail in shallow water was hoist the white braided rope and pull up the centerboard. Since we couldn't build up much speed, the heavy teak benches were mostly used for long conversations.

Dad, who was critically wounded in combat in the last month of World War II, had every reason to despise anyone with even a distant connection to the Japanese/German Axis. America was an enormously patriotic country back then and eight million men went to war because they honestly believed they could help save the world from evil. Sadly, no war ever saves the world. How the human species came to develop such hatred for one another is one of the bigger mysteries of life.

But for his part, Dad was a magnanimous, forgiving man. His job in the post-war reconstruction years was serving as the military governor of Japan's Honshu Province, Shiga Prefecture. Through 1949, it was his mission to open up food supply routes to families who were starving in the wake of the most devastating bombing in history. In his old steel army footlockers I still have the original hand-written notes from Japanese youngsters thanking him for giving them food and protection. The notes by children struggling so hard to be understood in English are priceless. It was during this time that I was born.

## First Taste of Racism

After moving the family back to this country in 1948, Dad became close friends with a gentleman of Japanese descent, George Kawaguchi. George had been swept up in the anti-Japanese hysteria that led to the imprisonment and impoverishing of thousands of American citizens in Japanese internment camps. After the war, George had dropped any resentment of America and had worked hard to put his family on some kind of solid financial footing. He was rewarded with Kawaguchi Travel, one of Seattle's most successful travel agencies in the 60s, 70s and 80s.

George's family and mine were frequent guests in each others' homes. One afternoon on our little 19 foot sailboat, I heard my dad say, "George, why don't you buy a house near us on Mercer Island?" I'll never forget what I heard.

"No one on Mercer Island would ever sell to a Jap."

At-twelve-years old, I was far too young to understand the implications of that comment. But I wasn't too young to read body language. My father's jaw dropped. His face fell. He looked like he'd been slammed in the head with an oar. I thought for a few moments that my Army war-hero father was fighting back tears. I think he gave some innocuous response like, "Oh, George." That memory was seared in my mind.

I do remember asking later what the incident on the sailboat was all about, and can still see Dad's anguish as he said, "Mercer Island property owners aren't allowed to sell to Japanese people."

My confusion was massive. My parents had always teased me about "being Japanese." As a post-war baby boomer, being born in Japan to white U.S Army parents gave me dual citizenship and interesting bragging rights among schoolmates. But here was Dad's best friend, a man with a Japanese surname, saying that he was racially restricted from ever living in this whites-only bastion, the Caucasian suburban community of Mercer Island. It was the first time I'd ever heard the term *restrictive covenant*. And I remember my father's growing anger as he pored over real estate documents and discovered that in development after development on Seattle's east side, real estate deeds dictated that property could only be sold to people of non-Asian lineage. Again, I was far too young to understand the implications, but in my naïveté I remember wondering if I could ever find myself being questioned about my own Japanese birth.

An even earlier source of confusion about relationships among human beings came while my parents were still in the military. At the Fort Sam Houston Army Base in San Antonio, Texas, Mom and Dad took me to see the Academy Award-winning movie, *Giant*. Elizabeth Taylor, Rock Hudson and James Dean starred.

The complexities of the plot were well above my head, but one biting scene burned in my eight year old mind. It depicted a Mexican family trying to order lunch in a rural Texas diner. When the owner refuses to serve them, hero Bick Benedict, played by Hudson, comes to their aid and tries to get the innkeeper to do the decent thing. After a vicious fistfight which the bloodied Benedict loses, the innkeeper tosses a lettered sign onto Benedict's prostrate body. It reads, "We reserve the right to refuse service to anyone."

I ached for that Mexican family. At that age, a young movie-goer doesn't really know what's real and how much is fiction. "Why won't that man serve lunch to that family and those children?" I asked my mother.

"It's his right," she explained. "The law says the restaurant owner can do that." The answer was unsatisfying and provoked a lengthy discussion about racism, the details of which have faded a bit from memory. But it's strange how some early impressions and emotions never fade. In dreams over the years, I've been Bick Benedict with a different ending, winning the fistfight against the café owner and personally cooking and serving lunch to that Mexican family. Many times I promised myself I would never live in a neighborhood or patronize a restaurant that refused service to some. Years later, I would find myself looking back with chagrin at the way life actually turned out.

One side note that may be important here: an annoying constant of life is the irritating self-righteousness of fellow sinners. They can tell you in intricate detail how to live, how to work, how to relate, but rarely do they want to disclose their own misdeeds. So it's an embarrassing admission to say that as a young adult, I once tried to buy my way into the country life in a beige house on someone else's former farm. It's where I first learned about Homeowners Associations. Those details will be discussed in suffocating detail later, but suffice it to say: if anyone was ever guilty of a sin against the land, I was doubly damned.

My penance is probably to spend the rest of eternity driving through fields marred by the same misdeeds I once committed. Somewhere, somehow, by some deity, I am undoubtedly condemned and no indulgence will ever buy my salvation. Perhaps, like Lazarus looking for a drop of water on his tongue, my destiny is to be an admonition for others. If so, then these words are written to warn just one other person about the consequences of "going beige."

## Not In Our Backyard!

Restrictive covenants and Homeowner's Associations have probably been around ever since the first Homo sapiens alpha male decided he didn't want a Neanderthal family moving in next door. "Neanderthals will just bring down property values," he must have argued around the fire pit at that first cave council. "They're not like us. They might carry diseases or knock up our daughters and knock us off our rung on the evolutionary ladder. They smell bad; they'll use our water holes. Neanderthals will just have wild parties and their kids will keep us awake on weekends. They won't keep their property up, and then the whole neighborhood will go Neanderthal. We'll be forced to move to caves farther out in the country."

One of the most mysterious passages in ancient literature might even refer to such a neighborhood dispute:

*Now it came about, when men began to multiply on the face of the land, and daughters were born to them, that the sons of God saw that the daughters of men were beautiful; and they took wives for themselves, whomever they chose. Then the Lord said, 'My Spirit shall not strive with man forever, because he also is flesh; nevertheless*

> *his days shall be one hundred and twenty years.' The Nephilim were*
> *on the earth in those days, and also afterward, when the sons of God*
> *came in to the daughters of men, and they bore children to them.*
> *Those were the mighty men who were of old, men of renown.*
>
> —Genesis 6:1-4

It seems that even before Noah's Flood, neighbors were bickering about the "wrong kind of trash" moving in next door. Although scholars debate the meaning of this Old Testament passage *ad nauseum,* a wilder interpretation is that God, Himself, was vexed at a nasty race called "the Nephilim." Their presence obviously violated whatever neighborhood covenants might have been in place at the time. Males from the "inferior" species lusted for daughters of the other and even got them pregnant a time or two, which was apparently anathema either to God or the human chronicler of the tale.

Surprisingly, mainstream science actually gives some support to this Bible story. Anthropologists, in fact, believe there were at one time two distinct species of bi-pedal hominids living side-by-side in the areas now known to be Europe, Eurasia and the Middle East. One species was the Neanderthal, a loutish, brutish animal. The other was Homo sapiens, a much more attractive, more delicate gentleman. Extensive genetic tests have shown that all humans alive today owe their existence to Homo sapiens. That's our lineage. For some reason, it was the Neanderthal race which died out. Despite a few, last, dying chromosomes on the family tree, no person on earth can be directly and genetically linked to that obviously tainted evolutionary dead-end, the Biblical "men of renown."

Studies on scores of fossils in the world's museums and universities, though, show that Neanderthals were actually physically superior to Homo sapiens. Theoretically it should have been the race that survived. A Neanderthal was said to be strong enough to pick up a Homo and throw him across the room. Although many scientists believe there must have been occasional interbreeding along the fringes of the two populations whatever DNA may have once been mixed never made its way out of the common gene pool. Every man, woman and child alive today is a product of that narrow keyhole of human evolution. It's also possible this conflict was mankind's first documented example of neighborhood racism.

From our earliest days we are taught that there are two primal instincts in the human psyche: self-preservation and species preservation. Self-preservation is the easier of the two to understand. When faced with a "fight or flee" situation, the glandular system pumps adrenalin into the bloodstream. The sudden surge in testosterone makes an otherwise-meek child suddenly daring enough to throw a punch at the schoolyard bully. Rare is the youngster who cannot instantly identify with the urge to put up his dukes and fling a fist at an offending jaw.

Species preservation is the tougher instinct to understand: the urge to mate with someone possessing a survival chromosome, the urge to pass one's genes on to a dominant receptor, be it blonde or brunette, the tendency to mate with a like-minded, cute double helix in the evolutionary stew. Woven into the fiber of our being is this drive to protect and preserve what's distinctively ours. We preserve our own, and repress the rest. Like it or not, science says that race consciousness is hard-wired into the human brain.

Broaching such a subject, though, is about as politically and socially dangerous as doing a country music line dance into a La Brea tar pit, but one cannot honestly study modern neighborhood development without occasionally gnawing on some distasteful carrion. Homeowners Associations, at least as they exist in this country, are firmly rooted in our nation's racist past.

After World War II, when GIs and officers began returning home to establish careers and start families, there wasn't a lot of conscious thought given to the need for setting up apartheid neighborhoods. Although the military was heavily segregated in the early years of the war, many minority servicemen had served with distinction. It wasn't uncommon to hear of acts of bravery that crossed racial lines.

One such story involved an unlikely hero named William Pinckney of Beaufort, South Carolina.[1] His primary duty was serving as a cook on the USS Enterprise. In 1942, he was below decks on the huge aircraft carrier when a Japanese shell left a gaping hole in the ship and exploded a magazine to which he was assigned. Many sailors were killed. Ignoring the heavy smoke and fire, Pinckney picked up a badly wounded white crewmate and carried him up a ladder to safety. He then climbed back into the burning debris looking for other wounded men.

Pinckney, for his heroism, was awarded the Navy Cross and a Purple Heart. A Navy destroyer now carries his name. Every sailor who walks on or off the USS Pinckney knows the story and sees the photograph of this black American hero. Despite the mutual inter-racial respect earned by many servicemen like Pinckney, the post-war years saw a return to the segregated ways of the past. Although those who had felt the sting of discrimination were keenly aware of its presence, many whites across the country were oblivious of the social barriers that kept minorities from access to basic human rights.

There were champions in the struggle for equal rights, of course. But there were also many moments when segregation and discrimination could have been ended at an earlier time. One such missed opportunity was a post-war court case that should have been a pivotal point in American history. For one reason or another, the timing was not yet right.

Seaman First Class William Pinckney was a cook onboard the USS Enterprise in World War II. He was below decks when a Japanese missile slammed into the top deck of the aircraft carrier. Pinckney, seeing that many fellow sailors were wounded, threw one of them over his shoulder and fighting back flames, he carried the wounded man up four decks. Then he went back down into the inferno looking for more victims. For his bravery, Pinckney was awarded the Navy Cross and a Purple Heart. In 2005, a Guided Missile Destroyer, the USS Pinckney, was christened in his honor.

—photo by U.S. Navy

## Restrictive Covenants Legal But Unenforceable

In 1948, the U.S. Supreme Court took up a case called *Shelley v. Kraemer.* It involved a legal dispute over a restrictive covenant in a St. Louis, Missouri neighborhood. Such covenants are contractual obligations on the homebuyer controlling any use or future use or sale of his property. Restrictive covenants are private contracts between the buyer and seller; they run with the land and are absolutely enforceable on future owners. Homeowners saw restrictive covenants as a way of defending white neighborhoods against the great influx of black families who moved into northern cities to escape their lives in the south. One study showed that 80 percent of all Chicago real estate was once covered by racial restrictions prohibiting blacks.[2]

One of those new black families, Shelley, tried to buy a row home in Chicago, Illinois. The Shelley family wasn't aware at the time that the house was accompanied by a racially restrictive

25

covenant written 37 years earlier. The 1911 covenant, signed by a majority of neighboring property owners, mandated that homes in the community not be sold to anyone of the "Negro or Mongolian race." One of Shelley's prospective new neighbors sued to block the black family from moving in, and the case ended up in the U.S. Supreme Court.

In a somewhat knock-kneed, thumb-in-mouth decision, the Court ruled 6-0 that government agencies could not be enlisted in enforcing a racially restrictive covenant. The covenants, themselves, however, were left standing.[3]

There's no question that *Shelley v. Kraemer* was a mile marker in the battle for civil rights. But if restrictive covenants were no longer enforceable in the courts, didn't that make the covenants useless? If white homeowners were no longer able to refuse to sell to a black person, wasn't that a huge civil rights victory? Apparently it was not, at least in the opinion of some observers.

In its decision the Court had principally relied on the 14th Amendment to the Constitution, which outlawed racial discrimination by government. Critics of *Shelley v. Kraemer* make a convincing argument that the decision fell far short of the massive civil rights victory it could have achieved. The 14th Amendment is aimed at the government's handling of civil rights behavior, whereas the 13th Amendment, the outlawing of slavery, is focused on private behavior.

By ending slavery, the 13th Amendment essentially gave blacks the private right or ability to own and use land and to make contracts. But the Supreme Court in *Shelley v. Kraemer* specifically said it was not going to outlaw racially restrictive covenants, which are private contracts between a buyer and seller. While the Court's action essentially made such covenants effectively unenforceable by government, it set up a system under which private Homeowners Associations would spend the next few decades wreaking social havoc.

The Shelley decision noted the Court couldn't restrict the Constitutional rights of citizens. Yet Constitutional rights are restricted all the time by the courts. The most notable example is the First Amendment's "freedom of speech" protection. When a lawsuit is settled, for example, one side or both sides are often contractually forbidden from discussing terms of the settlement. In other words, when the right to free speech is contractually suppressed, the courts will, indeed, enforce it. From a historical standpoint, the Shelley decision became a bit of an embarrassment to Constitutionalists.

In his 2005 award-winning paper, law Professor Mark D. Rosen argued that *Shelley v. Kraemer* was incorrectly decided, and that the case should be re-conceptualized to encompass the freedoms created by the 13th Amendment. He writes:

> The Thirteenth Amendment applies to individuals; it provides a basis for declaring the racially restrictive covenants themselves to be illegal, not just their enforcement. The Article's Thirteenth Amendment approach hence eliminates a perfectly noxious byproduct of the Shelley Court's analytics: the Court's conclusion that racially restrictive covenants themselves were perfectly legal. This is important. The covenants' legality not only has been an embarrassment to American jurisprudence, but a persuasive recent study has concluded that unenforceable restrictive covenants played an important role in entrenching racially segregated housing markets in this country.[4]

Yet another legal scholar, Richard R. W. Brooks, in his 2002 paper, *Covenants and Conventions*, argues that:

> The presence of extensive covenants in a community—even though they were unenforceable—served as a valuable signal

to mortgage lenders, Realtors and home-buyers of the traditional racial exclusivity of the community. In this manner, as well as discouraging prospective black buyers, unenforceable racial restrictive covenants played a key role in establishing perpetual segregation in northern cities like Chicago for many decades. In other ways, as well, the effects of these long-abandoned covenants continue to ripple through modern urban communities.[5]

Still, the Court's ruling for the first time dealt a partial blow to white developers and homeowners who were trying to keep neighborhoods "pure." And real estate developers began to realize they could not count on the government to help them maintain racially separate neighborhoods.

## The 1964 Civil Rights Act

In 1963, President John F. Kennedy and a bi-partisan majority in Congress were prepared to try to clean up some of America's racial divisions by passing the new Civil Rights Act. It was signed into law by President Lyndon Baines Johnson in 1964. The new law was a long-overdue correction of decades of discrimination. Although history trumpets it as a landmark decision, in its early years it, too, fell stupendously short of what it could have achieved.

"White flight" was a well-documented social phenomenon that occurred in many cities in the post-war years. As more affluent blacks moved into nicer housing on the outskirts of town, homeowners in previously white neighborhoods began hop-scotching into even more outlying suburbs in a transparent effort to avoid the prospect of living in mixed-race communities. There was growing fear in countless areas that property values would plummet when "the coloreds" moved in. The migration in some cities was dramatic. Even more dramatic was the timing of a plan that would institutionalize housing discrimination for decades.

## Legalizing Discrimination Again!

In one of history's more peculiar "coincidences," the Urban Land Institute and the National Association of Homebuilders came up with a new way to discourage minorities from invading white areas. The year, not surprisingly, was also 1964. Since the 1948 court decision had outlawed government participation in racially restrictive covenants, and since the 1964 Civil Rights Act outlawed racial discrimination in government, in schools, business and public places, developers reasoned that the law couldn't touch the membership policies of "private clubs" and "associations." They were right.

Private associations had amazing powers. They could keep out blacks, women, the disabled, people with green eyes, foreigners with long noses, essentially anyone they chose. Developers found that all the old restrictive covenants outlawed by the courts or by Congress could be resurrected and placed into the purchase agreements of prospective club members.

There was a secondary line of defense in some communities. As a condition of home ownership, buyers were obligated to join the neighborhood's private golf or tennis club. The common wisdom was that Negroes and Orientals weren't genetically pre-disposed to enjoy white sports and therefore wouldn't try to buy their way into such elitist real estate. Developers, of course, had not yet heard names like Arthur Ashe, Venus and Serena Williams and Tiger Woods. But for a time, it was a wildly successful tap dance around the Civil Rights Act. The modern day Homeowners Association was born.

Racially restrictive covenants and whites-only country clubs were extraordinarily successful in screening out blacks, Jews and many other minorities. Any objective researcher studying minority home ownership trends across America would have to admit that the results can still be seen today. In city after city, many upscale neighborhoods are almost exclusively white. In some Homeowners Associations consisting of hundreds, even thousands of homes, blacks are almost nonexistent.

In my Mercer Island through the 1960s, there wasn't a single black family out of a population of about 20,000 people. The lone exception was in 1965 when a family named Waterhouse moved in. Their son was enrolled in the Mercer Island High School, but he quit a few months later. We never knew why.

The impact of whites-only country clubs, communities and HOAs lasted throughout the last half of the 20th Century. One of the unexpected complications was in organized sports. In 1994, when 18-year-old Tiger Woods won the Jerry Pate Intercollegiate Golf Tournament, observers began noting that Shoal Creek in Birmingham, Alabama was a whites-only club a mere four years earlier. The PGA had to do some quick scrambling to check the policies of all the clubs on its circuit.

When Woods won the 1997 Masters at Augusta National Golf Club tournament, with its long history of excluding blacks and women, the PGA again faced a potentially difficult explanation. Except for a few black caddies, club staff, and Tiger Woods himself, golf was a white sport. But Woods was great. He drew huge audiences of whites and blacks, and his impact on private Homeowners Associations was as rattling as his golf score. Although he'd rather be remembered for his golf score, Woods fundamentally changed a number of institutions in America in the most positive ways possible. By becoming a sports hero, a man admired for his raw talent, he waltzed through many barriers, some of which he couldn't possibly have been aware.

Politicians made up another group which occasionally found itself entangled in awkward "whites-only" embarrassments. It happened on both sides of the political aisle from Republican Senator Strom Thurmond to former KKK member and Democratic Senator Robert Byrd. Maryland Governor Bob Erhlich took flack for raising 100,000 dollars at the whites-only Elkridge Country Club. Even President Bill Clinton faced unexpected questions after playing golf at the all-white Country Club of Little Rock.

"I should not have done it," Clinton said afterwards, adding to a lengthy list of personally humiliating situations after which he also could have said, "I should not have done it."

But in each case, sports figures and politicos ran up against a system often rooted in the racism and exclusivity that's simmered for decades in private Homeowners Associations. Vestiges of that bigotry continue even into the 21st Century.

One of the best news accounts exposing racially restrictive covenants was written in May of 1998 by *Seattle Weekly* writer Lawrence W. Cheek. He recounted his own experiences with a Homeowners Association, and recited some of the horrors faced by others. "Suburban Gestapo" one section of his essay was entitled. Cheek documented a number of cases of onerous and oppressive HOA tactics around the country, including the expelling of one resident from a retirement community because the homeowner broke HOA age restriction rules by taking a younger wife.[6] "Operating a home business" is another area where Homeowners Associations sometimes expel or fine residents for violations of rules. But the enforcement can be mindlessly arbitrary.

## Handling the Undesirables

Cheek's initial expose' began causing other reporters to examine the discriminatory language in old real estate deeds. In 2005, *Seattle Times* writer Lornet Turnbull reported on the efforts of residents of the community of Innis Arden to erase racially offensive language from the historic real estate records of the 500 or so property owners in that upper middle class community.[7]

The 60-year-old covenants were written into the records by developer Bill Boeing, one of the pioneers of Seattle's aviation industry. The covenants forbade white homeowners from selling or leasing property to non-whites. Negroes and Asians could only occupy homes in Innis Arden as domestic servants, not as property owners. Court decisions in subsequent decades rendered the covenants unenforceable and obsolete. But Turnbull reported that some homeowners were offended at the very existence of such racism in the official records. They circulated a petition to officially remove any reflection of the development's racial history so it didn't even appear on title searches. Such an "erasure" would require two-thirds of all property owners to sign notarized requests to remove the old clauses. After a year of trying, less than a third of the needed signatures had been collected.

A series of articles in Seattle newspapers condemned the existence of the covenants. A history professor at the University of Washington, James N. Gregory, wrote a searing guest editorial to the *Seattle Times*. He listed scores of communities, subdivisions and Homeowners Associations throughout the Pacific Northwest in which racial covenants still lived in public records. Typical of the language:

Laurelhurst Subdivision: "No person other than one of the White Race shall be permitted to occupy any portion of any lot in said plat or of any building at any time thereon, except a domestic servant actually employed by a White occupant of such building."

Broadmoor: "No part of said property hereby conveyed shall ever be used or occupied by any Hebrew or by any person of the Ethiopian, Malay or any Asiatic Race."

Greenwood: "No person or persons of Asiatic, African, or Negro blood, lineage or extraction."

South Lake City: "No person of African, Japanese, Chinese, or of any other Mongolian descent."[8]

Professor Gregory's *Seattle Civil Rights and Labor History Project* lists more than 120 similar covenants on real estate deeds in subdivisions throughout the Seattle area. He was at the forefront of a movement that convinced the government of Washington State to ease the process by which Homeowners Associations could erase such memories from public records.

While some might argue that "those who don't remember the past are doomed to repeat it" (Santayana), government officials in the State of Washington felt otherwise. On March 15th of 2006, Governor Christine Gregoire signed into law a bill introduced in the State Senate just two months earlier. The bill passed the Legislature on a unanimous vote. It allowed Homeowners Associations to petition for the erasure of racially restrictive covenants on a majority vote by an HOA Board of Directors. Many restrictive covenants, although unenforceable for decades, will remain forever on property deeds. But in the case of Homeowners Associations in Washington State, some now some have an increased ability to try to "forget embarrassing histories."

Erasing a history of discrimination, though, is not the same thing as erasing discrimination itself. Homeowners' Associations, by their very nature, are exclusionary organizations with covenants and by-laws built around carefully worded code that screens out *undesirables*. The exact definition of that word can be a constantly moving target.

Any prospective homeowner who would tend to lower property values is *undesirable*. An elderly person might be *undesirable*. A person of the wrong color could be *undesirable*. A family with a handicapped child can be an intolerable threat. Whistle-blowers or those known to have publicly opposed past HOA misdeeds most certainly are potential targets for some kind of removal from a neighborhood.

There are countless ways to encourage such "black sheep" to get on down the road. Any form of badgering can be applied. Overt racism, slander, public humiliation, arbitrary complaints about unwatered lawns or toys left on a front yard all work well to oust undesirable homeowners. If none of the aforementioned actions work to remove a targeted neighborhood bad guy, then the legal seizure of property is an incredibly effective and well-used final step.

A number of law firms around the country specialize in coaching Homeowners Associations on how to confront "riff-raff." Those law firms then sit on the periphery poised to "file-and-foreclose" at the first possible moment. It happens in state after state with stunning effectiveness and regularity, and now amounts to what some would argue is the largest transfer of wealth from private homeowners to trial lawyers in history. Property owners hit with such attacks invariably discover they are without legal rights, without legal advice, and often end up in court trying to represent themselves against batteries of HOA insurance company lawyers. Home after home has been snatched in a process that can only be described as bizarre.

One such "loser" was a family who was evicted from their home in Boynton Beach, Florida in 2003. Robert and Theresa Denson and their four children faced eviction for non-payment of HOA dues. They said that during a short marital separation, they had gotten behind on their bills.

"I figured the mortgage was more important than what was owed to the homeowners association, so I paid that first," Denson told reporters.

In the process of trying to catch up on bills, Denson became confused about whether the family actually owed their Home-owners Association a $1200 bill. Denson said he was under the assumption he had an oral agreement with the HOA president to make payments on the bill.

Fort Lauderdale lawyer Randall Roger, attorney for the Boynton Beach Homeowners Association, said there was no such deal. He filed a foreclosure action on the Denson's home in the fall of 2003. In December, he sold the Denson's $375,000 home at auction for a fraction of its real value.

"My job is not a pleasant one," Roger told a reporter from the *Miami Herald*.[9]

Attorney Roger probably could have added, "But it's extremely profitable."

In August of 2008, Nashville blogger Katherine Coble created a post called "My Homeowners Association Must Be Stopped." It recounted attempts by her Hampton Hall HOA to change the rules of her Homeowners Association to prohibit any property owner from leasing homes to renters. Each home in the association, according to those circulating the petition, had to be owner-occupied.

Despite the fact that such a rule-change monkeyed with the original property rights of each owner, the change was deemed legal. Had the rule changers possessed a little more courage they could legally have passed a new covenant saying "Negroes need not apply to become renters in this neighborhood," and it could have passed muster in court.

Coble wrote:

I served on the HOA board a couple of years back and the rental properties were the bane of our existence. I myself didn't mind the colour of the people's skin–but others did.

A couple of meetings before I quit, another board member frustratedly swore that the neighbourhood would be much better 'without all the n—ers.' He actually said that. He actually THINKS that. Never mind that there are Asian, Black and Hispanic owners *and* rental houses occupied by white tenants. Never mind that there are white owners who don't mow their lawns and leave their trash receptacles out front.

It's an attitude that feels perfectly justified in telling other people what to do with property they own. It's an attitude that hides racism that glorifies classism that is genteel in its barbarism. It's a greedy and disgusting attitude that is not satisfied with a seven percent per year increase in property values. It's petty and small. And it has to be stopped.[10]

Coble obviously sensed and discovered what many other HOA members have found. A Homeowners Association board can do whatever it wants. Laws against discrimination on the basis of race or disability are stunningly unenforceable when a private association is involved. If that means an unwritten code that bans Negroes from the neighborhood, so be it. *C'est la vie.*

Economist and public policy analyst Randal O'Toole in his book, *Best Laid Plans: How Government Planning Harms Your Quality of Life, Your Pocketbook, and Your Future*, acknowledges that developers have a strong interest in creating Homeowners Associations. But he points out a terrifying reality that in some cities, groups of homeowners can organize at any time and begin imposing enforceable covenants on their neighbors:

Houston permits residents of neighborhoods with no covenants to petition to create a homeowners' association and write new covenants. This requires approval of the majority of the votes in the neighborhood... like zoning, homeowners' associations are not perfect. They are somewhat tainted because covenants written in the early part of the 20th century explicitly forbade homeowners from selling to blacks and other minorities.

A more serious problem with homeowners' associations is that some have been overzealous in enforcing their covenants.

Houston inadvertently created another problem when it allowed homeowners' associations that won enforcement actions against their members to make the member pay the association's attorney fees and place a lien on the member's home until the fees were paid. This led to attorneys roaming neighborhoods looking for minor infractions and sending letters to homeowners telling them to fix the problem along with a bill for their services and a threat to put a lien on their homes if they did not pay the bill.[11]

In three short passages, O'Toole, a respected scholar with the Cato Institute, has perhaps inadvertently summed up a damning case against the entire Homeowners Association movement: foundationally racist organizations headed by overzealous board officers, backed by roving attorneys who seek and levy fines against homeowners, knowing that their legal bills are automatically paid by those facing foreclosure. One couldn't write a formula with more potential for abuse.

## Equal Opportunity Abuse

Racial discrimination against homeowners doesn't necessarily involve just white-against-black prejudice. HOA governance can be subtle and subjectively aimed at any race.

The city of Miramar is in Broward County, Florida. Blacks outnumber whites, and the city has one of the highest Jamaican populations in the country. In the 2000 census, homes averaged about $200,000 apiece.

In 2003, a fight over racial bias erupted in Franklin Farms, a community of 173 homes. The HOA board approved rules prohibiting homeowners from giving, selling or leasing their properties to any other person without prior approval from the board. Board officers refused to disclose what their criteria were for rejecting a prospective resident. In an October 2003 interview with the *Sun Sentinel*, board president Nancy Holloway was quoted as saying:

> It's a private thing. Race is not part of the application, but if you can tell what color they are by their name, that's fine and dandy.[12]

According to news reports, Holloway admitted that residents of Franklin Heights were never mailed a copy of the draconian new amendment to neighborhood by-laws until after it passed. More than 90 minorities who were members of the Franklin Heights subdivision signed a petition against the new rule, and they gathered signatures to begin a recall against Holloway and her husband. She told reporters:

> All I ever wanted for this community was to be the best-looking community that it could ever be. I am not a racist.[13]

Again, the attorney advising the Franklin Heights Home-owners Association is Randall Roger, a well known defender of the HOA movement in Florida.

Racism is a sore that has long festered in many American neighborhoods, in those who hide behind developers' covenants, it's especially rampant. Despite radical changes in the modern workplace, when perceived private property values are impacted, attitudes by some homeowners can reflect a loss of objective contact with reality.

Broderick Gamble thought he'd found paradise when he purchased a new home in a mostly-white development in the Dallas suburb of Arlington. In 2005, two days after he and his fiancé and four children moved in, his home was damaged by a fire. It was attributed by investigators to an iron that had accidentally been left on. Gamble, a handyman, began repairing the damage and rebuilding his home.[14]

On January 2, 2008, a midnight visitor used red spray paint to scrawl the words, "KILL" and "DIE NIGGER" on his white garage doors.[15] There were no suspects in the graffiti incident, but Arlington Police say the Gamble family had faced previous problems in the neighborhood.

Two weeks before the paint incident, the couple complained that a 66-year-old neighbor, Grace Snowden Head, had hurled racial slurs at them and used a two-by-four board to assault Gamble's fiancé. Head was arrested and charged with criminal trespass, assault and refusal to identify herself to a police officer. Three days later she was arrested again for felony criminal mischief after the couple accused her of jumping up and down on the family's car. Investigating officers said it was clearly a racial incident, and that the woman had refused to leave the couple's property even after being ordered by police to do so. "This is our home. We're not going to let anybody drive us away. That's what they wanted. But it's not going to happen," Gamble told reporters.[16]

Other neighbors had a different view. They criticized Gamble for not immediately removing the spray-painted ethnic slurs from his garage doors. They complained to city officials who ordered the Gamble family to clean up the slurs, but the graffiti remained for more than two weeks, as the neighborhood became increasingly agitated. Finally, two city workers showed up with paint cans and removed the graffiti without Gamble's permission or cooperation.

"I'm real disappointed," said next door neighbor William Cantrell. "If (the Gambles) had really wanted to ease the neighborhood tension, they could have done that earlier."[17]

One of the more startling stories in recent years revealing the racial sentiments of an HOA board involved a memo put out by the president of a Homeowners Association in Ocala, Florida. It was released immediately after Hurricane Katrina, the storm that decimated New Orleans and led to a mass exodus of half that city's population. The storm evacuees were largely black. Majestic Oaks HOA president Bob Watson told homeowners:

> The Majestic Oaks Subdivision residents are not to take victims from Hurricane Katrina into their homes. The Association is encouraging homeowners to simply donate money instead.[18]

When stories about Majestic Oaks made national headlines, Watson said the matter was "blown out of proportion." If so, then those winds continued to blow. Watson and his board were recalled from office. Under the glare of the national spotlight, Majestic Oaks residents were apparently uncomfortable with the word "intolerance" that was hurled at them from across the country.

## Fighting an HOA: Almost a Hopeless Task

A few scattered organizations have popped up which try to do battle with the draconian and sometimes racist actions of the HOA movement. Their task is almost hopeless. They're pitted against one of the largest, most lucrative legal lobbies in the world. HOA lawyers voraciously defend their clients against individual homeowners, regardless of the outrageousness of the underlying dispute.

One such protest movement in Texas is by "the National Homeowners Advocate Group."[19] It was started by a black couple whose home in mostly-white Kingwood, Texas was seized during a dispute over non-payment of a maintenance fee.

Johnnie and Harvella Jones were typical of the kind of "black sheep" that some Homeowners Associations try to weed out of their membership rosters. Like many newcomers to the HOA scene, the couple was unfamiliar with some of the rules of HOA life, the most serious of which is the late-payment of dues. More homes have been lost to that oversight, than any other. The Jones' write on their website that they felt membership dues were being illegally raised, and they protested by refusing to pay them. To aggravate matters, they began traveling to Austin, Texas to advocate for a Homeowners Bill of Rights before the State Legislature.

In the minds of some, the only thing more damaging to property values than the arrival of neighbors of the wrong color is activism. Activists of any stripe simply cannot be tolerated. They upset the apple cart. They attract attention. They sometimes bring about disruptive change. Activists, as a result, are often given "extra attention" by HOA boards.

The Jones family discovered that there is no court of appeals to which they could have brought their complaints of improper dues and fines. There is no court of last resort. In a situation where a peace-seeking board of neighbors could have appropriately sat around a kitchen table offering helpful advice, there was none. The board taking action against the Jones couple was simultaneously Judge, Jury and Executioner.

The incentive to rid the neighborhood of the Jones family was high. Not only could an activist be removed, the profit-motive in foreclosing on the Jones house was substantial. The lifeblood of HOA law firms is in seizing the assets of homeowners who are willing to gamble the family homestead on a moral principle. The Joneses thought they had a point to make about something they figured was illegal. The lawyers simply took their house.

The Jones family, minus their home, continues to advocate from a website called *TheNationalHomeownersAdvocateGroup.com*.

In past years, such advocacy would have been impossible. With the global Internet, Harvella Jones can continue to warn others about the consequences of fighting the Homeowners Association in Kingwood, Texas. Whether they'll actually ever win their battle is doubtful. But Harvella Jones does write on her website:

> Our organization receives calls from all over the state from homeowners complaining about foreclosures. We hear from senior citizens, handicap people and minorities. Just before Christmas, I received a frantic call from a black homeowner who was on a majority white board who had decided to foreclose on her home on New Year's Eve. I got a call from another black homeowner who was calling on behalf of her deaf brother who could not speak or hear and who was being foreclosed on January 2, 2007. This is just a small sample of the type of "some" foreclosures we hear about. They are not all black people, but generally speaking, the calls are coming from handicap people, senior citizens, minorities or other homeowners that board members want to control and/or eliminate from their "perfect neighborhoods."[20]

Jones is obviously not alone in her frustration. She says the only solution is for State Legislatures to enact a Homeowners' Bill of Rights which would severely restrict or prohibit home foreclosures or harassment on the flimsy grounds often claimed by Homeowners Associations and their lawyers.

She also wonders openly and often what it is about Mankind that causes one person to judge another's qualities by something as trivial as skin color.

## A Win Becomes a Loss

On very rare occasions, a homeowner actually wins against his Homeowners Association. Even then, the deck is stacked.

From a financial standpoint, a victorious homeowner usually ends up as the biggest loser. One such case involved a couple in Maricopa County, Arizona.

Bill Martin and his wife, Amy Amaro-Martin, bought a town-home in the mostly-white Sutton Place Improvement Association. The complex of about four dozen homes was built in the 1960s. Like many of their fellow homeowners, the Martins submitted plans to their HOA to renovate and improve their home.

In 2004, the HOA approved the couple's plans and the Martins borrowed against their home equity to begin the project. A few months later, complaints began pouring in. The stucco was wrong, the paint was wrong, the windows are wrong. "It was clear I was never going to be able to please these people," Martin told a reporter.[21]

In 2007, the Sutton Place Improvement Association filed a lawsuit against the Martins claiming the couple had violated their deed restrictions by deviating from their original architectural plans. But there were clearly other factors involved in the dispute. During the trial, one witness testified to hearing a board member say, "Black people shouldn't be living here."

After two years of litigation, hundreds of thousands of dollars in legal expenses, and four years after their original architectural submission to the HOA, the jury found in the Martins' favor, ruling that they had indeed been discriminated against. The couple was awarded $200,000.

Maricopa County Judge Craig Blakey ruled on May 29, 2009, that the Martins had not violated any deed restrictions and that any deviations from their initial plans were inconsequential. He ruled that the Martins had been treated differently than other residents who had remodeled their homes.

The Martins' attorney, Ashley Adams, said, "Juries in Arizona are tired of the power that HOAs have." He said the lawsuit by the Sutton Place HOA had financially ruined the Martins.

"They're not going to run me off," Martin told reporters.[22] Still, one wonders who actually won what appeared to be a frivolous and needless confrontation. The HOA was financially backed up by the multi-billion dollar industry that shields HOA board members from the financial damage of their arbitrary decisions. The Martins were on their own.

"I like my own HOA," many people will testify. "The board does its best to protect neighborhood property values and it does the best it can to improve life for all members of the community."

That's an interesting statement. Many Board members actually do try to do their best to promote community interests, and board officers who truly work to improve the lives of others are revered. But what are the chances that a community controversy of some kind could lead to a change in leadership, creating what some might describe as a "rogue board"? The chances are pretty close to 100 percent.

The very structure of Homeowners Associations gives them the ability to exert bully power on a completely arbitrary basis. Board members who fail to use their power to correct community problems are quickly voted out of office. The election of a single aggressive board member can completely change the makeup and feel of a neighborhood. Even the gentlest HOA board is a single vote away from going rogue. Many private homeowners have run up against this community buzz saw and suddenly found themselves homeless, or worse.

# 4
# The Ultimate Law
# of the Universe

*The law of unintended consequences pushes us ceaselessly*
*through the years, permitting no pause for perspective.*
—Richard Schickel

For centuries, scientists have insisted that the Universe must be a place of magnificent order, a life governed by natural laws that are as distinct, immutable, and unchangeable as light and dark. "Nothing can make sense," the reasoning went, "unless everything makes sense."

From Plato to Newton, and Maxwell to Einstein, great minds have tried to understand man's mathematical place in nature. While Plato orated, Newton calculated, Maxwell equated, and Einstein related, mankind gradually came to accept certain constants in life: that gravity is dominant, electromagnetism is strong, and the speed of light is ultimate. Life ought to be tidy, not messy. Even Albert Einstein whined, "God does not play dice with the Universe."

In an increasingly chaotic world, the intelligentsia eventually came up with a wild new package.

To make sense of an awkwardly termed "Chaos Theory," they tried to take all the complexities of life and jam them into some kind of general rules of order. The laws governing particles, waves and chaos all fit nicely within each other, except for one hitch: *people.*

From the exact moment Adam and Eve shared a fruit cocktail at the East Eden Garden Club, the mind of man has been in a state of functional decay. Human beings don't like God's laws. They don't like order. They appear to be governed, rather, by a law more rigid than any equation of science, the "Law of Unintended Consequences." At least as far as human behavior is concerned, this law has more relevance than the speed of light.

There probably isn't a human dispute in history that wasn't the progenitor and the product of unintended consequences. It seems the more people try to figure out how to live in peace with each other, the more they cannot. The more they attempt to "be fair," the more unfair they become. To re-state the ultimate law, then:

Nothing makes sense, unless nothing makes sense.

For the people who invented Homeowners Associations, that makes ultimate sense. And a majority of Americans who live in structured-life communities have been dealing with the unintended consequences ever since.

## Homeowners Don't Really "Own" in a Homeowners Association

Homeowners Associations are essentially private, members-only, non-profit corporations in which each homeowner signs real estate contracts which contain covenants or deed restrictions as a condition of purchase. Those deed restrictions vary from place to place, but they essentially provide property owners with "advice" on how to behave to maintain the community's overall property values.

Since the covenants run-with-the-land, they forever obligate and bind all subsequent property owners. Once those restrictions are in place, they are pretty much impossible to erase. The legal impact is that a homeowner never truly "owns" his or her land. The community owns it and for all intents and purposes "leases" it back to each subsequent purchaser. A monthly or annual fee is paid by each homeowner into the neighborhood treasury and those funds are managed by a board usually elected by the community. That board is given the power to handle mundane community chores such as neighborhood trash collection, maintenance of common areas, or the stifling of an annoying, barking dog.

City and county governments, of course, are more than happy to turn over such minor powers to these faux governments, or incorporations of private homeowners. Indeed, cities and counties increasingly mandate that all new developers incorporate deed restrictions as a condition of being awarded building permits. The arrangement looks perfectly benign. It reduces the burden on law enforcement while still allowing true governmental jurisdictions their usual control over such things as building permits, elections, taxation and maintenance of the infra-structure.

The problem with most non-profit corporations is that they have no police powers with which to force members to obey their "laws," or covenants. Such police powers, if ever actually granted, would have to be accompanied by the massive and grave responsibility of protecting each individual's Constitutional and human rights. True government bodies have a huge obligation to protect all citizens by fair and equal enforcement of the law.

## The Power of Foreclosure

But Homeowners Associations have figured out how to carve out for themselves an impressive enforcement mechanism that's so massively powerful, any police agency in existence would salivate (if such agencies could actually do such a thing as salivate) over the right to use it. It's scarier than an arrest, more frightening than incarceration, far more intimidating than facing stocks and pillory, uglier than a public whipping, even more hideous than a sentence of death by firing squad. "What power is this?" one might ask. *It's the power of foreclosure*, the power to arbitrarily confiscate property, thereby completely shattering the life of any homeowner (and his descendants) whose infraction may be as minor as say, owning a dog greater than 26 pounds, leaving a trash can unattended, being of the wrong race or religion, or underpaying an annual HOA bill by 78 cents.

True government agencies have to ensure that each and every action they take against a citizen is mindful of not only the U.S. Constitution, but of 240 years of court rule and precedence. Government has an extreme obligation of transparency, openness, equal protection, equal and fair administration of justice, observation and protection of the right to vote, the right to worship, the right to speak out, the right to congregate, and a myriad of other rights which fill entire law libraries with their books, their pamphlets, their decisions and discourse.

Above this entire framework of protection against the excesses of government is a massive court system where an aggrieved person can ask for his case to be heard. Although far from perfect, this court system theoretically allows the average person a chance to be heard not once, but twice, and thrice and even more times before various bodies of law. Again, in theory, somewhere in that labyrinth are multiple layers of protection for someone seeking justice and that person may actually have a fighting chance of finding it.

So what kinds of protections are available to a member of a Homeowners Association?

What's that again?

In case there's any misunderstanding, here's a repeat of the rights of a property owner in America's system of Homeowners Associations:

The silence is thunderous.

Welcome to the weird world of the HOA, the CID, the POA and the Co-op, where life, liberty and property are in the hands of your neighbors, neighbors who are unconstrained by the law, unsympathetic to your requests for fairness, and in a massive number of cases across the country, too busy or too apathetic to get involved in neighborhood affairs.

The typical HOA is governed by an elected (and sometimes unelected) board whose responsibility it is to meet, collect and allocate money, maintain the common areas and pass rules designed to manage the behavior of members. These boards for the most part are not obligated to protect or respect any human or civil rights. The only factor at play when an HOA board begins making decisions is the will of the majority on the board.

There is no court system to decide whether a board's actions are illegal or unconstitutional. In fact, in many neighborhoods across the country, rules are being enforced that are arbitrary and outrageous. And in nearly every state, the courts are refusing to reign in misfeasance and malfeasance of board members. The U.S. Constitution is unrecognized as a controlling legal authority over these private non-profit corporations. That's right, the U.S. Constitution is not recognized by the HOA.

If a Homeowners Association board suddenly decided it wanted to ban guns, for example, no Second Amendment arguments by gun owners could be raised. If an HOA board decided it wanted to enter each member's private residence and rummage through his or her private tax returns, Fourth Amendment arguments could likely be raised in vain. Each homeowner, by signing real estate documents which acknowledge in advance the surrender of Constitutional rights, permanently gives up his or her ability to claim future legal protection.

Although the examples above seem absurdly hypothetical, Homeowners Associations in many places have incredibly suspended such Constitutional privileges as the right to free speech, religion, and the right to bear arms. There is no question, that over the years, most Americans have become accustomed to the idea that speech is fundamentally protected. But when an HOA board decides that the display of certain political opinions is not in its best interest, it can actually prohibit expressions of non-permitted thought, even on what most homeowners might consider their own private property.

## Unequal Protection of the Law

For proof, one needs look no further than a 1996 court decision in Pennsylvania. The court ruled that a condominium association was within the law when it removed some political yard signs from the private property of a homeowner. It said:

> The courts of this Commonwealth have vigorously defended the rights which are guaranteed to our citizens by both the federal and our Commonwealth's constitutions. *One of the fundamental precepts which we recognize, however, is the individual's freedom to contractually restrict, or even give up, those rights. The Cappuccios contractually agreed to abide by the provisions in the Declaration at the time of purchase, thereby relinquishing their freedom of speech concerns regarding placing signs on this property.*[1] (Emphasis by author)

An even more closely watched court case in New Jersey came to the same conclusion: that a group of homeowners called *"The Committee for a Better Twin Rivers,"* would not "better" the community by always allowing member residents to express political opinions. The court's 2007 decision found that *private homeowners had given away their free speech rights by joining the HOA.* There were no protections against government, because the court didn't feel that the HOA constituted a "government:"

The ***minor restrictions*** on plaintiffs' expressional activities
are not unreasonable or oppressive, and the Association *is
not acting as a municipality.*[2] (Emphasis by author)

Oddly, in another case just one year earlier, the same New
Jersey Supreme Court ruled that it was perfectly acceptable
for political activists to harangue shoppers in privately owned
shopping malls. In other words, the owner of a private shopping
mall was acting as a government and was thus bound to protect
free speech, but an HOA which actually imposes a myriad of laws,
regulations and taxes on homeowners is not really a government,
thus homeowners who live in such places have no Constitutional
right to free speech. You can display signs and hand out literature
to shoppers, but you can't put up a political sign in your bedroom
window.

The bottom line is that a homeowner who thought he was
protected by his Constitutional right to express a political opinion
was personally and financially punished by his neighbors for
doing so. His private property was trespassed upon, his personal
property was seized, and his family's finances were decimated.
The basic human rights this homeowner thought he possessed
had no more value than the chits and chads from an office paper
shredder. Wise observers expect this decision to be reversed in a
future case.

The court decisions beg an interesting question. What if a
Homeowners Association board decided to remove only the
political signs of one particular candidate or a ballot issue it
opposed? Try another: what if a board decided it didn't want
racial or religious minorities in the neighborhood? If a Homeowners Association does not have to abide by an individual's
Constitutional right to express a political opinion, why would it
have to respect any Constitutional guarantee, including that of
equal protection? If absurdity is best demonstrated by being

absurd, then let's explore this thought experiment one wicked step further:

> You, Mr. Minority, will be allowed to purchase a home in our community if you will sign a legally binding contract that you will not use racial discrimination as a defense, if we decide at some point to throw you out of the community based on your race.

Obviously, trial lawyers will fume and thunder at the hyperbole, but fuming and thundering is just shtick. In the American tort system, "shtick" is also known as "billable hours." It's doubtful many lawyers would take on such a case pro bono.

Since the courts allow homeowners to voluntarily, albeit unknowingly, contract away Constitutional rights, do homeowners have any protection against the potential mayhem? The answer is a disappointing one. An HOA board is, for the most part, above the law. It does what it wants. The courts have almost no relevancy to Homeowners Associations. There is a stunning lack of knowledge of an even more stunning lack of rights among people who buy into an HOA. And there is an awesome cloud of lawyers who've earned their wings flying above the growing gaggle of dysfunctional Homeowners Associations just waiting for the right time and circumstances to float down and begin feeding.

## Scientology? Go'wan!

A private members-only, non-profit corporation can exert almost Gestapo-like control over its membership. To demonstrate whether such a claim is even remotely close to the truth, the author asks the reader's indulgence as we take a crazily and seemingly unconnected trip through a court case that, on its face, has nothing to do with Homeowners Associations. It does, however, involve another kind of members-only, non-profit corporation, one that has been followed by decades of controversy. It's also instructive, in that it has possible implications for anyone who's involved in the HOA system. The court case is called *Wollersheim vs. Church of Scientology*. Many in the news media described the case as "Scientology's war against the Internet."

> They're raiding my house! The Church of Scientology is raiding my house, and the federal marshals are just standing outside letting it happen!

The frantic August, 1995 call to a Denver television reporter came from Lawrence Wollersheim, a man who described himself as a refugee from the cult of Scientology. Wollersheim had joined the church in California in 1972. Through a seven year period which he described as "a trip into Hell," he says he underwent years of what the church calls "auditing." While hooked up to "e-meters," devices that are little more than crudely fashioned polygraph machines, church members are quizzed about their sins, their lusts, any mental aberrations they may have experienced in this life, or in previous lives. Only through confession of such sins can a prospective member rise in the ranks of Scientology.

Wollersheim claimed the auditing sessions caused him extreme psychological and emotional damage. After extracting himself from the church, he and several other ex-members including Dennis Erlich, Arnie Lerma and Robert Penny, decided to use the burgeoning power of the Internet to expose the church's secrets, its flaws and a number of suicides committed by young Scientologists during auditing sessions.

Wollersheim and his anti-Scientology associates set up a network of discussion groups and websites (Wollersheim's was called *FACTnet.org*), which offered Internet users an online database of Scientology's "secret papers." Among the supposedly copyrighted secrets was an odd bit of wisdom only learned by upper-level church members. The secret involved a peculiar science fiction story written by L. Ron Hubbard, the founder of Scientology. The main character was "Xenu," who was said to be the warlike god of a "galactic federation" of planets.

When the "federation" became overpopulated, so the story went, Xenu flew all the excess beings to the planet Earth, chained them to volcanoes, and blew them up with hydrogen bombs, thus turning all the creatures into little spirit entities called "thetans" which now infest all humans. To rid oneself of these so-called "thetans" upper level Scientologists have to go through "clearing exercises." Never mind that the sophomoric Xenu tale could not pass a single scientific falsifiability test, it's still revered as doctrine by many Hollywood luminaries and church members like John Travolta, Tom Cruise and Priscilla Presley.

Since Scientology is famously aggressive in stifling its critics, the ex-members knew they'd be targeted and would undergo massive harassment. So their database of church papers was mirrored on servers around the world. If one discussion group was taken down in the U.S., another would pop up in Norway, or Spain or any of a number of countries where former church members lived. The anti-Scientology group communicated anonymously through an Internet re-mailer in Finland who stripped all routing information from emails, making it difficult for church lawyers to track down the critics. Like the old arcade game Whac-A-Mole, no matter how many times one enemy was smacked down, another would pop up and thumb his nose by offering downloads of the "secret" papers.

One ex-church member, Steven Fishman, took another step to ensure the public had access to the Xenu tale. He put the entire 61 page story into an affidavit in his own lawsuit with the church. The "Fishman Affidavit,"[3] as it became known, was mirrored on

*FACTnet.org* and was downloaded by hundreds of thousands of computer users.

Top level Scientologists and their lawyers went ballistic. Armed with civil writs of seizure, the church staged a series of raids to try to shut down the sites of its critics. Federal marshals and local police were ordered to stand by to preserve the peace. Scientology lawyers accompanied by gun-toting private detectives then rummaged through the private homes and personal belongings of church critics in Virginia, Colorado and California.

They seized computers, hard drives, documents and any other potential evidence involving alleged claims of copyright infringement. Wollersheim complained that he was in bed with his girlfriend when the church bashed down his front door. A federal judge in Denver eventually ordered that Wollersheim's belongings be returned to him. Still, the ex-church member complained to reporters that for a period of months, Scientology lawyers had complete access to every word, every memo, every letter, and every email he had ever sent or received. His entire thought life, he says, was under the control of the church.

The World Wide Web was still in its infancy in 1995 when the Scientology squabble made headlines across the world. Most reporters didn't even use email then. TV stations and newspapers were only vaguely familiar with the term "website" and "UseNet." Most media outlets, surprisingly, had little or no Internet or Web presence. But Wollersheim and his associates were Internet pioneers who turned their fight against Scientology into the Web's first genuine scandal. The unintended consequence was that millions of people around the world only became familiar with the Internet because of the Scientology scandal. Some of the controversy and more lurid details of the fight are still memorialized on the Internet in such UseNet chat groups as *Alt.Religion.Scientology*.

Wollersheim eventually won his lawsuit against the church, and still rants about its abuses on *FACTnet.org*. But he says the legal expenses and the mental trauma of the court case far outweigh the amount he was eventually awarded.

Many observers of the case were surprised to learn that a members-only, non-profit outfit like Scientology could waltz unescorted into someone's private home and begin searching through and seizing that homeowner's personal belongings. In the Wollersheim case, *Scientology got that permission from a federal judge.* But across the country, tens of millions of Americans have unwittingly signed real estate documents which essentially give their neighbors the right to trespass and confiscate without any judicial oversight at all. Growing numbers of homeowners are discovering to their dismay that neighborhood covenants far outweigh any rights recognized by the U.S. Constitution. Homeowners have been laid just as bare as Wollersheim found himself on that day in 1995.

## Cults and HOAs: Cut from the Same Cloth?

There are amusing parallels between religious cults and the typical Homeowners' Association. Evaluating such a seemingly ridiculous leap, however, takes a moment of open mindedness on the part of the reader. But consider this: Cult leaders (feared by all members) occasionally release oracles (arbitrary changes in the religion or the CCRs), dictate how members are to live their daily lives (mandatory changes in personal behavior), and then administer harsh punishments (shunning, lawsuits, expulsion) to those who fall short of the "community goal" (permanent state of beigeness).

Cults and the HOA movement are both based on total fictions: the former with its belief in myths like Xenu, the latter with its belief in the myth that an HOA keeps property values high. Both institutions are characterized by capriciousness and a lack of fair and equal treatment of members. Religious cults never have constitutions which protect members from abuse of power. Neither do Homeowners Associations. Ever.

Giving our odd simile one final stretch; America's founding documents are based upon what government is not allowed to do. Homeowners Associations (and cults) are based upon what the members are not allowed to do. Without the Constitutional protection of personal rights, a vacuum is created. Since nature abhors a vacuum, into that void dives a dictatorship, every time. Not even the act of calling an HOA (or cult) a "democracy" will save it from dictatorship by the majority. With the exponential growth of Homeowners Associations, Constitutionalists have little reason for optimism.

The lesson for homeowners here is to approach any non-profit, members-only corporation with caution and with awe. Contracting away one's Constitutional rights can have profound implications not only on personal freedom, but on the psychological and financial well-being of any homeowner or community entering the system. *The power granted to Scientology to raid private homes and seize incredibly private documents is the same power that is granted and can be wielded by the boards of Homeowners Associations, with or without judicial oversight.*

A single election, a single new board member, a single vote cast by the few remaining participants in an increasingly apathetic populace can overturn the balance of a neighborhood and lead to massive changes in the livability or economic viability of a community.

One vote can instantly change the board from passive to punitive, from genteel to rogue. It's frightening to think that the Constitutional protections our founders worked so hard to enact are just one breath away from a reduction to dust. How fragile is our republican way of representative government! How very, very fragile!

There's no safety net, no court of last review, no call to reason through which a community can be protected from caving in upon itself. In a single tragic moment, an entire neighborhood can get branded in the real estate world, and property values can plunge as great numbers of prospective homebuyers decide, "No, I'd rather not live there. I've heard something about them." A brand is a difficult thing to build. The structure of Homeowners Associations does not lend itself to creating and improving brands. No corporation can build a brand while it's tossing around threats to damage or destroy a percentage of its own members. It's hard to think of clinking champagne glasses or wishing one another "Happy Holidays!" in a community where threats of lawsuits are flung about like cow pies.

## Beware the HOA Lawyers

Many HOA boards have been historically lenient and understanding but in recent years, on the advice of their law firms, others have learned to govern with all the subtlety of a sledgehammer. Law firms that specialize in representing HOA boards are increasingly advising clients to litigate even the slightest deviation from covenants with all the ruthlessness of Attila the Hun. "Give 'em a warning," Attila advises. "Then pop them with a lien on their homes. If they don't come around, sell their homes at auction for a couple thousand bucks. Buy them back at auction and slap their equity right back into the HOA's general treasury. No harm, no foul. Smooth as silk."

*Since your shade of gray is one tone lighter than what we approved, we're either going to take your house, or charge you $5000 bucks (including attorneys fees and collection costs).*

*Since your trash can was left out an hour after dark, you'll pay a ten thousand dollar attorney's fee, or lose your house to foreclosure.*

*Since you parked your vehicle on your driveway on August 23$^{rd}$ instead of moving it into the garage, your fine is $3000. Pay it, or we'll lien your house and sell it at auction.*

It happens over and over again.

One great tragedy here is that federal agencies don't investigate this kind of abuse as racketeering. It fits all the classic characteristics of RICO activity. In Scientology, the fallback position is that "we're exempt because we're a religion." In Homeowners Associations, the fallback position is that "every participant willingly signed away his or her access to Constitutional rights in order to join a nice community." That argument has worked for decades for groups like Scientology. But for the HOA movement, there's growing resistance that could someday re-write the social experiment that has led to a massive amount of conflict in America's suburban neighborhoods.

Because understanding this core issue is so important, permit this writer a chance to wade a little deeper into this bug-infested swamp.

## Beware the Developer

Since the early 1960s, homeowners across the country have been blithely surrendering constitutional rights to private real estate developers in exchange for the right to buy into upscale communities where all other residents have mutually agreed to surrender all their rights to the "common good." Developers promise prospective home buyers that the covenants are benign. The covenants, they claim, only exist to keep the occasional homeowner from adding an extra room to the house without first getting permission.

On its face, the trade sounds reasonable. The homeowner gets a vague promise of higher property values in exchange for accepting life under the supervision of a corporate board. The corporation vaguely promises to always be a benevolent dictator. The homeowner contractually agrees never to challenge the dictator's judgment, and also agrees (inevitably buried deep in the fine print) to pay all court costs should any future conflict arise.

Since the original developers have just a single motivation, that of selling all their properties and skidaddling before the ruse is uncovered, they have every interest in looking just as compassionate and accommodating as possible.

"Move to Wild Valley Estates," the deep-voiced radio announcer intones, "where life is good, and your family is safe."

"Look, Mom! There's a deer!" a child exclaims.

What the developers' radio ads never tell prospective homeowners is that when the last home site is sold, the benevolent dictatorship is handed over to a committee of homeowners who now have a different motivation. The new board members are not interested in promoting neighborhood friendliness and selling properties. Their interest is in maintaining the status quo regardless of the net cost to the sense of community. Since that's best done by homogenizing the neighborhood and stifling any sign of dissent or individuality, there's no longer a need for gentle salesmanship or old fashioned neighborliness.

In case after case, HOA boards have adopted the exact ham-fisted authoritarianism the original developers sought to avoid. Instead of dictatorial benevolence, those neighborhoods become what can best be described as heavy-handed fiefdoms.

Still, for a multitude of homeowners, the sacrifice of personal rights in order to "join the cult" seems fair enough. Surrender a few Constitutional rights, pretend they didn't matter to you anyway, live in a nice place, and make a few thousand extra dollars from a future property sale. For those joiners, that sort of personal emasculation has worked well. But growing numbers of others have begun chafing at the bit when they realize how the draconian and arbitrary nature of some HOA boards has become, and how hollow the original promises of financial returns really are.

## Power: the Ultimate Aphrodisiac

As Lord Acton once warned, "Power corrupts, and absolute power corrupts absolutely." And the resulting power of some boards has been devastating to property owners who've lost all their life savings to abusive HOA teams in extremely minor disputes.

The people who rise to the top of Homeowners Association governance are invariably inexperienced at leadership. They are often retired, unemployed or underemployed fellow homeowners who have too much time on their hands. There are few rewards for all the hours of unsalaried work. HOA board members are able to rise to their positions principally because American neighborhoods are massively apathetic in their voting habits.

The typical homeowner who can afford to live in an HOA-controlled environment is generally too busy trying to earn a living to worry about micro-managing the affairs of neighbors. Thus, board members who spend the time it takes to campaign for office are often elected with vote totals that reflect a tiny percentage of the overall community membership. The tragic result is that officers on many HOA boards are at times the least-qualified to serve. Their motives for serving are often suspect.

"Can an attorney who's an HOA board member handle a homeowner's case and be paid by the board at the same time?" asks one member of a California Homeowners' Association who spots an obvious conflict-of-interest.

- In Hallandale Beach, Florida, a contractor and a former board officer were arrested and accused of kickbacks that may have run in the millions of dollars.[4]

- Yet another homeowner complains that the president of his HOA is a former felon who was convicted of taking kickbacks during the Reagan administration.[5]
- Still another raises questions about a past conviction of money laundering and kickbacks by a management company hired by his own HOA.[6]

But the biggest motivation for serving as an HOA board officer, as weird as it seems, may be purely chemical. There's a magnificent intoxication that comes from holding a public office in which one has extreme power over others. Scientists have long known that there are discernible changes in brain chemistry when one human being assumes a dominant position over another. Stimulated neurons in the brain "fire" a sodium ion, which then starts a chain reaction of similar "firings" in adjacent neurons. The resulting chemical, dopamine, is a powerful and addictive stimulant closely paralleling the kinds of brain changes that take place during the act of copulation. It's not unusual, then, for politicians to talk about the achievement of power as "being better than sex."

Even the astute former Secretary of State Henry Kissinger, when asked why a beautiful actress as Marlo Thomas would take up a relationship with someone as homely as he, replied, "Power is an aphrodisiac."[7]

Here's an interesting thought experiment: ask the man who serves as president of the local HOA board if he would trade his two year term on the board for a two year prescription for Viagra.

"You wouldn't trade? No?"

Case closed.

The previous few paragraphs may give you a new way of looking at the male appendage who sits astride a rogue Home-owners Association board. He is not necessarily there because he has, as Scripture calls it, "a servant's heart." He may just have a hard-on. And woe is the homeowner who crosses horns with this animal during the annual rut.

How powerful is an HOA board? Even the President of the United States is constrained by the limits of the Constitution. Senators, Congressmen and Judges are all constrained by the Constitution. Governors, and state legislators are not only constrained by the U.S. Constitution, they also have to abide by all the mandates of their respective state constitutions. Mayors and city councilmen are bound by charters. The lowest trash collector's contract with a municipality contains language about ethics. Each plumber, electrician and framer must abide by building codes and ethical standards.

From the top of government to the bottom, the behavior of each and every human being with any position of power is governed, regulated, overseen, and double-checked with only one exception: the boards of Homeowners Associations. Newly elected board members are often stunned to find out that there are no limits to their powers. Their mandate is to enforce the local covenants which were developed to benefit the original developer, but most boards are given (or often assume) full reign to interpret the rules as they see fit.

Another of Lord Acton's famous quotes: "Great men are almost always bad men."[8]

History and common sense have shown that private corporations are at best, incapable of recognizing the existence of human and Constitutional rights. Few would question that corporations can control such things as speech, behavior and privacy. But the power of a Homeowners Association corporation goes even further. Each board

> **HOA boards know that homeowners have little recourse or way of appealing a capricious decision. It's no wonder that certain people gravitate to leadership on an HOA board. It's Nirvana.**

member is protected by an insurance policy which every home-owner agrees to uphold and finance before any property purchase is ever finalized. HOA residents must hold an offending board member harmless of all liability, in addition to paying for the attorneys' fees on both sides should a future dispute ever arise. In other words, regardless of how outrageous and illegal a board's conduct, a homeowner who has the gall to file a lawsuit is duty-bound to pay the bills, often without regard to which side prevails. For an officer of the board, that is heady power, indeed.

Many Homeowners' Boards would find it difficult or impos-sible to operate if their actions were ever opened to public scrutiny. The official neighborhood newsletter rarely, if ever, honestly explores issues in a dispute. Homeowners are only given one side of a story. They're often mystified at why their board uses community funds to file a lawsuit against some hapless homeowner who leaves his garbage can out an hour after the mandated deadline.

In Communist dictatorships like those in Cuba, China, or the former Soviet Union, all news dissemination is through the government-owned media. Viewpoints that conflict with the official government line have virtually no chance of making their way to the public. American Homeowners Associations enjoy the same luxury. The news is written or approved by the same board members who create the news in the first place. Small town news-papers are often criticized for being beholden to the commercial establishment. But an HOA newsletter is exponentially worse. Despite being financed by mandatory dues, the typical home-owner has no access to explore or read contrarian views. Tragically, the major casualty of "HOA journalism" is truth.

## Importance of the Fourth Estate

In a true representative democracy, elected officials bear a heavy burden to administer justice as fairly and as evenly as possible, primarily because they're subject to constant media scrutiny. Since most of an HOA board's discussions happen away from the eyes and ears of other homeowners, personal corruption, conflicts of interest, and dishonesty are not uncommon. Board members are immune to all but the most heinous of allegations, and criminal indictments of corrupt HOA boards are rare.

A vigorous and independent news media is historically what leads to a just state. In his 1840 treatise, *On Heroes, Hero Worship, and the Heroic in History*, Thomas Caryle wrote:

> Burke said there were Three Estates in Parliament; but, in the Reporters' Gallery yonder, there sat a **Fourth Estate** more important far than they all. It is not a figure of speech, or a witty saying; it is a literal fact,—very momentous to us in these times. Literature is our Parliament too. Printing, which comes necessarily out of Writing, I say often, is equivalent to Democracy: invent Writing, Democracy is inevitable. Writing brings Printing; brings universal everyday extempore Printing, as we see at present. Whoever can speak, speaking now to the whole nation, becomes a power, a branch of government, with inalienable weight in law-making, in all acts of authority. It matters not what rank he has, what revenues or garnitures: the requisite thing is, that he have a tongue which others will listen to; this and nothing more is requisite. The nation is governed by all that has tongue in the nation: Democracy is virtually **there**. Add only, that whatsoever power exists will have itself, by and by, organized; working secretly under bandages, obscurations, obstructions, it will never rest till it gets to work free, unencumbered, visible to all. Democracy virtually extant will insist on becoming palpably extant.[9]

Without a free news media able to assess and criticize, Caryle and Burke told us government is nothing more or less than a tyranny where the worst injustices take place. Sadly, that's the state of many Homeowners Associations today. With occasional exceptions many constitute a complete subversion of justice.

The 18th Century novelist, Henry Fielding further observed:

> None of our political writers ... take[s] notice of any more than three estates, namely, Kings, Lords, and Commons ... passing by in silence that very large and powerful body which form the fourth estate in this community ... The Mob.
>
> Without "the mob," the citizens looking in and inspecting the actions of the Parliament, there was no justice, just a dictator willing to exert power against the people.
>
> With, however, the mob looking in, injustices are exposed, excoriated and laid open for all to see.[10]

So, what are the extremes of an out-of-control Homeowners Association? Although there are too many to count, a case in Texas provides a wonderful example of not only the absurd, but also what happens when public scrutiny is used to peel open the absurd.

KB Home is one of the largest homebuilders in America. Its five billion dollars worth of business and 25,000 new homes a year puts the company squarely on the Fortune 500 list. It's typical of other developers which scrape open a field, plant a thousand homes, require each new resident to sign draconian deed restrictions, sell the remaining few properties, and then leave the local Homeowners Association to its own devices. The CC&Rs (Covenants, Controls and Restrictions) created and imposed by KB Home are widely used as a model by other developers across the nation.

In 2003, Rick Casey, a columnist for the *Houston Chronicle*, caught the homebuilding giant planting some fascinating language in its deed restrictions. In a column headlined: "Buy a

House and Shut Up," Casey noted several clauses which every prospective member of a Homeowners Association should commit to memory:

> No sign of any kind or character, including (a) any signs in the nature of a 'protest' or complaint against Declarant (KB Home) or any homebuilder, (b) or that describe, malign or refer to the reputation, character or building practices of Declarant or any homebuilder, or (c) discourage or otherwise impact or attempt to impact anyone's decision to acquire a lot or residence in the Subdivision shall be displayed to the public view.
>
> Any home builder or their agents shall have the right, without notice, to remove any sign, billboard or other advertising structure that does not comply with the above, and in so doing shall not be subject to any liability for trespass or any other liability in connection with such removal.
>
> The non-payment of such fine can result in a lien against said Lot, which lien may be foreclosed on ... by the Declarant or any Owner in the Subdivision.
>
> Moreover, no Owner may use any public medium such as the 'Internet' or any broadcast or print medium or advertising to similarly malign or disparage the building quality or practices of any homebuilder, it being acknowledged by all Owners that any complaints or actions against a homebuilder or Declarant are to be resolved in a private manner and any action that creates controversy or publicity for the Subdivision or the quality of construction of any homes within the Subdivision will diminish the quality and value of the Subdivision.[11]

Breathtaking. Every person buying into a KB Home neighborhood was essentially forced to sign restrictions that were forever stamped on their deeds that said:

1. You cannot protest poor workmanship on your home.
2. You cannot warn other prospective homeowners about your neighborhood.
3. You cannot stop neighbors from trespassing and removing your belongings.
4. Your home can be seized and sold at auction by any neighbor.
5. You cannot complain in any public forum if you feel you've been raped.

While that last point is probably hyperbole, it doesn't miss the bull's eye by much. In the case of Casey's *Houston Chronicle* article, the proverbial "ship hit the span." Phone calls were made, protests were lodged, and denials were placed in every possible forum.

Spokespeople for KB Home claimed they weren't trying to suppress the free speech rights of any homeowners. They promised to drop all such restrictive covenants in future developments, "It's the right thing to do," they said.[12] But any homeowner who'd already bought into a KB Home property with such restrictions was bound by them.

As Casey noted in his follow-up column in the *Chronicle*, "once subdivisions are built out, enforcement of deed restrictions is turned over to Homeowners Associations. It takes no large stretch of the imagination to foresee an association enforcing it."[13]

Unintended consequences. They can be bizarre.

# 5
# Closer Screwtiny

*The Bible tells us to love our neighbors, and also to love our*
*enemies; probably because they are generally the same people.*
—Gilbert K. Chesterton

T he drive-up approach to the exclusive neighborhood of
Edgewater Point in Westchester County, New York is
memorable. It's one of those unique private communities on the
eastern seaboard that few people get to see in person. A red-tiled
guard shack stands at the neighborhood's only entrance. Just
28 homeowners live on this half mile long spit of land that
juts out into Long Island Sound just offshore from the town of
Mamaroneck. The expansive properties have private swimming
pools, tennis courts and putting greens. The Hampshire Country
Club is just a couple of miles to the north. Twenty miles to the
south across the gleaming waters of Long Island Sound is the
Manhattan skyline.

What are these one-acre homes worth? If you have to ask,
you don't need to know.

The sand spit was developed in the early 20th Century by
railroad baron Henry M. Flagler and the two roads that split
the current neighborhood still bear his name. An advertising
brochure for the community once bore the notation "Peace and
security. Romance and charm. A garden spot in the sea for the
homes of a fortunate few." The current occupants are obviously
men and women of wealth and privilege.

Even among the wildly wealthy, it turns out that common, vulgar neighborhood spats over property lines are nothing new. They boil up tempers and destroy friendships, sometimes even shredding the reputation of a neighborhood forever.

All was quiet in Edgewater Point until the late 1990s when longtime resident Melvyn Kaufman decided that the neighborhood was not following its own HOA regulations. Kaufman was a well-known Manhattan real estate developer. In 1958 he moved into the home at 1320 West Flagler Drive. Kaufman, who had built a number of Manhattan office buildings heralded for their distinctive and innovative designs, knew a thing or two about real estate. He knew how to create and maintain value.

But in his own Edgewater Point neighborhood, Kaufman became disgusted at the number of homeowners who were obviously violating neighborhood covenants that were written into deeds more than 80 years earlier. The covenants required certain types of construction, controls over how property was utilized, and generally tried to maintain the look and feel of a neighborhood. In 1997, Kaufman became a member of the board, where he tried to push his ideas of bringing neighbors into conformity, possibly by hiring a professional management company. His suggestions were repeatedly rejected.

Kaufman even mailed out copies of the covenants to each of the Point's 28 neighbors, reminding them of their responsibilities as Edgewater Point property owners and encouraging them to take action against violators. But other members of the board turned a deaf ear on his complaints. Kaufman was just a troublemaker and a curmudgeon they decided. He ended up quitting the board in frustration.

But that was just the opening round of Kaufman's battle. He began filing a series of lawsuits, one of them against a next-door neighbor who was building a stone pier without the required permit. He then sued the City of Mamaroneck for not taking action against the pier-builder. He sued a neighbor for running an illegal home business, i.e. renting out another property she owned across the street. There were eight lawsuits in all, each one connected in some way with forcing the community to obey its own covenants. The most interesting one filed by Kaufman was against the Edgewater Point Property Owners Association, itself.

Legal beagles everywhere were intrigued. Nowhere in New York could they find case law where a homeowner had sued to force an HOA to become stricter in its enforcement of covenants. It was always the other way around. The lawyers began predicting dire consequences across the country if HOAs could be required to enforce the restrictive covenants written into their deeds.

The community was emotionally split wide open. The anger in Edgewater Point was so thick neighbors said they could feel it on the streets. This "Heaven on the Sound" had become for some a hell-on-earth, especially for homeowners who faced having to pay legal bills for what they thought were Kaufman's frivolous lawsuits.

"They're obligated to enforce these covenants," Kaufman insisted. On the other side, an attorney for the HOA insisted that Homeowners Associations could choose whether or not to take action to enforce restrictions.

Edgewater attorney William H. Mulligan, Jr., argued that the Edgewater Point Property Owners Association had no obligation whatsoever to enforce its own covenants. "There isn't a duty (by the HOA) to sue," Mulligan said. "The Association isn't a police force." Surprisingly, a Westchester County court agreed and dismissed Kaufman's case.

As New York lawyers reviewed Kaufman's lawsuits and his multiple appeals, some observers were troubled. If HOAs were not obligated to make sure homeowners adhered to their deed restrictions, then what motivation did homeowners have to abide by them? If enforcement was completely arbitrary, didn't that give weight to the argument that some HOAs only enforce covenants as a means of harassing certain unwanted homeowners? The Equal Protection clause was enacted as a restraint on government. But when a *de facto* government or a "private government" that's unconstrained by law possesses the power to selectively badger, fine and foreclose, doesn't that create the same injustice writers of the Constitution tried to prevent?

Going one annoying step further, if a black family decided to move into an exclusive white subdivision, could an HOA board swing into action, suddenly deciding that certain covenants had to be enforced to preserve property values? If there is no obligation to enforce, no obligation to enforce equally, and no legal constraint on the purpose or forms of enforcement, at some point could an HOA's actions begin to look a lot like uncontrolled and arbitrary harassment?

With tens of millions of Americans moving into covenant-controlled "private government" compounds, the implications are breathtaking.

## Your Lawn Is Not "First Class Quality"

In early 2002, the Pebble Creek Homeowners Association in New Tampa, Florida went onto the property of members Edward and Billye Simmons at 9769 Fox Hollow Drive, ripped out their lawn and replaced it with new sod, then charged the couple $2212 for the work. Although the Simmons couple owned the home, they were leasing it to Ada Phillips, a single mother of four foster children. Phillips is black.

Pebble Creek had warned the Simmons family that their lawn was not "first-class quality" as mandated by deed restrictions. The lawn, like many others in the neighborhood, had been yellowed by the ongoing drought in the southeast. The HOA claimed it had the right to trespass onto the Simmons property to complete the work. Simmons said the HOA had completely overstepped its bounds and had no right to take the actions it did.

There were other complexities in the case. To replace the lawn, the HOA hired a man who had done previous work for the association. The man was Michael Meggison. At the time, Meggison also happened to be vice president of the Pebble Creek Board. HOA president Michael Carricato denied there was any conflict of interest in hiring a fellow board member to do such work.

"He's been our contractor for seven years. We're happy with the quality of his work."[1]

They must have been. Meggison had done some lucrative work for the association, in one year alone taking in more than $109,000. Edward Simmons was outraged at the unasked-for lawn replacement and refused to reimburse the association. Pebble Creek sued.

A series of stories about the troubled Homeowners' Association was done by *St. Petersburg Times* reporter Michael Van Sickler.[2] There were resignations. There were community protests. Board members and community volunteers resigned or were replaced. Members of the association complained about the massive amount of turmoil and anger among homeowners. But the Pebble Creek lawsuit against Simmons just chugged on through the courts.

In February of 2006, the case against Edward Simmons went to a jury. It ruled that Simmons had to pay the Pebble Creek Association the $2,212 cost of replacing the lawn. The Simmons' legal expenses were well in excess of $100,000. Because the jury granted any kind of victory to Pebble Creek, the Simmons family was also on the hook for another $100,000 to $250,000 in legal fees to cover Pebble Creek's expenses. The Simmons family probably ended up paying up to a half million dollars to protest the new sod that was placed around their home. But justice was done.[3] The jury had spoken. Another American family who had tried to protest HOA injustice was ruined.

## Harassment: the Name of the Game

When Homeowners Associations are involved, some of the bloodiest battles in American life can occur. Two disagreeable neighbors don't generally form a Homeowners Association. But the moment a third neighbor enlists in a corporate agreement, the majority rules. That hammer can be brought down as forcefully and as harshly as necessary against the lone dissenter, and a multitude of homeowners have lost their homes and life savings because the majority simply wanted them gone. At first glance, it almost sounds like a democratic form of self-governance, but in every sense of the word, it's Democracy on steroids. It's fascism, the absolute dictatorship of the majority.

In 2006, a couple living in a four unit townhouse in Jefferson County, Colorado were targeted by three neighbors who decided the couple's smoking habits were intolerable. Colleen and Rodger Suave had purchased their home several years earlier. As lifelong smokers, they had adjusted to society's evolving rules on smoking in public places. But they figured their home was a sanctuary where they could indulge their bad habit. They were wrong. In an attempt to appeal the HOA's action, they took their case to court.

Unfortunately for them, the judge found herself bound to uphold the HOA's covenants. When the Suaves had signed their real estate papers they had unwittingly abandoned any protections of the Constitution, and in fact had handed over their rights to a non-profit HOA corporation.

District Court Judge Lily Oeffler ordered the couple to stop smoking in their town home. They could light up on the sidewalk (about fifteen feet in front of their neighbors' windows) but they couldn't do so in their home. The newly enacted HOA covenant prohibited members from creating a "nuisance," and a majority of members decided to act against this one.

"We never dreamed this kind of thing could happen," the Suaves told reporters. "We've owned this for five years. They didn't even tell us they were voting on a no-smoking rule. How can a homeowners association control your behavior inside your own private home without even telling you about it?" The answer is that it's done all the time. The Suaves admit they were naïve about the power of Homeowners Associations, but they learned an exorbitantly expensive lesson. Don't mess with the HOA.

While the self-righteous, healthy, non-smoking crowd will have no sympathy for the Suave couple, one could replace the word "smoking" with almost any characteristic or behavior and run afoul of an HOA covenant someplace. No redheads. No pickup trucks. No blacks. No Jews. No uttering of passionate sounds during sex. Any behavior, race, relationship, or personal habit that a majority thinks can lower property values can be banned. And those bans can be arbitrarily enforced.

## Can They Really Do That? Oh Yes, They Can

Another odd case appeared in Gunnison County, Colorado at the Red Mountain Ranch Subdivision. The subdivision includes a number of millionaires who've built mansions in the mountains. But one mansion was "too rich" for the other homeowners. The monthly minutes from the meeting of HOA October 4th, 2007 are posted online:

> Angela explained the association had filed a lawsuit against a homeowner for violating the covenants by building a home in excess of the maximum 7,500 square feet. She said the exterior of the house was very similar to the plans submitted to the association but the interior floor plan use had been

changed and the basement was living space instead of the mechanical area approved by the association.

Rod explained that future discussion would focus on how to abate the covenant violation by filling in or blocking off specific areas of the house. He confirmed that it would be possible to bring the house into compliance with the covenants but that penalties and attorney's fees would also be sought.[4]

Translation: the Red Mountain Homeowners Association caught some stupid shmuck trying to secretly finish off his unfinished basement. They sued him, and a possible settlement in the case involved his agreement to "seal off" certain areas of his home. And, of course, he'd be forced to pay all the legal fees.

While the particular individual at the center of the Red Mountain case is not somebody with a stellar reputation in legal circles, the fact that any Homeowners' Association has the power to force an "unwanted" resident to completely seal off certain portions of his home is awesome. This man's home is completely hidden from public view by mountain vegetation and elevation. The actual size and footprint of his home did not increase with his interior work. He was literally finishing his basement. No other property owner could possibly have been impacted. But the interference by his neighbors will cost him tens, possibly hundreds of thousands of dollars. And, he'll have to pay his homeowners association's legal bills which could run into the hundreds of thousands.

Often, in the process of banning supposedly unacceptable residents, the act of community shaming is enough to drive an offending family from their home. There's no Homeowners' Bill of Rights. Each owner of each housing unit has signed a clause in his or her real estate papers that essentially acknowledges that the will of the corporation supplants any rights the homeowner might think he has under the U.S. Constitution. When a contract is signed with a Homeowners Association, the new homeowner has for all intents and purposes contracted away and surrendered any claim to traditional legal justice.

Many new homeowners have been stunned to discover how powerful those contracts are, and how easily a property owner can be legally libeled, slandered, sliced and diced. Countless homeowners have lost lawsuits, life savings, and reputations because of an inadvertent breach of some obscure rule that would never be imposed in a non-covenant controlled neighborhood. Others have lost their homes simply because an HOA board decided to enact a new rule far outside the scope of the original covenants. Those invasive, arbitrary rules have the same force of law as the ones recorded in the initial deeds.

## A Kiss Is Just a Kiss

One well-publicized and oft-quoted case involves a woman in a condominium association in Santa Ana, California. According to most accounts, Helen Garrett was shocked when she learned that her association had distributed a notice to her neighbors that accused her of "...kissing and doing bad things for over an hour..." in her car in the driveway of her condominium unit. It warned her about significant fines if she was caught engaging in such behavior in the future.

While most people might have enormous admiration for a 51 year old grandmother's ability to love life in any seat of any vehicle, the allegation was ugly and Garrett was appropriately fuming. She threatened a slander suit and scurried for a lawyer. The story was picked up by several national newspapers and run ad nauseum. Eventually, the association acknowledged it had misidentified Garrett and apologized, theoretically ending the dispute. But it failed to end her anger, it failed to pay her legal bills, and failed to prevent the story from being published and re-published by many authors many years later.

Helen Garrett may actually have gotten off easy. Had she taken an emotional distress lawsuit to trial she most likely would have lost, after spending hundreds of thousands of dollars. Association boards are invariably defended by a multi-billion dollar insurance industry that specializes in quashing lawsuits by homeowners. Garrett would have been hit with even more outrageous allegations, this time by HOA insurance attorneys whose behavior during the trial process is immune to legal action.

The discovery process in an emotional distress lawsuit against an HOA is one of the ugliest, most vexing things that can ever befall a human being. Garrett, had she pursued her case, would have been asked under oath about her sexual habits, her affairs, she would have been forced to identify past partners, describe her drug and medication use, her medical records, her confidential discussions with intimate friends, pastor or advisors. Her employer would have been subpoenaed to produce Garrett's personnel file, testify about Garrett's personal habits at work, attractions to co-workers. Garrett's previous sex partners would have been ordered to testify as well.

To complete the destruction of her character by HOA insurance lawyers, depositions containing marvelously lurid questions, allegations and personal details would have been well-circulated among her neighbors. Those depositions, no matter how despicable or slanderous, are all public record and can't be suppressed. The HOA and its attorneys would have turned her case into salacious neighborhood pornography. And the lawyers who carried out the final injuries to her reputation would have had complete immunity. The people who actually did the worst damage to her character would have been well-paid and left unscathed.

In the end, Garrett would have been outspent by the HOA insurance lawyers. The absolute last objective in the process would have been a determination of the unfairness of the original HOA slander. The goal, although attorneys won't generally admit it, would have been to bleed her finances, savage her reputation, finally offering a paltry settlement to end her misery.

Or it could have been worse. Had a judge or jury ruled that Helen Garrett had not proven her case against the HOA, the insurance company lawyers would have filed a lien against Garrett's home to pay the HOA's legal expenses. As unbelievable as it sounds, the covenants most homeowners sign when they buy property and move into an HOA require the homeowner to pay the HOA's lawyers if a damage claim is not proven. Helen Garrett, just by trying to protect her reputation, would have been eviscerated.

Finally, the destruction of Helen Garrett's reputation would have been memorialized in every legal seminar, on websites, in books and magazines, and waved in the faces of future home-owners who might deign to file a lawsuit against the excesses of an out-of-control HOA. It's a heavy hammer, indeed.

Garrett's "kissing and doing bad things" horror was in 1991. Twenty years later, Homeowners Associations are still pulling outrageous stunts and slandering often innocent members. Entire insurance companies and law firms have grown up around the specialty of foreclosing on homes where the owners have committed minor infractions of HOA rules.

## When a Public Shaming Backfires

Disputes in Homeowners Associations run the gamut, each one sounding more outrageous than the last. In December of 2006, Lisa Jenson lived in the Loma Linda development near Pagosa Springs, Colorado. To celebrate the holidays she hung up a Christmas wreath outside her door. The wreath was innocuous enough, but two little evergreen branches in the center turned the wreath into what looked for all the world like a peace symbol out of the 1960s. Jensen insists the peace symbol had no special meaning beyond the fact that she favored world peace.

A couple of Jensen's neighbors, however, decided this Christmas wreath was one of the most evil things ever inflicted on the good people of the Loma Linda Homeowners Association. A few even speculated it was at the least anti-war, unpatriotic, and at the most, some kind of secret symbol of witchcraft.

HOA president Bob Kearns ordered Jensen to remove the wreath immediately, or face fines of $25 dollars a day. She was miffed, and swore she wouldn't knuckle under to a knuckle head. Word of the incident began spreading among other residents in the area. A local newspaper picked up the story, then the national media. Across the country, outrage against Kearns and his Homeowners Association began growing. Phone calls poured in, photographers showed up at Jensen's door to take pictures of the offending wreath.

Other families in Loma Linda and Pagosa Springs started fashioning and displaying peace-sign Christmas wreaths on their own homes. At one point, there was even a downtown parade of people protesting the harsh and nonsensical harassment by the HOA. As the story was repeated, Bob Kearns and the Loma Linda Homeowners Board became community laughing stocks, the butt of jokes on national talk shows, and subjects of coverage on the news wires.

"It was all a misunderstanding," a letter from Kearns finally said, in a transparent attempt to disentangle himself. The Homeowners Association board resigned in embarrassment. Jensen's growing fine was dismissed.

Linda Jensen's well-timed use of the news media was, if not a stroke of genius, at least lucky. The HOA had tried to shame her with her obvious impudence and wickedness and had every intention of ultimately costing her thousands of dollars. But when the media painted a bull's eye on the buttocks of Jensen's neighbors, it was a perfect example of the Law of Unintended Consequences at work.

The firestorm over Linda Jensen's alleged lack of patriotism was not unique. Other homeowners around America have found themselves being fined and sued over their own acts of "extreme" patriotism. After the terrorist attacks on New York and Washington on September 11, 2001 and during the subsequent wars in Iraq, Afghanistan, many homeowners began flying American flags to show their support of U.S. troops fighting overseas. Flying "Old Glory" is about as old as Betsy Ross's Philadelphia Upholstery Company. It would take a stretch of imagination to think that anyone's display of the Red, White and Blue would be considered an illegal act of political heresy.

Homeowners Associations have waged war against any member who dared show an American flag in public. "Un-American! Offensive!" these HOAs declared. "Displaying the American flag is an unconscionable violation of covenants! It brings down property values! Besides, the colors aren't on the list of approved "earth tones!"

One homeowner after another was hit. Letters of warning, daily fines, and lawsuits were *de rigueur* for HOAs everywhere. In fact, from the numbers of neighborhood disputes over American flags, one might even think they rank higher than barking dogs as a source of community outrage.

In Georgia's Avery Park Community Association, homeowner Roy Johnson noticed that the State Legislature had passed a law called "The Freedom to Display the American Flag Act." The 2005 law prohibited neighborhood associations from outlawing the flag. In a show of patriotism, Johnson put up a 20 foot flagpole in his front yard and hoisted the Colors.

"I have family members in the Armed Forces," Johnson told reporters. "My dad was in Vietnam; my grandfather was in World War II. I'm extremely patriotic."

Avery Park's law firm hit Johnson with a letter saying he was going to be fined 25 dollars for every day the flagpole was in his yard. The issue was not his display of the American flag; it was the construction of the pole. Johnson tried in vain to negotiate with his Homeowners Association, but he was told the matter was non-negotiable. The new state law prohibiting flag bans didn't happen to mention flagpoles, so Avery Park and its lawyers decided residents should only be allowed to fly flags from angular porch brackets.

"I'll take this all the way to the Supreme Court," Johnson said.

HOA lawyers must have salivated. Such an appeal could have eventually cost hundreds of thousands of dollars, Johnson would have more than likely been outspent by insurance attorneys, and the Atlanta-based Weinstock & Scavo law firm would have been in a position to foreclose on Johnson's home to cover its legal fees. Johnson wisely chose to accept a confidential settlement even though it severely restricted his flag-flying rights.

Florida's Village Walk Homeowners Association was another HOA where a flagpole prohibition was enforced by a militant HOA. After Governor Jeb Bush signed a law prohibiting heavy-handed anti-flag rules, Mary and Jeff Gardner put up a 15 foot pole in their yard. They, too, got a letter saying they were being assessed daily fines by their neighbors. After word leaked to the press, fifty people, many of them veterans, gathered to stage a public protest against the Village Walk board. The story garnered even more coverage by television and print media.

Association president Paul Feuer showed up to try to interfere with the protestors in an effort to get across the HOA's point of view. Again he said, "It's not the flag, it's the pole," leaving protestors pondering two things: why would any homeowner ever want to buy a property in Village Walk? Second: why would anyone want to be an HOA president?

## Sue, Sue, Sue

Being heavy-handed and ham-fisted is almost a prerequisite for getting elected to the board of a Homeowners Association. Around the country in neighborhood after neighborhood, lawsuits are threatened, filed or provoked. One study estimated that three-quarters of all neighborhood associations are involved in active lawsuits at any one time. Some of the lawsuits can only be categorized as beyond bizarre.[5]

In 2006, Pamela McMahon of Long Beach, California, was forced out of her home by a condo association, whose rules mandated that when a resident takes a dog through the lobby of the condominium, the dog must be carried. It could not be walked on a leash. Because McMahon was elderly and got around only with the assistance of a cane, she was unable to carry her cocker spaniel through the lobby.

Her explanations about her disability fell on deaf ears. The association began assessing daily fines against McMahon whenever she traveled through the lobby with her dog. In frustration, she finally moved from the building. The association and its attorneys won.[6]

An even more bizarre quandary: would a Homeowners Association actually file a lawsuit against a seven year old child for some offense against neighborhood fascism? Without even a hint of sarcasm or satire, the answer here would be "yes." One such legal assault was launched by Colorado's Ken Caryl Ranch Homeowners Association against a little girl named Brianna Kuck and her mother Nancy. The details are almost too painful to discuss.

Little Brianna was concerned about a family of ducks that would occasionally waddle across a busy road that cuts through the neighborhood. She did what any responsible (and adorable) seven year old girl would do. She hand-lettered a sign that read "Caution, Baby Duck Crossing."

In many neighborhood associations, children are about as welcome as ticks on a picnic blanket, and this precocious youngster prompted an allergic response by the HOA that could rival any arachnid bite on earth. No anaphylactic kit here. No, the solution was a huge fine by the community and a vow to take Brianna and her mom to court.

"Ken Caryl hates baby ducks? And little girls?" the media cawed.

"It's too late," said Dave McMahon, president of the Ken Caryl Homeowners Association. "If we let one person put up a sign, then more people will want to put up signs. The Kucks will have to pay a thousand dollar fine. If they don't pay, we can place a lien against their home."

Lawyers were hired, thousands of dollars were spent. In the intense glare of the media spotlight, an embarrassed Ken Caryl came up with a compromise of sorts. Brianna could put up her sign on rare occasions when ducks were actually present. But the ultimate loser was a neighborhood that now has a reputation for stirring up HOA rage, and savaging the innocence of seven year old children.

Across the country, Homeowners Associations are battling a crime wave of unprecedented proportions. The perpetrators are generally young, ranging in age from five to ten. The illegal substance they're peddling to unsuspecting neighbors and friends is lemonade. HOA after HOA has forbidden the practice, and they're not above using strong-arm tactics to wipe out the illicit trade.

Should you fall for the argument that the above paragraph is hyperbole, then we'll name a few of the actual "criminals": Jessica and Kayla Cohen of North Palm Beach, Florida, and

Megan Jensen of Bella Veranda Homeowners' Association in Las Vegas, Nevada. While there's really no room for five and six year-olds in local jails, the youngsters' parents are no doubt being pursued for allowing their children to cross the HOA's line-in-the-sand. After all, many HOAs across the country have strict rules against anyone operating a home business.

Tragically, wonderful days of childhood innocence have been forever impaled on the javelin point of political correctness. There's no sadder existence than one without a real childhood. In the new atmosphere of structured HOA life, allowing a kid to set up a sidewalk lemonade stand is almost tantamount to hiring Charles Manson to run the neighborhood day care.

Nancy and Brianna Kuck hold the "duck crossing" sign that got them fined by Colorado's Ken Caryl Homeowner's Association. They say it was a bitter experience for both of them. Inset picture shows Brianna at a much more innocent age.
—photo by author

The obvious violation of covenants would cause fur to fly, the accusations to be hurled. Sooner or later, some black-booted, self-righteous board member with a Himmler hiss would slap the kid's parents with a cease-and-desist order, lawsuits would be threatened, the official shaming would begin in the monthly newsletter, and the board meetings would excoriate the offending family. When pundits and philosophers start pondering the why's and wherefore's of the loss of innocence, the answers are probably a little bit more tragic than most listeners would like to hear.

Life evolves, of course, and the only thing that never changes is change. Still, one can't help but mourn the loss of childhood simplicity. If, indeed, there are "many mansions" in whatever kingdom exists after life passes on, then God may have a spider-infested crawl space reserved for those who've spoiled childhood innocence.

## Afford It or Die, Paint It or Pay

The heartlessness of some HOAs knows no bounds. But many's the homeowner who's learned of the blood-in-the-water phenomenon when community mores are violated. At 69, Doris Vieregg must have felt so when she was confronted by the Colorado Highlands Ranch Homeowners' Association. She had been recently widowed and was struggling to keep up with bills. The HOA threatened a lawsuit against her saying she was in violation of covenants because her house had not been recently painted. There's probably no question her house needed paint. There's probably no question she was outside of accepted neighborhood standards. The painting had to be done. But the letter from Highlands Ranch offered only two options: either paint the house or pay 7000 dollars.

"It's not that I ever said I don't want to do it, it's that I can't afford to do it," she told reporters.

After stories in the local media, Doris got her champion. Two Colorado business owners stepped forward and told the widow not to worry; they'd take care of the house painting for free. The Mark IV Painting Company showed up with ladders and employees to handle the work. The Diamond Vogel Paint Company offered to donate the supplies. Somewhere in Heaven, there may even be a reward for the kinds of people who come forward to help widows in times of distress or persecution. Perhaps here on Earth, these two companies will get also get some extra business because they helped out a widow who was being threatened with ruination by her neighbors.

Theoretically, that should have been the happy ending. But the legal process against Doris Vieregg continued.

"I thought that was the end of it and I thought I had been embarrassed and humiliated enough," said Vieregg. It wasn't over. The Highlands Ranch Community Association said Doris Vieregg still owed either $450 in legal fees and fines, or the threatened lawsuit would stand.

Colorado is a state with a long history of self-reliant pioneers. In days of old, where communities actually worked together for the common good, a case like Vieregg's would have had a far different conclusion. A small crowd of neighbors would have quietly gathered on a Saturday morning, the crowd would have made repairs on the widow's house, caulking and painting and replacing damaged trim. By evening, the men would have finished all the work on the house, while the women were spreading out red and white checkered tablecloths over makeshift picnic tables.

As the men put down their paintbrushes, they would all have been seated together, a prayer would have been offered, and the workers would have eaten their fill of salad and fried chicken while listening to the warm-up strains of a dance band. Then, over beer and wine, the workers and their families would have begun singing and dancing, and partying as another neighbor's home was saved. They would have celebrated well into the evening, while a grateful widow thanked the Good Lord for her neighbors.

But times have changed, *times have changed*. Under the new paradigm, neighbors are your enemies, not your friends. And the presence of a dance band would probably have led to yet another fine, one for creating a public nuisance.

## Your Neighbor Ain't Your Friend

Increasingly, bloggers, talk show hosts, commentators and news agencies are beginning to take note of some of the more egregious actions of Homeowners Associations. In July of 2008, syndicated radio talk show host Neal Boortz took a well-aimed gut-punch at the management company of the Little Suwanee Pointe Subdivision in Lawrenceville, Georgia in a post entitled "Homeowner's Associations—Gotta Love 'Em":

> Another wonderful tale of a homeowner's association. Don't you just love them? How in the world do home and condo owners so often seem to manage to select the most power-hungry and irrational neighbors to serve on these boards? Could it be because the more sane homeowners want nothing to do with the association and wouldn't run for office if the perks included a private plane? So often we find the people serving on these boards are petty little people who have never wielded any power their entire lives and are now enjoying the experience, or just the opposite—people who were powerful at one time, lost that power and now miss it.[7]

Boortz then included a copy of a letter written to a homeowner by the Liberty Community Management Company, warning the homeowner that he had just fourteen days to stop his dog from urinating on his lawn:

Robert XXXXXXX
2425 xxxxxxx Court
Lawrenceville, GA 30043

Monday, July 28, 2008

Re: Violations at Little Suwanee Pointe Subdivision—Notice 1: Warning of Violations

Dear Robert,
As you may know, the goal of Liberty Community Management and your HOA is to enforce the covenant standards for the Little Suwanee Pointe subdivision set in place by your Homeowners Association, maintaining your property value and the overall appearance of the neighborhood. Please be advised, the following violations were noted at your property:

> It has been reported that your dog has been allowed to urinate on your lawn, causing the lawn to be destroyed. Pets should not be allowed to urinate on the grass and should be directed to an area where there is no turf such as in pine straw beddings. We hope to have pet stations installed within the community in the near future to try and resolve this issue.
>
> Please address the above issues before your next community drive-through, which is scheduled in approximately fourteen (14) days. Thank you for your cooperation with your HOA in their efforts to maintain the covenant standards in your community. If you are in need of a copy of your governing documents,

please visit our website at www.Libertycm.com. If we
can assist you in providing any information regarding
your community covenants or you have questions
regarding your violations, do not hesitate to contact
us using the information below.

Regards,
Compliance Department
Liberty Community Management, Inc.
P.O. Box 2082, Loganville, GA 30052
(770) 466-6331—Violations@LibertyCM.com[8]

The stunning thing to keep in mind as one reads the so-called
"Nazi-gram" to this homeowner is that he most likely can face
fines of thousands of dollars, and eventual foreclosure of his
house should he not re-grow his grass within the two weeks
mandated by this HOA. There is no neutral court-of-appeal, no
objective hearing process. Should the immediate corrections not
be made to the subjective liking of the HOA board, this homeowner could be yet another to lose his dream home in his beige
covenant-controlled community.

There's no shortage of nightmare stories involving actions
against homeowners by their boards. But one case was so bizarre
it was featured on the Paul Harvey show on October 8, 2008. It
produced an avalanche of websites and outraged blog posts.
One blogger even posted the home phone number of the HOA
president whose actions caused the controversy.

The story was first published in the *Seattle Times* and the
*Tri-City Herald*, and involved the Oak Hill Country Estates
Homeowners Association in Kennewick, Washington. Oak Hill
is a new development of 47 lots, most of them still in the possession of developer Chick Edwards. His family first homesteaded
the property in the early 1900s, and Edwards is now trying to

sell off the property as two-and-a-half acre lots. He has created a Homeowners Association, and like other real estate developers, he requires each buyer to sign extensive HOA covenants and deed restrictions.

In 2007, a new resident to the neighborhood was Burke Jensen, an employee at Energy Northwest. Burke is also a U.S. Navy reservist, and a few months after he moved in, he was activated to serve with his military unit in Kuwait. Because his wife was pregnant at the time, she and the couple's young son went to stay with other family members on the East Coast until her baby was delivered. Their Kennewick home would be unoccupied until one or the other of them returned.

In the Fall of 2008, Edwards notified Lt. Jenson that he was in violation of the HOA covenants which demanded that all land-scaping be completed within a year of the certificate of occupancy. Jenson's landscaping plans, of course, had been interrupted by his sudden activation to Kuwait, but he was warned that he was about to face a lawsuit by the HOA.

When news of the story broke, Edwards, the developer, told reporters, "I don't give a [expletive] where he is or what his problem is. I still own (these properties), so I am the Home-owners Association. This clown gets to do what he wants, and I'm as mad as hell."[9]

Jensen's attorney informed Edwards that the Federal Service Members Civil Relief Act makes it illegal to take any civil action while a member of the Armed Forces was overseas on active military duty.

But the developer may be able to take action in another way. In Lt. Jensen's absence, the officer wanted to try to find a tenant who would rent the house until his family could return. It would help cover the mortgage payments, of course. Chick Edward's response was that the HOA covenants prohibit any commercial use of the house. "He doesn't get to rent it."[10]

# 6

# "We're Lawyers and You're Stupid"

*I don't think you can make a lawyer honest by an act of*
*legislature. You've got to work on his conscience. And his*
*lack of conscience is what makes him a lawyer.*

—Will Rogers

Snatching land that belongs to someone else is at least as old as the written word. From the time of the ancient Exodus, the Israelites were warned by Jehovah against taking someone else's property:

*Do not move the ancient boundary stone set up by your forefathers.*
—Proverbs 22:28

And again:

*Cursed is he who removes the ancient boundary stone.*
—Deuteronomy 27:17

Yet again in the Ten Commandments:

*Thou shalt not covet thy neighbor's house, thou shalt not covet*
*thy neighbor's wife, nor maid servant, nor his ox, nor his ass, nor*
*any thing that is thy neighbor's.*
—Exodus 20:27

It seems that God, Himself (or at least, Moses), laid down the law about respecting the historic property rights of others.

## Land Takings: Yes, They're Legal

While Moses was apparently Mankind's first lawyer, he kept things pretty simple. There's not much in the Ten Commandments that's difficult to understand. But in bringing such a magnificent document down from the mountain, he created an age-old profession of solicitors who can interpret, rationalize, justify and argue all 31 flavors of murder, theft, blasphemy and adultery.

The legal profession thrives on making the simple complex. It also seems to have a bottomless grab-bag of ways to twist the old wisdom and game the system, all on billable hours of course. In the view of many people, modern civil law has less to do with protection of personal rights than with carving up someone else's property for personal gain. Many people believe the American legal profession, because of its long history of arbitrarily and intentionally damaging the innocent for profit, is in desperate need of an ethical and moral overhaul.

The profession could never survive without its ability to take another's property by whatever means necessary. Grabbing land, moving the boundary stone, is the profession's stock in trade.

Some of the more extreme legal land-grabs go by such diverse names as eminent domain, and non-judicial foreclosure. One such case of overreaching happened on the eastern seaboard in the early 1990s. The last name of the plaintiff is a familiar one in that part of the country and possibly deserves a short ancestral history.

South Carolina is married to its Colonial past. In some towns, among the more common names in the phone book are "Lucas," "Cotesworth" and "Pinckney." The names and the history go back to the early 1700s when 16-year-old Eliza Lucas was turned loose by her British father, Lt. Col. George Lucas, to take control of the family's three plantations. As a self-taught botanist, this young teenager began experimenting with the production of indigo. In fact, after she shared her newfound knowledge of the process with fellow Carolinians, indigo became the south's second largest export, bringing a fortune into the southern states.

Eliza Lucas (later Eliza Lucas-Pinckney) apparently didn't mind bucking the establishment and taking extremely unpopular actions. She was among the first who insisted that slaves be permitted to learn to read. She personally tutored several of her father's slaves so they could become teachers themselves and educate the children of other slaves. So important were her contributions to the foundling republic that when she died in 1793, George Washington asked to be one of her pallbearers.

Another branch of the family, Jonathon Lucas I and his son, Jonathon II, invented and improved the rice mill. This invention, too, had a major role in building the southern states into an agricultural powerhouse. Thomas Jefferson signed the original parchment patent for the device. Two hundred fifty years later, a descendant of the Lucas clan helped shake up the establishment in another way. His contribution to society was to attack one of the most odious provisions of law; the ability of a government agency to arbitrarily confiscate the property of a private citizen without compensation.

"Eminent domain" is sometimes said to be one of the most misused and abused principles in American law. The idea that the "King" can expropriate private land for his own personal use goes back more than a thousand years. The Magna Carta attempted to ameliorate that damage by requiring an immediate payment for property seized by the King. But in ensuing centuries, the rights of landowners under English common law were subject to continuing erosion.

The applicable concept was, "If the King needed the land, you didn't." It was a frequent exasperation for American colonists, for example, to be permanently escorted off their land by the British government, with no compensation whatsoever. So when fore-father James Madison began stitching together the Constitution's Bill of Rights, he tried to limit the ability of the government to seize land from private citizens in the 5th Amendment:

> No person shall be… deprived of… property, without due process of law; nor shall private property be taken for public use, without just compensation.[1]

Under Madison's vision, there existed a limited ability for government to seize property *for public use*, but only *for public use* and only after *just compensation* was paid. Bureaucrats from the most powerful federal gorilla to the lowest HOA prosimian have been trying to chisel away at those protections ever since. A 20th Century court victory by a South Carolinian named David H. Lucas shook bars on the cages of a lot of primates.

## He Won, But He Lost

In 1986, David Lucas (no direct relationship to this author) bought himself a couple of vacant beachfront building lots on the Isle of Palms, one of the barrier islands. He planned to build two homes. At the time there were no restrictions against building there, and in fact the residential neighborhood was well established.

Two years after his purchase, the South Carolina Legislature enacted the "Beachfront Management Act." Despite the fact that Lucas's two lots were in the middle of a row of expensive water-front homes, Lucas was told he no longer had the right to build on his property. His two lots, for which he had paid 975,000 dollars, were rendered essentially worthless. Without the ability to obtain a building permit, their only value at this point was to improve the view for a couple of Lucas's millionaire neighbors.

The two lots owned by David Lucas on the Isle of Palms are on each side of the "cube house" in the center of the photo. Once Lucas was ready to build, the State of South Carolina decided that Lucas's lots were "unbuildable."
—photo courtesy of Prof. William A. Fischel, Dartmouth College

David Lucas (shown with beard) returns to the area years later. He says his court costs were three times what the land was worth. He says, "You can't really beat the government. It just spends you to death."
—photo courtesy of Prof. William A. Fischel, Dartmouth College

Lucas, pointing to the Fifth Amendment prohibition against uncompensated government "takings," asked the state to reimburse him for what amounted to an "inverse condemnation." The message to him by the system was essentially, "Get lost."

Lucas sued, claiming that the government had rendered his property valueless and that the action by the state agency was unconstitutional. A state court agreed, and awarded him 1.2 million dollars. The case was, of course, appealed. The South Carolina Supreme Court reversed it, essentially again telling Lucas to "Get lost." In the initial Beachfront Management Act, the legislature had determined that any "new construction in the coastal zone threatened a valuable public resource," therefore Lucas's plans to build two new homes in a row of previously existing houses amounted to "a harmful or noxious use." As such, the state felt Lucas didn't have to be compensated under the Fifth Amendment's takings clause.[2]

Lucas, with the assistance of Charleston attorney Jerry Finkel, appealed the case to the U.S. Supreme Court. This time, he won on every point and the U.S. Supreme Court for all intents and purposes told the State of South Carolina to "Get lost."[3] By a 6-3 vote, the state was ordered to compensate Lucas for taking his land.

Through five separate courts, Lucas finally "won" his victory against the system. Lucas said later that the victory was pyrrhic, which was a massive understatement.[4] Through the wonders of the American system of justice, Lucas was forced to spend three million dollars trying to recoup his original one million. In a case where South Carolina was ordered to make a victim whole again, this injured victim was taken to the cleaners over and over. Lucas discovered, like many other targets of land theft, that the "just compensation" clause in the Fifth Amendment has been rendered largely meaningless by the legal system.

The odds are massively stacked against the victim of a government land-grab. There's really no true way to obtain "just compensation" for the financial, mental, emotional, physical and spiritual anguish from such a run-in with government. This kind of battle is beyond true healing. The time spent worrying, the hours of sleep lost, can never be compensated.

One major hitch in the Lucas case was that the court noted the loss of value to his property was total. As long as Lucas still had the right, say, to pitch a tent on his property (in the words of one Justice), his loss would not have been total and he probably would not have won any compensation at all. Had some lower court along the way ruled that the amount of Lucas's loss was only 95 percent, he could well have lost the entire case.

In fact, this apparent loophole in the Supreme Court decision is almost a roadmap for government exploitation in the future. Leave the victim with five percent of his property value, and the uncompensated land-grab can go forward.

In a sad but predictable footnote to the whole Beachfront Management debacle, the State of South Carolina did not return the property to Lucas. It did not continue to insist that there was great public concern in preventing construction of new homes on the Lucas lots because of some perceived noxious and dangerous use of his property. In fact, the state finally decided that the best use of the two beachfront lots was actually for the construction of private homes. It sold Lucas's land to a brand new developer who built his own home on one of Lucas's former properties.[5] The irony was massive. The slap-in-the-face was obvious.

"He got a great deal," said David Lucas.

## Take from the Poor, Give to the Rich

Although the Lucas case provided a slight respite from abusive takings by government, a Supreme Court decision thirteen years later allowed the government to go in an opposite and far more breathtaking direction. This case was called *Kelo vs. City of New London*. Instead of taking a property for "public use," the new case seized private property for the **"public purpose"** of turning it over to a private developer.

The so-called "public purpose" was to raise the local tax base and thereby increase the amount of collectible taxes. Certainly, eminent domain has been used to clear blighted areas in the past, but the Kelo case didn't involve blight. It did amount, though, to the state becoming a "reverse Robin Hood," taking from the poor to give to the rich.

At first, the Kelo case just looked like an everyday garden variety land-grab. The City of New London, Connecticut, was in economic decline in the late 1990s. Many of New London's neighborhoods were depressed; people were moving out, the tax base was declining. City fathers were thrilled when the Pfizer Corporation, the pharmaceutical giant, proposed building a huge commercial facility in the older, lower-income Fort Trumbull neighborhood. Some of the homeowners there were not quite as enthusiastic.

New London began buying out the neighborhood's approximately 115 property owners to make way for huge resort hotel and conference center. The developer also planned to build lavish new retail and residential space. The tax benefit to the city was obvious. The benefit to the private developer was that he'd be offered cheap land, which would rapidly be transformed into one of the wealthier parts of the state. Homeowners in the area saw it another way. They were in disbelief that their homes could actually be seized and turned over to a private developer just because future property use might generate higher taxes. Fifteen of the property owners led by plaintiff Susette Kelo filed suit.

Ralph and Susette Kelo had purchased their little salmon pink home near the corner of East Street and Trumbull in 1997. A year later a real estate agent came to their door asking them to sell the home. When Kelo refused, the agent warned her that the city planned to condemn her property under eminent domain and that Kelo and her family stood to lose everything. Unbeknownst to Kelo, the agent was actually a representative from New London who'd been hired to begin clearing out remaining homeowners to make way for the private developer.

"Give up. The government always wins," the agent told her.[6]

Kelo and the handful of neighbors decided to fight. They held community meetings, they wrote protest letters, they appeared before the city council. They filed a lawsuit which ultimately became the 2005 Supreme Court eminent domain case that shocked the nation. In a 5-4 decision, the U.S. Supreme Court ruled that private land could indeed be legally seized on behalf of a private developer.

Susette Kelo, standing in front of her "little pink house." The City of New London, Connecticut, seized a neighborhood of more than 100 homes under eminent domain and bulldozed them to turn them over to the pharmaceutical giant, Pfizer. The drug giant planned to build a huge convention facility which the city felt might bring in more tax revenue, a decision that dismayed property rights advocates. Pfizer never built its project and the land still stands vacant. Pfizer faced unrelated legal troubles and ended up pleading guilty to civil and criminal charges and paying the largest criminal settlement in American history.
—photo courtesy of Institute for Justice

The "public use" clause in the Fifth Amendment could be construed, according to the court, as a "public purpose." Because the city's tax base would be increased by the new development, the public was the beneficiary, the purpose was fulfilled, therefore the land grab was legal. But even a cursory look at the decision shows that almost any property could be seized at any time by any public entity for any purpose.

In the minority dissent, Supreme Court Justices Sandra Day O'Connor and Clarence Thomas expressed dismay at the majority's ruling. O'Connor wrote:

> Any property may now be taken for the benefit of another private party, but the fallout from this decision will not be random. The beneficiaries are likely to be those citizens with disproportionate influence and power in the political process, including large corporations and development firms.[7]

Justice Thomas was even more disappointed.

> Something has gone seriously awry with this Court's interpretation of the Constitution…. Allowing the government to take property solely for public purposes is bad enough, but extending the concept of public purpose to encompass any economically beneficial goal guarantees that these losses will fall disproportionately on poor communities. Those communities are not only systematically less likely to put their lands to the highest and best social use, but are also the least politically powerful.
>
> If such "economic development" takings are for a "public purpose," any taking is, and the Court has erased the Public Use Clause from our Constitution.[8]

Constitutionalists across the country were also stunned. Was it really possible that government had suddenly subsumed that much power, and that the right to own a piece of ground was just a mirage? The reinterpretation of property rights so that they existed up until public purpose was invoked, essentially meant that no citizen had an unfettered right to own property. With a little imagination, a "public purpose" could be established for seizing anyone's land at any time. The Court decision amounted to one of the most massive government power grabs in two hundred years. The complete cancellation of the right to own property was chilling.

The Kelo case cemented the legality of seizing a homeowner's property on behalf of a private interest. Again, a reminder of the wording of the U.S. Constitution's Fifth Amendment:

> No person shall be... deprived of... property, without due process of law; nor shall private property be taken for public use, without just compensation.[9]

Despite the "just compensation" clause, the Kelo family lost everything. Their neighbors lost everything. And the voice of the City of New London's secret agent who showed up at the Kelo doorstep will echo forever, "Just give up. The government always wins." Put another, probably more appropriate way, the citizen always loses. Even if an attempted government taking is an abject failure and is eventually overturned by the courts, by the time a citizen's case is heard he or she has invariably been spent into oblivion. The citizen who beats City Hall has a difficult time healing the battle scars. Just give up. The U.S. Constitution doesn't say what school children are taught it says.

The protection against arbitrary government "takings" was nice while it lasted. More than anything else, the right to own a piece of property was the glue that kept our society hanging together for 230 years. But change happens. It's the only unchanging fact of life.

Kelo and her neighbors suffered one final indignity, compliments of the City of New London. It was sort of a parting shot at the mostly elderly residents who had fought the seizing and razing of their homes. New London informed them they would each be hit with a bill for five years worth of back rent, dating back to the moment that the City had first offered to take their homes under eminent domain.

For her part, Susette Kelo has continued her fight against what she believes is extreme abuse of eminent domain. She has given speeches across the country and testified before Congress. Her plea to the country is contained in multiple YouTube videos which show pictures of the city of New London bulldozing her neighborhood.[10]

The Kelo case did end up having some unintended consequences. Outrage around the country was high. It has been identified as one of the most despised rulings of the U.S. Supreme Court. The national media began reporting on other abuses of eminent domain. Many other people began coming forward to tell their own horror stories of losing homes and businesses to government entities that were turning confiscated land over to private developers. In poll after poll, a majority of Americans agreed that the process of eminent domain needed to be re-examined to increase protections for private citizens.

But who really lost? Susette Kelo certainly did, as did her community. The bulldozing of the neighborhood left the City of New London with a smaller tax base. And the Pfizer deal collapsed, with the pharmaceutical giant deciding not to buy the land after all. Today that former neighborhood is a barren weed-choked lot, a bigger eyesore than anything that pre-existed here.

Instead of being a low-key under-the-carpet land-grab, Kelo became a *cause célèbre* and a rallying cry for those concerned about government overreaching. More than 40 state legislatures and even Congress started looking at ways to modify or control the eminent domain process to see if there were fairer ways to handle such cases in the future. Across the World Wide Web, activists spread stories of eminent domain abuses. The Institute for Justice began providing legal help for those who'd lost their land, and even offered an eminent domain survival guide.[11]

## Public Condemnation and the Municipal Bulldozer

The Castle Coalition, a public policy group, put out a study called *Public Power, Public Gain*. Attorney Dana Berliner compiled a state-by-state look at eminent domain abuses in which municipalities were virtually grabbing land left and right and handing it over to "friendly" private interests. She found more than 10,000 cases of such government-mandated transfers of wealth! In the report's forward, law professor Douglas Kmiec wrote:

Government is instituted to protect property of every sort... and for this reason, that alone is a just government, which impartially secures to every man, whatever is his own. This precept of justice was embodied in the Fifth Amendment's protection of private property, where by constitutional text, property can be taken only for public use and upon the payment of just compensation. For reasons that are more regrettable than rational, the courts have greatly relaxed the public use requirement. Inevitably, this invites the taking or eminent domain power to be misused either by inefficient or corrupt application or both.

The extent of this abuse is widespread, but until recently, largely unaddressed in part because isolated landowners confronted with costly and cumbersome condemnation procedures seldom have the legal or political wherewithal to stand against the winds of power… these owners wish only for what Madison said our Constitution guarantees—the protection of property.

When projects are carried out heavy-handedly and unnecessarily, not through voluntary transaction, but coercion, the protection of property is eroded and our bedrock freedom to decide upon our own course is worn away.[12]

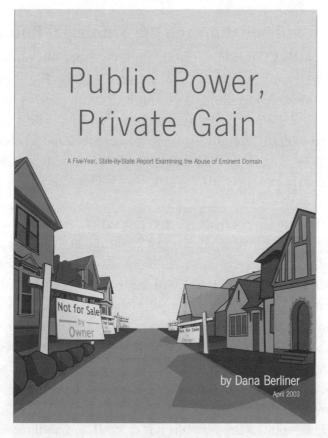

A study done by Dana Berliner that showed the vast number of ongoing eminent domain actions going on across the country.

—photo courtesy of Institute for Justice

While the Kelo case was dramatic for the public wrath it provoked, there are many other such cases that generally fly under the radar. One interesting, pending eminent domain threat is tucked away in the open fields of southeastern Iowa. In 2001, members of a small religious cult began buying up farmland about eighty miles southeast of Des Moines. They bought dozens of farms, about three thousand acres in all and incorporated as Maharishi Vedic City.

In their town and University, the cult teaches such things as transcendental meditation, Vedic vibration and "yogic flying." Members believe they can literally fly through the air for long periods of time while in altered mental states. Video of such "flying moments" by TM practitioners shows people with crossed legs hopping up and down on mattresses.

Although the religious sect now owns a huge tract of land for its 400 members, it has been pressing a nearby farmer, Bob Palm, to sell his 149 acre family farm. He is unwilling to do so. Since Maharishi Vedic City is incorporated as a city, officials say they have the power to condemn Palm's farm under eminent domain. The sect says it wants to turn Palm's land into a park. Judging from land-grab stories across the country, they may be able to do just that.

Historically, property-grabs have been accomplished in a number of vulgar ways, including the following:

- In the old west, lynchings, racial and otherwise, were done as a means of taking private land.
- Denial of water rights is a well-used method of snatching someone else's property. Without water, of course, land has no value.
- Denial of physical access is yet another form of confiscation (although many states now have laws which mandate access to otherwise landlocked properties).

## Many Means to the Land-Grab End

It's impossible in a book like this to detail all the ways a landholder can be deprived of his property. As stated earlier, private property ownership is so fundamental to our identity as Americans that all other rights are subservient. In fact, our noble Constitution crumbles into dust if that great right is not observed, respected and even reverenced. If the ownership of private property is surrendered to government, what have we left?

The Institute for Justice is battling another form of land-grab that's been passing just beyond the borders of consciousness for most Americans. When the collapse of the housing bubble began crushing the life savings of many homeowners across the country, some decided their only alternative was to rent out their properties until the financial climate improved. Housing prices were so depressed, that the only chance at survival for some homeowners was to advertise for a lessee who would help make mortgage payments and keep their properties out of foreclosure. It worked for millions of homeowners who wanted to try to salvage their investments. It also worked for renters who'd been driven from their previous homes by predatory lenders.

But "City Planning" is another way that private property is secretly redistributed. A class of planners called "30 Percenters" showed up in a number of communities in Minnesota. They argued that "renters" are less stable than "owners." They began teaching that neighborhoods in which more than 30 percent of the residents were renters were basically unhealthy. There was a government "fix" of course. That was to force all prospective landlords to be licensed. The legal ratio was 70/30 owner occupied to renter occupied. If less than seventy percent of a given city block was held by resident owners, the city would refuse to issue further licenses. It was a flat denial of rental income to people who'd worked hard to preserve their properties. And it was a government "taking" just as clearly as the David Lucas case was a "taking" in South Carolina.

The results were disastrous. The "30 percent law" didn't keep owners in their homes. They just went bankrupt, throwing many more homes into foreclosure. The thirty percent brainiacs moved their social experiment from Winona to Mankato, and from Northfield to West St. Paul, Minnesota.

Ted and Lauren Dzierzbicki are plaintiffs in a "takings" case in Winona, Minnesota. That's one of a number of towns trying to limit the percentage of rental homes in any single block. It's called the 70/30 rule, 70 percent owner occupancy vs. 30 percent rentals.

—photo courtesy of Institute for Justice

Ted and Lauren Dzierzbicki were caught in the middle of this Marxist piece of work. They own a house in the City of Winona which they tried to put up for sale. Conditions in the housing market were so bad, they could not find a buyer. They felt their only alternative was to find someone who would rent their house until the economy improved. But, 30 percent of the homeowners on their block were already licensed as landlords. The Dzierzbickis were stuck, forbidden from renting out their home. The law had essentially deprived them of all property value and they faced letting their vacant home go into foreclosure. In a major sense, their property was ripped away from them without due process and without any benefit to the public.

The Institute for Justice came forward to file a lawsuit on behalf of several families caught in this vice grip of government theft. They argue the 30 percent law is clearly unconstitutional. The law does the city no good. It does the property owners no good. It does the targeted city block no good since it increases the number of home foreclosures. And it does the renters no good because they now find that the law of supply and demand has raised the cost of rental housing city-wide.

To aggravate the tormented housing market even more, in 2011 the FHA and a growing number of lenders began secretly applying the 30 percent test to Homeowner Associations. Many potential buyers of HOA homes discovered that promised bank loans just didn't materialize if too many people were renting homes in a community. Since many of the renters were minorities there were many parallels to the old red-lining laws of the 60s and 70s. Once again, institutional racism reared its ugly head. In terms of home sales, some HOAs became toxic. But that's often what happens when a government decides the Free Market is incapable of regulating itself.

Red-lining was insidious. Lending institutions would literally draw a red line on a map encircling entire neighborhoods where a large number of minorities lived. For those who had homes or businesses within the red-lined areas, loans of any kind could be next to impossible to obtain.

## Look, Ma! Isn't that Man Squatting?

One of the most abused of all land grab schemes involves an age-old concept called "adverse possession" or "squatter's rights." By following a certain set of rules established by state law, a squatter can claim ownership of another person's land simply by announcing he has "made use of" the land for a prescribed period of time.

The history of adverse possession is a long one, set out in the Magna Carta and upheld through centuries of English common law. It essentially creates a mandate for landowners which says "use it or lose it." If a longtime property owner doesn't take aggressive, affirmative steps to use, protect or develop his property, he could likely discover one day that his property has simply been handed over to someone else. Many a property owner who has just wanted to keep his land open, pristine and undeveloped has lost it because of the presence of a squatter.

Most states require that a squatter make use of the land for a prescribed period of years, before claiming adverse possession. For example in Colorado, a squatter can claim ownership of land after 18 years of supposed continuous use. Some states like Utah require only seven years.[13] Theoretically, a squatter's use has to be visible and adverse to the interests of the true owner. But that's also the source of some of the law's biggest abuses.

## We Live Next Door! Fork It Over!

"Outrageous, absolutely outrageous," Denver attorney Dan Caplis said about such a land-grab involving two well-known political figures in Colorado. The controversy made headlines around the country.

Caplis and a fellow lawyer, Craig Silverman, are well-known on the Colorado legal scene. They are also some of the best-known broadcasters in the Rocky Mountain region, even recognized at one point by a writer for the *New York Times*. Caplis is notoriously conservative and Silverman is far more liberal.

In addition to practicing law, the two men have long hosted a radio talk show where they comment and debate local and national politics. They rarely agree on much. But for several months during 2007 and 2008, their talk show focused on a controversy over a land-grab in which the claimant, a retired judge, won ownership of his next-door neighbor's land. Caplis and Silverman seemed to be in rare agreement that the adverse possession case was a rank abuse of the law by a lawyer and judge who knew better.

Judge Richard McClean is a prominent figure in Democratic Party politics in Colorado. He was a city councilman, a Mayor of Boulder, and was later named a Boulder County District Judge. His wife, Edith Stevens, is also an attorney who was once head of the Boulder Democratic Party.

For at least twenty-five years, Judge McClean and Edie Stevens have lived in a home on Hardscrabble Drive, a Southwest Boulder neighborhood known as the Shanahan Ridge Subdivision. The neighborhood looks up at the spectacular Flatirons mountain range, a 300 million year old rock ridge that marks the exact point where the Rocky Mountains rise out of the Great Plains to meet the western sky. It's an exclusive neighborhood where a small home site with an unobstructed view can cost a million dollars or more.

McClean and Stevens don't have any neighboring homes between them and the mountains. There is one property owner however who bought a plot of land next to the McClean home. Don and Susie Kirlin bought the property in 1980. The Kirlins' current residence is just down the street, but they say they had always planned on building their ultimate retirement home on their view property on the edge of the development.

In the fall of 2006, Kirlin, a former airline pilot, began making moves to build his Shanahan Ridge dream home. He hired a contractor to put up a split rail fence to mark the property line. Within a few hours, he was hit with a restraining order. Judge McClean and Edie Stevens planned to claim that they owned 34 percent of the Kirlins' building lot under the theory of adverse possession.

The McCleans claimed that for more than twenty years they had used a path through the Kirlin property to reach their backyard. They argued that they had continuously walked over the Kirlin property to access a woodpile, and that they had sometimes hosted parties during which houseguests walked across the Kirlin property.

It was apparently a slam-dunk adverse possession claim, and indeed, after a short court case Boulder District Judge James Klein ruled that Judge McClean now owned a third of the Kirlin's property. Since the Kirlin lot was only 55 by 80 feet long, the purported walking path cut right through the property's only possible building envelope, making the Kirlins' lot unbuildable. Kirlin had lost his million dollar home site. Judge McClean's property, in theory, had just gained a million dollars in value.

The news media went wild. In a matter of hours, the dispute went from a regional sensation to a national news story. The Kirlins appeared on the Caplis-Silverman radio show. National Public Radio did a lengthy report on the controversy. Members of the neighborhood began picketing the McClean home, and a Boulder singer-songwriter began performing satirical songs about the "McClean land-grab." The Kirlins asked the state judiciary oversight committee to review circumstances surrounding the case.

113

The famous "woodpile" that made headlines across America. Judge Richard McClean, whose home is in the background, claimed adverse possession of his next-door neighbor's land. He claimed he had a right to take his neighbor's land because he supposedly accessed a woodpile on the adjacent lot for at least twenty years.

—photo by The Denver Post

"The code of ethics says an attorney will not use his knowledge of the law for personal gain over people who don't have that knowledge," Kirlin told reporters.[14]

Kirlin was wrong. Judge McClain and Edith Stevens won.

"I can't understand why either of them would be willing to do something so wrong," talk show host Dan Caplis said. "I don't care if you're ACLU or John Birch, you shouldn't have your property taken by people who trespassed on it."[15]

Caplis was wrong. It's done all the time with the blessing of the courts.

In fact, one doesn't have to stray too far down the streets of Boulder to find several dozen parallel adverse possession cases. And one doesn't have to imagine too wildly that the same kinds of circumstances exist in cities across the country. A second Boulder case was much less high-profile than the McClean-Kirlin case, but nevertheless, noxious.

In 2006, Dana Marshall purchased a home in the 2200 block of Mariposa Avenue, not too far from the Kirlin/McClean controversy. She tore down an aging fence in her backyard that ran alongside a creek that separated her property from her neighbors, Mohammad and Gay Salim. Testimony indicated that the fence had been built in the 1960s when the neighborhood was new. The fence was apparently just inside of Marshall's property line and was under her control; therefore she felt she had the right to remove it.

Salim filed an adverse possession lawsuit, claiming that the longstanding existence of the fence had essentially become a demarcation of the two neighbors' common property line. His lawsuit demanded that he be awarded the four inches of land between his property and the fence, and that Marshall be forced to rebuild the fence. Salim testified that he had continuously used the four inches of land, occasionally made repairs on the fence, and had even sat on the disputed land with his back to the fence while meditating.

The court ruled in his favor.

## Consequences: Intended and Unintended

Outrage against the Salims was almost as intense as the rage against Judge McClean. It's possible that without the McClean case as an immediate precedent, community reactions might have been more muted. In any event, after the Salim decision, both he and his wife felt compelled to issue a press release to further explain their actions. He said the fence had always been a privacy issue, since his bedroom windows faced in the direction of the Marshall house. Salim testified that had he tried to rebuild the fence four inches closer to his house, the City of Boulder would have required a hydrology study, since the creek that ran between the two houses was in a flood zone.[16]

Both neighbors did interviews with the media, in which they each tried to rationalize their respective sides in the dispute.[17] Still, with the hundreds of thousands of dollars that were spent in the case, the fury that will always exist in this neighborhood, the quality of life that's now been lost, a rational person might think a less adversarial settlement could have been reached.

"Good fences make good neighbors," said the poet. Actually, they don't. Robert Frost was wrong. Fences lead to lawsuits. Fences finance the college educations of lawyers' kids and help them buy expensive cars. Some future poet may pen a more applicable poem that says something like "good surveyors make good neighbors." But then, again, the revised line doesn't have just the right meter to enrich the literature.

The existence of an adverse possession threat ultimately leads to extremely awkward situations—such as, the mandated obligation of a property owner to take specific steps to stop his neighbor from trespassing: "Get off my property! Get out of here! Don't come back!"

Those shouts are not exactly the kind of language one would expect in a neighborhood where homeowners could be using their energies to try to find common bonds. It's tough to go to the annual Christmas party and engage in "holiday chatter" with people who've aggressively thrown each other off their respective properties. But the law on adverse possession actually requires such aggression. Many a landowner has discovered too late that by not loudly protecting his boundaries, he ends up losing the right to enforce them.

The controversy over the two adverse possession cases in Boulder, though, may actually have had several unintended consequences. The Colorado State Legislature took a long hard look at the law of adverse possession and voted to tighten the reins on when and how it can be used. One major change in the law will now require a squatter to pay the full price of whatever land is taken in an adverse possession action.

Sadly, the revision is still weak enough to be monstrously ineffective. In the vast majority of adverse possession cases the legal fees on both sides far outweigh any benefit that comes from fighting over the small bits of land involved. So again, the net result of a new law is to provide full employment for law firms.

One benefit of the McClean-Kirlin fight and the Mohammed Salim case is that a number of average citizens began to be educated about the existence of laws that support and even encourage squatting on someone else's land. The Kirlins, for example, created a website that recounts their ordeal and the loss of their land to Judge McClean. It includes extensive coverage of the law of adverse possession.[18]

Finally, an intriguing lesson is that public outrage really can impact the outcome of private disputes. In the customarily mellow atmosphere of an often-stoned Boulder populace, community anger against the retired judge and his lawyer wife continued to grow. The hate mail kept coming. The couple reported that they were subjected to death threats and ugly comments on the street. A pending lawsuit by the Kirlins produced aerial pictures which appeared to show that the alleged McClean "footpath to the woodpile" may have actually been a recent creation.

In November 2008, Judge McClean and Edie Stevens suddenly announced that the case had been settled. The McCleans said they would be satisfied by just squatting on 15 percent of their neighbors' property, which would give to the Kirlins' a small building envelope on which a future home could be built.

117

The Kirlins released a simultaneous statement saying they, too, were satisfied with the settlement because they could at least put their land on the market. After all the bad blood between these two families, the thought of them living side by side is unfathomable.

McClean and Stevens, of course, could have acquiesced and given back all the land they took from the Kirlins. Perhaps the 15 percent settlement helped these two lawyers save face. And bank some extra dollars.

In any event, an enormous amount of money was wasted over the right to own a small piece of undeveloped property. *Until the legal system truly finds a way to make an injured party whole again, "justice" will continue to be an empty word, not an achievement.*

But the biggest land grab of all occupied the attention of all Americans when homeowners across the country found themselves sliding into a black hole that seemingly had no bottom, and no way back out. The end of the first decade of the new Millenium had taught many homeowners a new meaning of the term, "underwater."

# 7
# Bang, Bang, Crash!

*If the people are afraid of the government, that's tyranny.*
*If the government is afraid of the people, that's liberty.*
—Thomas Jefferson

The worldwide economic crisis of 2008 and 2009 shone a spotlight on yet another form of land taking, one that every homeowner has learned to live with and even grudgingly respect: the right of a mortgagee to seize property when a homeowner fails to make payments. The reasons for that great crash in mortgage and financial markets are massively complex and will be analyzed and debated for decades.

**A simplistic but probably accurate view is that the collapse had its roots in political mandates in the 1970s and mid-1990s which forced mortgage companies to lend money to economically unqualified families.**

## Redlining Made Illegal

The 1974 Equal Credit Opportunity Act, the 1977 Community Reinvestment Act along with other government refinements forced banks and mortgage companies to increase amounts of money made available for risky loans to underprivileged borrowers. For years, lending institutions had avoided writing mortgages in neighborhoods where higher percentages of borrowers had defaulted on past loans. The process of "redlining," as explained earlier, made it more difficult for minorities or lower-income families to obtain mortgages at reasonable rates. Red lines, drawn in ink around predominantly lower-income areas, showed neighborhoods where loan seekers were more likely to default because of certain "ethnic propensities," such as higher unemployment, greater under-employment or higher rates of crime.

Because of the disparate impact on minorities, redlining became illegal. Banks and mortgage companies were threatened with stiff penalties for refusing to lend money in previously redlined areas. Over a period of years, the government created increasingly aggressive rules to ensure that the less-fortunate had the same access to mortgages as those in higher-end neighborhoods. The ligature around the necks of lending institutions caused many to make loans in cases where borrowers were deemed risky, at best. Poor-risk applicants were not required to put up collateral or down payments on home purchases. Often, high-risk borrowers were not even asked about credit histories. Others were allowed to claim welfare payments, food stamps or child support as recognized streams of income.

"Provide affordable housing" was the mantra that became ingrained in the language of American politics. "Every family has the right to an affordable home" was the winning rhetoric in campaigns across the country.

In hundreds of thousands of cases, mortgage agents were instructed to refrain from asking applicants if they had legal residency, and so-called sub-prime loans were issued to families who not only were in the country illegally, but who had no known ability to pay back loans of any kind. *The federal government essentially guaranteed the repayment of all bad loans, and mortgage companies and real estate firms became intoxicated with the knowledge.*[1]

## Invest in Real Estate: You Just Can't Lose

Private home and commercial real estate prices were rising crazily in the 80s and 90s in almost all parts of the country. "You can't lose money buying a home," prospective buyers were told. Year after year, values were skyrocketing. The advice *du jour* was "Don't get left out of the boom, lock down a piece of real estate now!"

It was a heady time for lenders. In massive advertising campaigns, homeowners were told they could get loans of 120 percent of their actual home values, even with bad credit. In case after case, mortgage company salesmen pointed to a 20-year history of annual increases in the price of American homes.

"Your property will gain an average of 10 to 17 percent in value each year," they said. "You can pay off your five-year interest-only mortgage with the future increase in the value of your house!"

Agents of one major mortgage company, Countrywide Mortgage, slyly handed the following chart to real estate investors in at least one major metropolitan city. It showed the annual increase in home values and the implications were obvious.

| Year | Average Increase in Value |
|------|---------------------------|
| 1992 | +5.10% |
| 1993 | +8.13% |
| 1994 | +8.53% |
| 1995 | +8.76% |
| 1996 | +6.53% |
| 1997 | +6.43% |
| 1998 | +10.56% |
| 1999 | +17.21% |
| 2000 | +9.74% |
| 2001 | +7.55% |
| 2002 | +4.73% |

Mortgage brokers told wide-eyed future homeowners that a $105,000 home in 1992 had risen to $243,000 in 2002. That trend, they promised, could only continue. A 120 percent loan-to-value, it was reasoned, should fall to just 30 or 40 percent loan-to-value over a mere ten years. After all, borrowers were told, even Will Rogers reasoned that real estate prices could only rise because "land is the only thing they're not making anymore."

The homebuilding industry went crazy, too, throwing up millions of new homes, the overwhelming majority of them in newly created Homeowners Associations surrounding more densely populated urban areas. There didn't seem to be an end to the stream of customers willing to buy into the dream.

For several years beginning in about 2004, federal officials and real estate experts began warning of an impending "real estate bubble" that could crash the U.S. economy. No one was really able to define exactly what such a financial implosion might look like, but the "housing bubble" became part of the public consciousness. The term was printed in newspapers, repeated on newscasts. Still, exuberant investors ignored the wisdom that irrational speculation almost always precedes economic disasters. The drunken policies of the mortgage industry continued, too. The "ninja loan" was one of many terms used by insiders to refer to penniless borrowers who were still able to obtain home loans: "No income, no job, no assets."

## Looming Consequences

Bad loans were re-packaged with good ones and sold as "derivatives" to the secondary loan market. Poisonous loan packages were so intermingled with "the good, the bad and the ugly" that even institutional investors had no ability to calculate the real risk of the securities they held. Investors with extremely conservative investment goals were persuaded to put their money into what were essentially ponzi schemes. Like all pyramid schemes, the whole structure was destined to collapse when investors became aware of the unsupportable weight above them.

When the economy began decaying and housing prices started falling instead of rising, many sub-prime borrowers realized their mortgage debts were higher than the actual appraised value of their homes ("underwater" in the parlance of the industry). It made no sense to make payments on a 400,000 dollar home loan when selling the house would only bring in 300,000 dollars. Home-owners simply walked away, leaving their homes to the banks. The growing numbers of foreclosures began toppling one financial institution after another. Entire neighborhoods collapsed, along with the investors who had created them.

As the crisis rippled through the economy, the list of casualties grew: Bear Stearns, Lehman Brothers, American International Group (AIG), Merrill Lynch, Countrywide Mortgage. Businesses from the smallest to the largest found they couldn't borrow money at any price. The "perfect storm" continued with real and threatened bankruptcies by General Motors, Chrysler and many others. Trillion dollar bailout proposals were slammed together by a panicked White House, and re-written by a dysfunctional Congress in what amounted to the first-ever nationalization of entire industries by the federal government. State governments from California to Nevada to New York announced that they were near bankruptcy with billions in debt and no ability to generate new revenue.

Plunging home values and entire neighborhoods faced with foreclosure meant that property tax collections couldn't keep up with government spending. A corresponding international drop in gasoline prices combined with fewer travel miles meant plummeting gas tax collections. Frightened consumers spent less money, shutting down streams of sales tax collections. The perfect storm left no community untouched.

Homeowners Associations were hammered as well, sometimes twice as hard. In gated neighborhoods from Florida to California where developers had not yet sold all their properties, builders declared themselves bankrupt and walked away. Half-finished neighborhoods, unbuilt clubhouses, and algae-filled swimming pools further devalued the properties of homeowners who'd been persuaded to buy into the myths of covenant protection. Hapless homeowners were not only underwater themselves; they started ignoring HOA dues, fees and fines. Homeowners Associations across the country were forced to raise dues on other members to make up for plunging revenues. Un-mowed lawns and "For Sale" signs made some developments in California, Nevada and Arizona feel like ghost towns as financially-strapped homeowners fled their mortgages.

**As more and more owners tried to file for bankruptcy, some Realtors began to recognize the new difficulty of selling properties within HOAs. More astute Realtors began steering clients completely away from HOA controlled neighborhoods.[2]**

The collapse was a perfect demonstration of "chaos theory" at work. The theory holds that every physical event in nature, no matter how tiny, ultimately has some kind of an impact on every other particle in the Universe. "A butterfly's wings flapping in the tropics," the theory explains, "ultimately contribute to air currents which could theoretically wind up contributing to hurricanes elsewhere on the planet." Causality, therefore, is as infinitesimally small as it is potentially catastrophic.

A corollary is the 14th Century proverb passed down through generations:

> For want of a nail a shoe was lost, for want of a shoe a horse was lost.
> For want of a horse a rider was lost, for want of a rider a battle was lost.

For want of a battle the kingdom was lost,
and all for the want of a horseshoe nail."[3]

If chaos has no boundaries, then the obvious economic parallel has to be drawn; one missed payment on a single bad mortgage somewhere could have been the triggering event for the collapse of the entire world economy. Or a single frivolous HOA lawsuit in some obscure neighborhood on some mid-west prairie could have created the tipping point. Conversely, if two warring neighbors at some point in time had decided to detoxify their relationship, could their decision to reach a mutual peace have led the way to a chaotic wave of random acts of kindness? Perhaps, but that would be too good to hope for.

The etymology of the word "mortgage" is fascinating. It can be traced back through most romance languages to ancient Latin. The word "mort," or "mortus" means death. "Gage" or "gaige," in old French refers to the word "pledge" or "grip." Mortgage. Death Grip.

Although in most cases such a grip probably referred to the clench that a lender has on a borrower, another intriguing locker-room crudity often used in the mortgage business is, "If you owe the bank 100,000 dollars, the bank has you by the balls; if you owe the bank 10 million dollars, you have the bank by the balls." Because of the awesome size of the 2008 mortgage meltdown, the testicular grip was as deadly for one side as it was for the other. For the first time in nearly 80 years, lenders and borrowers were in a mutual death grip, each destined to take the other to its knees.

## Even in Disaster, the Constitution Governs...

While the 2008 financial disaster was bizarre and painful, it cannot go unsaid that American citizens who lost homes to banks, were at all times protected by rights enumerated in the U.S. Constitution. In hundreds of thousands of loan foreclosures, not a single person lost his property because he was a member of the wrong race. No woman lost her home because of her gender. Homes were not lost because a family member was too old or too disabled. No one who lost a home was denied access to the courts. The rights of free speech and free assembly were never shut down by a mortgage company. No person lost his or her right to vote in an election because of a missed house payment. Even as financial institutions were crumbling, an almost perverse amount of care went into ensuring that all individual rights under the U.S Constitution were observed, honored and for the most part upheld.

This elevated concern over Constitutional rights also hovers over the two major forms of land confiscation discussed in the previous chapter. As unfair as eminent domain and adverse possession can seem to victims of such land-grabs, Constitutional law is still the controlling authority. For example, even though minorities are often disproportionately impacted by eminent domain, no man loses his house in such an action simply because he is black, disabled or the wrong age. And adverse possession, as fundamentally evil as it seems, is not generally done to rid a neighborhood of a minority, or someone of the wrong age, religion or gender. As counterintuitive as it seems, in most land-grabs enormous care is taken to avoid even the appearance of Constitutional impropriety.

## ...Except in HOAs

The one exception, of course, is the takings by *de facto* governments called Homeowners Associations. The HOA movement was blatantly and notoriously created to screen out minorities and the disabled. And many Homeowners Associations routinely use their unique access to the lawsuit industry to rid themselves of certain people who get through the initial barriers. There's a growing mountain of evidence that shows a desperate need for national reform in all flavors of property confiscation. And there's no shortage of examples.

"I can't even visit my husband's grave. Because of my Homeowner's Association, I'm essentially housebound." The Arizona resident, Marlene Bagarazzi, says she is elderly and retired. She is confined to a wheelchair but has tried to stay as vibrant and active as possible. Her van is equipped with hand controls which allow her to drive to and from medical appointments 25 to 30 miles away.

Bagarazzi found a home she wanted, right in the shadow of Superstition Mountain. While doing her due diligence, she noticed that the CC&Rs in her neighborhood didn't permit vans and pickup trucks. She explained her medical problem to the developer, who told her he would grant her an exception for her handicap van, and it was written into the title work. With the promise in writing, Bagarazzi moved into her new home and became a member of the Gold Canyon Tesoro Homeowners Association, a community of several dozen gleaming stucco townhomes.

"I thought I got a good deal. It's why I moved in here," she said. "They even put up a sign on the street that said 'Handicapped Parking Only'."

But almost from the beginning, she says she felt the neighborhood's animosity. Letters began arriving from the HOA, saying that her handicap van was not allowed in the neighborhood and that it would be towed if she continued to park it on the street outside her home.

Bagarazzi produced her purchase agreement to show HOA officials that the original developer had given her written permission for her handicap van. Apologies were issued by the board and the matter was apparently put to rest. But before long she says she began receiving threatening letters again, ordering her to get rid of the van or lose it. "You cannot park your van near the common area," she was also told. "You are forbidden from using the common area."

"I thought the common area was for the convenience of members of the community. People who play golf can walk on it. People can walk their dogs on it. Children going to school can walk on it. But they've forbidden me from going out my back door into my common area. They shouldn't do that just because someone doesn't like me using a cane or a wheelchair."[4] Finally, in an effort to end the apparent harassment campaign, Bagarazzi turned to Mesa attorney Clint Goodman.

Goodman says he emailed the management company which represented the Gold Canyon Tesoro Homeowners Association. It refused to budge. Goodman reminded the manager that the Association was in violation of Arizona law by discriminating against Ms. Bagarazzi because of her disability. The manager, Goodman says, responded within minutes saying the HOA was right and Goodman was wrong.

"HOA Management companies are not regulated," says Goodman. "It causes serious problems for many HOAs. Managers need no training or credentials to run multi-million dollar operations. A high school dropout can become the self-proclaimed manager of a Homeowners Association. He can run up tremendous legal costs for individual homeowners. Those homeowners have no knowledge of the huge special assessments they're hit with until they start getting their new monthly bills and realize they have to pay some kind of massive legal settlement because their representative got them into a big unwinnable lawsuit."

On Bagarazzi's behalf, Goodman filed a lawsuit against her Homeowners Association. Month after month, the case dragged on. The Homeowners Association filed a series of motions, each one delaying the eventual resolution of what should have been a cut and dried, day-one agreement. At one point, according to Goodman, the HOA offered to settle and allow Bagarazzi to park in her handicap space, but they refused to cover her growing stack of attorney's bills. Bagarazzi rejected the settlement unless her expenses were covered.

There were more delays as motions and counter-motions were filed.

The HOA then threatened to file abuse of judicial proceedings if Bagarazzi didn't accept the previously offered non-compensation settlement. That was rejected. The HOA moved to dismiss the whole case. That was rejected.

Finally, the case that never should have made its way past the first email ended up in front of a judge. The court rejected the HOA's arguments, issued an order to allow this handicapped woman to park in her handicap spot, and awarded Bagarazzi her legal fees and costs. Tens of thousands of dollars later, this elderly lady is now permitted to live among all those "compassionate" neighbors who had harassed her mercilessly over her disability. Bagarazzi, according to an acquaintance, has since suffered a series of heart attacks and medical setbacks.

## The Need to Reign in the Rogue HOA

Goodman has lobbied the Arizona Legislature to come up with some kind of system that would prevent rogue Homeowners Associations or management firms from manufacturing frivolous disputes among neighbors. In one interview in the East Valley Tribune, Goodman explained why he felt state governments need to begin controlling some of the abusive practices of HOAs:

> Like it or not, Arizona is no longer a place where people enjoy free use of property. We're not trying to abolish HOAs entirely,

but they pose threats. Some HOAs amend or selectively enforce community documents to single out individual homeowners and unfairly restrict their rights. HOAs far too frequently target specific individuals and use HOA powers to harass them. We've seen this frequently. In some situations, HOAs amend their community documents so as to interfere with basic, fundamental, real property rights. As far as I am aware, there is not a single state in the country that subjects HOAs to the same Constitutional due-process requirements as state and local governments, even though they fulfill traditional governmental functions of taxation, regulation and enforcement. HOAs have become very powerful; at times more powerful than government itself.[5]

As an attorney who represents homeowners against HOAs, Goodman says he could talk for hours about outrageous cases where the boards of Homeowners Associations are recklessly out of control. In one such case, he says a board president directed a board officer to kill neighborhood cats. Cups of milk laced with antifreeze were left on the steps of homeowners who were known to be keeping cats against HOA regulations.

Goodman says a more frequent complaint involves homeowners who are illegally denied access to financial records of the HOA:

The boards will often deny a member permission to see the books. Sometimes we find that it is because someone has pocketed some money and is trying to cover it up. I sue homeowners associations all the time because they don't disclose financial records. Lack of accountability and a widespread lack of interest in tougher HOA laws have (created) a setup that's ripe for fraud and financial shenanigans. It seems like the main purpose of HOAs has backfired.[6]

Goodman says he doesn't necessarily support the creation of a Homeowners Bill of Rights, but he says there's definitely a need for some kind of regulation. He likens the current Homeowners Association scene to the kind of mess that existed in interstate trade and commercial regulation before the states adopted the Uniform Commercial Code.

"Unfortunately, I think we've dug ourselves into a big hole here." Goodman is a lone voice in the legal community, a voice calling for massive reform of an abusive industry.

## The Mortgage Crisis and the "Underwater World"

The 2008-2009 mortgage crisis claimed lots of victims all over the country both inside and outside of Homeowners Associations as stressed homeowners walked away from their mortgages. One organization that tracks such conditions is *Zillow.com*, a Seattle-based real estate research firm that lists property values of tens of millions of homes across America. It also lists cities with the highest number of "underwater homes." It named Modesto, California as the country's hardest-hit. According to *Zillow* and to *Forbes Magazine Online*, in May of 2009, 81 percent of the homes in Modesto with mortgages taken out in the previous five years were "underwater." Housing prices there have dropped 57 percent since 2005, a massive collapse in personal wealth for tens of thousands of families.[7]

Modesto, like many other cities in California, is filled with Homeowners Associations which were theoretically supposed to protect members from decreases in property values. So what happened?

Over the years, the ability of HOA boards to defend their "beige neighborhoods" by aggressively foreclosing on "non-conforming residents" may have looked good to most members. Prospective homeowners were comforted by the thought that "bad people" would be quickly screened out. Savvy Realtors, of course, left the interpretation of that concept up to the imagination of clients. In years of national economic strength, HOA boards could ignore complaints that the bully tactics were illegal or unfair.

An occasional foreclosure on a "problem family" had little impact on a neighborhood's overall property values. In the late 1990s and early 2000s a typical Homeowners Association didn't have more than one or two foreclosures on the books at any one time. In fact, the knowledge that HOAs aggressively pursued foreclosures was a pretty good selling point by local Realtors who bragged that a particular HOA would actively get rid of "undesirables."

But the mortgage and banking collapse began shifting the paradigm. When the bad times hit, homeowners discovered that foreclosures of any kind actually had a huge impact on nearby property values. Entire neighborhoods were poisoned by excess bank foreclosures. HOAs, of course, felt the pinch as their dues collections went down. To shore up their faltering budgets, HOAs counter-intuitively filed foreclosures of their own to shore up their sagging maintenance budgets. Combined with the bank foreclosures, though, the HOA actions rendered many neighborhoods absolutely toxic in terms of attracting new buyers.

Economists and real estate experts began churning out reports that quantified the impact of even a single foreclosure on surrounding property values. Some were very interesting and instructive.

One study was done by the Center for Responsible Lending, which says it has offices in North Carolina and California. It reported that on average, one foreclosure would cost nearby homeowners an average of $7,200 apiece in home value. It calls its estimates of the spillover impact on nearby homes "conservative."[8]

Even well before the economic collapse, a previously discussed study by a Washington University Professor shows that a single home foreclosure dropped all nearby home values by at least one and one-half percent.

Other studies have turned up the same kinds of results. The Woodstock Institute, which has analyzed property values for 35 years, reports that a single home foreclosure can reduce the value of all other homes within an eighth of a mile by one to two percent.[9] It's not hard to understand how multiple foreclosures or reckless HOA foreclosures can exponentially poison a neighborhood.

## A Beanie on Your Side

But the most thorough ad hoc study ever done by an interest group involved an examination of the actions of Homeowners Associations is in Harris County, Texas. At 80-years-old, Beanie Adolph is a keg of dynamite. One of her sons is an attorney. Another son runs a website design service, and Beanie has worked with both of them to wage a decade-long fight against Texas Homeowners Associations from a website called *HoaData.org*. Their research has terrorized Homeowners Associations from Houston to Austin, and they've actually had some success in bending the ears of a few concerned legislators.

Perhaps Beanie's biggest accomplishment was creation of a database of 25,000 real estate transactions in Harris County over a period of years. The raw statistics show some eyebrow-raising results. It appears that the aggressive filing of lawsuits by HOAs did not have the impact of increasing property values. Just the reverse occurred.

In neighborhoods where lawsuits and foreclosures were rarely filed, property values *seemed to rise twice as fast* as in neighborhoods which were aggressive in protecting covenants. Beanie also tracked which attorneys were filing most of the lawsuits and discovered that the vast majority of those actions were filed by a tiny handful of attorneys, who she names.[11]

So, here's a word to the wise: if you're planning to buy a home in Harris County, Texas, one of the first questions you should ask is: who is the attorney for *this* Homeowners Association? If he or she is on Beanie's list, would you want to shop elsewhere? Would your home, your net worth and your sanity all be at risk?

Knowing all of the above information, knowing that one too many foreclosures turns an idyllic, gate-protected Shangri La into a graffiti infested ghost town, with uncut grass and weed-infested lawns, why would the boards of HOAs choose such dire times to begin throwing homeowners out and confiscating their homes? Why not come up with a gentler means of collecting dues, neighborhood fund raising projects, more reasonable liens for the amount due without the vulgar attachment of attorney's fees, debt collection fees and late charges? And why take a neighborhood where people talk to each other and celebrate holidays together and transform it into a realm of terror where no one wants to answer the doorbell? Some of the most interesting questions on earth apparently have no answer.

# 8

# "Nigger Roy" of Russell Gulch

## (The Warning Shot from the Federal Bench)

*Though the mills of God grind slowly, yet they grind*
*exceeding small; though with patience*
*He stands waiting, with exactness grinds He all.*
— Friedrich Von Logau ("Retribution")

Roy Smith, Gilpin County's most famous modern day gold miner, standing in front of his 19th Century mining hut.

— photo by The Denver Post

Ah, my good friend, Roy. How in hell did your odd story end up in a screed about Homeowners Associations? There's just no good way to tell your story without throwing caution to the wind, and putting the burden on the reader to find a way to cut through the language. The current politically correct word wasn't used in your now-famous court case, nor in the decision of U.S. Federal Judge Wiley Daniel. In fact, the use of the racial slur was fundamental to the ultimate outcome of your case. As such, this author will also decline to substitute the socially mandated code word.

"I'm Nigger Roy. That's what they call me, Nigger Roy."The 1993 phone call to a Denver TV reporter came from Roy Smith, a would-be gold miner who owned several historic claims in an area known as Russell Gulch, near the 19th Century gold fields of Central City, the so-called "richest square mile on earth." It's also one of the world's most fascinating neighborhoods.

When gold was first discovered in the area in 1859, more than 60,000 fortune-seekers poured into Colorado from all points of the compass. They dug, they panned, they sluiced, they sometimes committed murder to steal one another's claims. Underneath Central City, Blackhawk, and Russell Gulch is a labyrinth of thousands, possibly tens of thousands of mineshafts and tunnels. Some go straight down into the ground, others bore at odd angles back into the hillsides. Some mineshafts intersect with others, going hundreds, even thousands of feet into the crust of the earth. There are areas where so many shafts were dug, that the weakened rock sometimes collapsed onto whoever happened to be underground at the time. The famous Glory Hole marks one spot where the honeycomb of tunnels was so extensive that a mining entrepreneur in the 1920s found it profitable to collapse the entire mountain into a massive crater, and reopen the huge pit as a strip mine.

Gold is heavier than other metals. If a shovel full of alluvial soil is dropped into a sluice box or a gold pan and sufficiently washed or agitated with water, the particles of gold filter down to the bottom. A good find is immediately obvious. The flecks of color sparkle on the bottom of whatever device is used, and for some mystical reason that discovery never fails to stir some primitive emotion in the human soul.

Typical 19th Century mining cabins that dot the hills of Central City, Black Hawk and Cripple Creek. Would-be gold miners still move into these ghost towns in an effort to find veins of the precious yellow metal.

—photo courtesy of Robin Pejsa

Covering many of the mineshaft openings in Gilpin County are weathered old cabins, shacks built right over the entrances so that miners could continue their work even when the Rocky Mountain weather turned frigid. Some of those 150-year-old shacks are standing today. In fact, modern treasure hunters occasionally move into the abandoned cabins to follow a gold vein discovered more than a century earlier. It was into one of those rickety old cabins Roy Smith moved when he first arrived in Colorado from the Mississippi Delta in the 1980s.

## Roy Smith's Demons

Smith was the only black man in Gilpin County, a sparsely populated county of mostly ghost towns and piles of old mine tailings. He was well-known among the county's 350 or so white residents as an eccentric loner who faced some communication and mental challenges. Most people living in those pockmarked and deserted hills could be considered eccentrics. But Smith was tormented by demons of another sort. He claimed he was constantly being attacked by other residents of the area because of his race.

Smith acknowledged he was considered by many in Gilpin County to be a little strange. Like others who lived in the cabins that freckled the hillsides of Russell Gulch, Smith claimed he was actively trying to find gold. It's not known if his attempts at placer mining ever produced any of the precious yellow metal. But Smith's conversation with the TV reporter was not about gold mining. It was about his neighbors.

"Ever since 1988, I've been beat up and left for dead. They catch me, beat me at night when there's nobody around."

Smith claimed he was constantly being terrorized by racists who called him names, burned him, hanged him upside down. On another occasion he said that as the racists attacked him, he was pulled out of his bathtub naked and hung by his heels from a tree. Yet another time he complained that someone tried to run him off the road. Each story of abuse was a little wilder than the one before but he always seemed to be able to show corresponding injuries. Still, to believe some of his complaints, a listener had to stretch his or her imagination.

Smith made repeated complaints to various police and sheriff's departments. Time after time, deputies were dispatched to investigate. Each time his complaints were discounted because of his purported mental problems. Investigators said his reports had no credibility. At one point Smith was even charged with filing a false police report.

Smith may have been inarticulate and uneducated, but he was not too dull to understand the sting of bigotry, and he eventually ended up in contact with a Denver civil rights attorney. John Holland was a vocal and aggressive defender of victims of social injustice. He and his legal partner had won some famous decisions on behalf of the downtrodden. Roy's case was a tough one but after some consideration, Holland decided to tackle it.

## Roy Smith vs. the County Sheriff

A former Colorado state patrolman working as an investigator for the Holland law firm found evidence that Roy Smith really had been sporadically insulted or abused by at least one neighbor. That neighbor acknowledged to investigators and to the news media that he wouldn't mind dislodging Smith from his Gilpin County properties. The desire to own someone else's land wasn't unusual in Colorado's nightmare of tangled mining and real estate claims. Errors in 19th Century surveys plague property owners even today, and appropriating a neighbor's land by whatever device or strategy is almost a sub-text in the state's history. Miners are notoriously aggressive toward one another's claims. But what eventually became the focus of Smith's federal lawsuit wasn't a covetous neighbor; the suit was filed against the Gilpin County Sheriff's Department.

Attorney Holland had discovered sheriff's department records in which investigators had recorded the complainant's name as "Nigger Roy." That was prima facie evidence of improper treatment of Smith. It demonstrated a callous disregard for the equal treatment and adequate investigation of Smith's complaints. Under federal civil rights law, that kind of discrimination is actionable.

Ultimately, Holland won for Smith a 700,000 dollar judgment against the county. The case even attracted some national network news coverage, after ABC's *20/20* did a 1998 report on Smith's ordeals. When network newscasters try to report on a local or regional story, facts are sometimes embellished. But the main part of the story got through; that Smith's complaints were thoughtlessly and illegally handled by county officials.

"Stuff was done to Roy Smith," said another Gilpin County family who'd rather not be named. "There was bar talk. There was a couple of guys who'd make sure Roy's life was miserable. They admitted it. Even with his lawsuit, he got a bum deal. He might have been crazy, but we know for sure stuff was done to him. It's too bad."[1]

But Smith did win. U.S. District Judge Wiley Daniel called it, "the most appalling and reprehensible record I've ever seen."[2]

Smith may not have found the gold he was seeking in the mineshafts and tunnels under Russell Gulch. But his supporters say the stand he took to demand acknowledgement of his basic human dignity was far more valuable than any material riches he might have discovered underground.

Most residents of Colorado would insist that it is not a racist state. Like many parts of the country, it has some stains on its past with any number of historical injustices done to one race or another over the years. Most racial problems in Colorado didn't involve discrimination against the black community, but were focused instead on the wave of European immigrants who poured into the state between 1870 and 1920.

Fifty million Europeans swept into North America during that great turn-of-the-century people migration. Many of those arriving in the Rocky Mountain region were Italians who had entered the country through the Port of New Orleans and had worked their way north looking for jobs in the farmlands, the smelters and mining operations.

## The Black Hand

When the 1920s ushered in Prohibition, the state was rocked by a years-long series of gangland slayings that seemed to accompany the Italian immigration surge. Rum-running, gambling and extortion were all firmly rooted in the new community and enforced by its far more violent fringe. The "Black Hand," as it was called, was the criminal element that was imported along with its harder-working law-abiding community.

The gangsters got their name from a trademark often used in the commission of their crimes, the drawing of a black hand on letters demanding extortion payments from fellow immigrants. The extortion letters led to popular use of the term "black mail," and a number of Black Hand kidnappings and murders were committed against the state's immigrants. On occasion, the list of victims included police officers and prosecutors who had tried to take action against the racketeers. As the gang continued to flex its muscles, the brutality and the sheer numbers of slayings stunned the public. Newspapers across the country contained frequent coverage of Black Hand murders. To combat the immigrant crime wave, an old organization with a violent past raised its ugly head.

In the aftermath of the American Civil War, tattered remnants of the Confederate Army had arisen to try to solidify white supremacy in the southern states with the creation of a group that called itself the Ku Klux Klan. Using a variety of intimidation tactics, the group had originally sought to suppress Negroes and northern state "carpetbaggers" from involvement in southern politics. The Klan's stated mission was to protect the interests of white Americans against the Republican Party. As the Klan grew from a small southern organization to one with a national political presence, it had helped re-build and solidify the Democrat Party's dominance in the southern states. Several post-war laws passed by Congress in the 1870s suppressed the Klan's violent influence, and its importance subsided. In fact, the Klan all but disappeared from American life. Four and a half decades later, all of that changed.

## Re-birth of the KKK

Membership in the Ku Klux Klan was widespread in the 1920s. It claimed to be a different organization than its racist days after the Civil War. The Klan organized auto races and even held an occasional Ku Klux Klan family day at local amusement parks.

—photo courtesy of the Denver Public Library

The early 1920s saw a reintroduction of the Klan in Colorado. The "reorganized" group was trying hard to change its image away from the racist organization of the past. Its new mission, leaders said, was to support law enforcement and the temperance movement, restore civil order, and get like-minded people elected to office. To that end, the organization vowed to help combat the new wave of bootlegging and gangland murders.

The state's newly resurrected Klan chapter was the largest in the western half of the country. One estimate indicated that for a brief period in the early 1920s, one out of every four Colorado adults was a member. Prohibition allowed the organization to gain a foothold as an open, high visibility movement that ended up getting a number of Klan members elected to local and state offices in several western states. It included prominent citizens, including Colorado Governor Clarence Morley.

Colorado Governor Clarence Morley was elected largely through the support of the Ku Klux Klan. Morley's growing unpopularity led to his ouster. A decade later he was convicted of mail fraud and sentenced to five years in Leavenworth.
—photo courtesy of the Denver Public Library

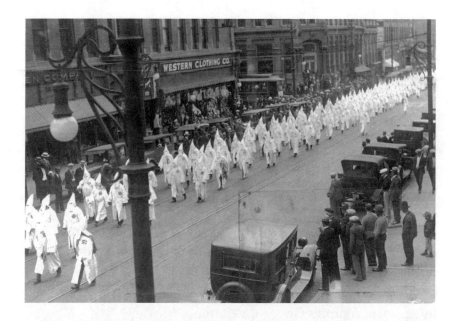

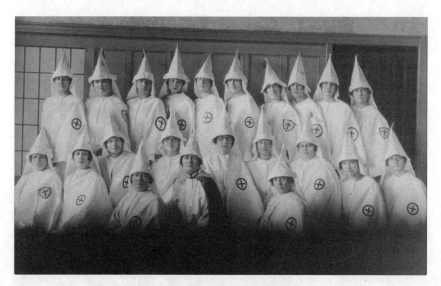

After the Klan's re-emergence in the 1920s, its members were very open about their membership. Ladies of the Klan were sometimes photographed in their attire. Mass public marches were held on city streets in support of Klan members running for office.

— photos courtesy of the Denver Public Library

Klan activities were often quite public: its members didn't always hide behind the white masks which in later years became so offensive to American sensibilities. In fact, Klan attire was at one point considered quite benign. Mass marches by the group were staged through Denver, Pueblo and Canon City in support of state and local politicians. The group even occasionally leased out a nationally known entertainment and amusement park where it conducted its annual Ku Klux Klan Family Day. Historic photographs show ridiculously-clad KKK members filling all the cars on the park's famous Ferris wheel. Yet another shows the hooded lady members of the KKK Ladies Glee Club.

But despite the election to public office of a small number of acknowledged members, Klan violence combined with several public corruption scandals caused the organization to quickly lose popularity. Across the country, members quit by the hundreds of thousands. During a five year period, national Klan membership dropped from six million to about 30,000. By the 1930s, the organization simply stopped being a factor in American politics.

The fact that the Klan gained any kind of foothold in the Rocky Mountain West was, in itself, a bit of an anomaly. Colorado was a rough and tumble place built on trapping, gold and silver mining, prostitution, and the great cattle drives that happened before the introduction of barbed wire fencing in the early 1880s. Blacks and Hispanics were always an integral part of the region's cowboy and mining heritage.

Cattle drives in the post-Civil War years were hot, dusty, miserable affairs. Each cowboy was responsible for 250 to 300 head of cattle on the 1000 mile trek from Texas to the rail lines across Missouri, Kansas and Colorado. In 1866, entrepreneur Charles Goodnight and a partner, Oliver Loving, established a cattle drive route through the deserts of New Mexico and Southern Colorado to Denver. An estimated 5000 to 8000 black men, many of them former slaves, worked as cowboys alongside their white counterparts. The Black History Museum estimates that one out of every three or four cowboys was black. Photos of old west cowpokes show that the world of 19th Century cow hustling was pretty integrated, with white, black and Mexican cowboys working side by side in an atmosphere apparently devoid of racism or prejudice.

Charles Goodnight

Oliver Loving

After the Civil War, Charles Goodnight and Oliver Loving discovered a new route for driving cattle from Texas to Denver and Cheyenne. It became known as the Goodnight-Loving trail.

—photos courtesy of Denver Public Library

Though not typically pictured by Hollywood filmmakers, black cowboys may have comprised up to a third of all cowboys in the old west.

—photo courtesy of Denver Public Library

One of the first miners to strike it rich in the Rocky Mountain gold fields was a black man named Henry Parker. There were other regional heroes, too, including Dr. Justina Ford, the west's first black female doctor. Yet another early character in regional history was "Stagecoach" Mary Fields, a former slave born in 1832. She later became a hard-drinking, pistol-packing woman who fancied herself the guardian of a group of white nuns who had established a convent in Cascade, Montana. She drove a stagecoach through the worst kind of weather, making sure the convent was adequately supplied with all its needs. A stage driver faced all sorts of dangers from sudden Rocky Mountain blizzards, to marauding Indians, to stage robbers who'd take anything of value. But six- foot-tall, cigar-smoking Stagecoach Mary had a reputation for pulling her pistol at the slightest provocation. She also won more than her share of bar fights. In fact, the Great Falls Examiner once reported that she broke more noses than any other person in Central Montana.

Stagecoach Mary Fields was a former slave who migrated to the Wild West. Smoking handmade cigars, she never turned down a good bar fight.
—courtesy of The Archives of Ursuline Convent, Toledo, Ohio

## Civil Rights and the Rise of "Beige Neighborhoods

With a history rich in examples of races generally working in harmony, the old west is possibly one of the last areas of the country where racism or separatism would be tolerated. Yet as the modern American Homeowners Association movement evolved after the 1964 Civil Rights Act, Colorado, Utah, New Mexico, Nevada and Texas became well-known for their creation of large numbers of "beige neighborhoods." Real estate developers had no motivation or interest in building "inclusive communities." People who invested in the white suburban "look and feel" of a neighborhood paid higher prices and were subtly promised the covenants would keep it that way. Unlike the pioneer days when racial differences were acknowledged and accepted, homeowners under the new paradigm embraced the HOA movement.

For decades, most of these new neighborhoods or private government compounds actually maintained a racial purity that defied common logic. But there's no mistaking the regimental feeling where every house is exactly alike, no flower pots on the porches, no tricycles on the walks, no oil spots on the driveways, no personal expressions of individualism. Many residents seeking life in these bleached private government compounds don't have trouble adjusting to the enforced symmetry they offer. For them, life in an HOA is idyllic and doesn't need to be changed.

Homeowners Associations, as envisioned by the private developers who invented them, were created for the ostensible purpose of supervising and maintaining "common areas" within each development. The common areas could be the sign at the front entrance, a community swimming pool or clubhouse, certain parks or open spaces scattered around the neighborhood. Imposing dues on residents to maintain such community benefits seemed perfectly reasonable. But the concept is as fundamentally flawed as it is fraudulent. History has long shown that bleached neighborhoods have little to do with making the necessary collections to support common areas. They are all about being bleached.

The fact that small boards of elected officers are allowed to not only enforce the rules, but to enforce them selectively, reinterpreting and embellishing them at will, is a constantly steaming cauldron waiting to burst. Stir into the brew the fact that these officers often have unlimited discretionary budgets, the ability to change rules and impose new fees and fines at will, unlimited access to legal help, and total immunity from any personal civil liability: it suffices to say that dictators in the meanest banana republic would die for such powers. It would take super-human ethics to resist such temptations.

## "Constitutional Rights Don't Apply Here"— Go Read Your Deed

The powers to harass, to fine, and to foreclose all add up to an "unspoken code" that may as well read:

- Don't stand out from the crowd.
- Don't have a political opinion.
- Don't be of the wrong race or ethnic group.
- Don't have a disability that makes others uncomfortable.
- And don't ever disagree with a board member who has control over your fate and fortune.

The annual "Spring Cleanup Day," during which volunteers stroll the neighborhood looking for covenant violations, takes on a sinister new meaning. It immediately reinforces a class warfare mentality between the "in-crowd" and the "outs." The enforcers, most often HOA elites, walk through the neighborhood in judgment of all those who are not part of the in-crowd. The blue tricycle on a board president's sidewalk doesn't attract the same demerits as the purple trike on the local black family's front yard. The grass seems longer, the weeds a little thicker on the single mom's lawn. When victims of uneven enforcement suddenly discover that they're the only ones being targeted, it's an uncomfortable moment of realization:

We don't recognize equal protection here. Constitutional rights don't apply here.

For many, it's a stomach-turning moment. Aggrieved home-owners who stand up at the annual HOA meeting and spout, "I know my rights!" are appropriately laughed at. There are no rights. Although the verbiage in most property documents is not always clear, HOA board members can properly respond: "Go read your deed."

An appropriate question, then: with all the recent progress made in civil rights, with the warm-and-fuzzy feeling of having elected the nation's first black President, with blacks, gays, the elderly and the disabled ensconced in virtually every aspect of civil life, is there really such a thing as discrimination anymore?

Go read your deed.

Really?

Go read your newspaper.

From Rybolt's Reserve, a Homeowners Association near Orlando, Florida, this covenant language: "Any lessee... shall be limited to leasing a lot... to, and occupied by, one family at a time... one adult natural person together with that person's spouse."[3] The limitations in that deed could have massive implications.

From Frisco, Texas, homeowner Jim Greenwood's brand new F-150 pickup truck was banned from the Stonebriar Homeowners Association while Cadillac Escalades, a Lincoln Mark LT and Hummers were permitted. The message could only be interpreted "You're too low-class to live in Stonebriar, Jim Boy."[4]

In Boca Raton's Casa Del Rio Condominium, the board refused to allow a resident to install electronic locks on her door. Josefina Fontanez is a thalidomide victim, born with no hands and no legs. She must use her mouth and her teeth to open deadbolts and door handles on her apartment. An electronic lock would make a world of difference to her quality of life, but in Boca Raton at least, the disabled apparently don't have the same rights as the able-bodied.

Service dogs for the handicapped? Banned in state after state.[5]

Accommodations for disabled youngsters? Totally unwelcome.[6]

Modifications for families with an autistic child? Hit the road, Jack.[7]

A Jew? Wrong answer. Get a life. Go back to your own kind.[8]

Wrong race? Butt out, black guy! Don't bring down our home values, please![9]

In Baytree Plantation in Myrtle Beach, South Carolina, the manager of an HOA padlocked a swimming pool, closing the pool to members of a black family who were holding a family reunion, while white families were allowed to continue using the pool.[10]

In Orange Grove, Florida, a mixed-race couple is faced with the seizure of their home for late payment of dues. Thomas Canuelas is white, his wife is black. The stated crime was non-payment. But in many HOAs, the outcome of a case like this is almost pre-ordained.[11]

## Legal Liabilities for HOA Members

In many insidious ways, HOA boards, and sometimes even a single HOA official can take actions which put the entire community at serious financial risk. The owner of a home in the all-white Jet Mobile Home Park in Palmetto, Florida, planned to sell her home to a friend of 30 years. Gail Bucci told a reporter for the Sarasota Herald-Tribune that a member of her HOA board warned her on the phone, "You are not moving a black guy in."

Jet Park has 300 homeowners, the vast majority of whom undoubtedly knew nothing of the attempt to keep out the prospective buyer. Bucci and her intended buyer, Reginald Alleyne, thought they had followed all of the HOA's rules, filling out applications and meeting with the president of the board. But shortly after that meeting, Bucci was told she wouldn't be allowed to sell her home to Alleyne.

"They just didn't want him in there because he's black, period," Bucci told reporters.[12]

The part of the story still untold is whether Alleyne will file a damage suit against each and every member of that mobile home park for its apparent policy of racial discrimination. Many of those homeowners who'd never dream of keeping out a prospective buyer because of race could actually discover they owe tens of thousands of dollars in judgments and legal fees because of a finding of discrimination. One stupid move by a single HOA board officer can have profound financial implications for all.

In San Diego County, the Lakeshore Villas Homeowners Association was fined 150,000 dollars by the state after it refused to accommodate a terminally ill disabled man in September of 2010. Board representatives removed his wheelchair ramp from his designated handicap parking space. He was, as a result, virtually imprisoned in his home for ten weeks. One idiotic move by an HOA official, and that 150,000 dollar fine in addition to hundreds of thousands in legal fees will be owed by every resident of the community. Individual homeowners may not have known anything about the case, but each of them is still fully liable.[13]

## Racist Troubles "in Paradise"

Perhaps there's better treatment for rich and famous minorities in million dollar gated communities? Four black families who live in multi-million dollar homes in the Southern Highlands country club compound in Las Vegas Valley might beg to differ.

The black homeowner who created the most controversy was Steven Ferguson, a well-to-do businessman whose presence in Southern Highlands has generated an enormous amount of fuss among his rich neighbors. He bought his Las Vegas mansion in December, 2001, becoming the first black man in the exclusive gated community. His 90,000 dollar membership fee gave him access to a country club that advertises: "Only a few can claim membership in such a prestigious and exclusive golf club. Admired by many, experienced by a privileged few."[14]

But soon after his arrival at Southern Highlands, Ferguson discovered he had not moved into the sanctuary he'd long been seeking. The first indication of problems, he said, was a crude photo pinned to his front door, a photograph of a lynched man accompanied by a note that read:

THE ONLY GOOD NIGGER IS A DEAD NIGGER! GET YOUR BLACK ASS OUT OF SOUTHERN HIGHLANDS![15]

It was the kind of offensive note that educated and cultured whites and blacks generally ignore, most likely the work of misguided teenagers trying to shake things up and shock a few people. Still, Ferguson made a complaint to the head of his Homeowners Association.

A few months later, Ferguson was denied access to the golf course for which he had paid the required 90,000 dollar fee. Southern Highlands, according to Ferguson, sent him a hand-delivered letter saying he had resigned and that his resignation had been accepted. He sent a letter back, saying he had not resigned, and asked to be put back onto the club membership roster. He was reinstated, and suddenly ejected a second time.

Finally, Ferguson, believing he'd broken no rules worthy of expulsion, filed for an injunction. Federal Judge James Mahan granted the injunction, reinstating Ferguson's membership. Once again, Ferguson was thrown off the course, this time after being told his credit card was not valid. With the help of the Las Vegas chapter of the NAACP, Ferguson went forward with a federal lawsuit.

There were more eggs and rocks thrown at Ferguson's home, and more racist notes left at the house. He claims his front door lock was filled with super glue. He made police complaints about each incident.

"I don't want this to happen to anyone else," Ferguson told reporter Cathy Scott. "My father once told me it's like a wild dog. If you take off running, they'll keep chasing you."[16]

Southern Highlands HOA president Garry Goett told the media, "We think Mr. Ferguson is just trying to embarrass and intimidate us with these false claims, and we're just not going to yield to the pressure. As president of the club and as an owner, the club documents grant me considerable authority to deal with membership and member issues which includes, but is not limited to, recalling a membership at any time for any or no reason whatsoever."

The reporter who worked on the Ferguson story wrote that she drove up to the entrance gate to the exclusive compound and asked permission to go to Ferguson's home. The guard told her, "Who?"

"Steven Ferguson."

"Scott Ferguson?" the guard asked.

"No, Steve Ferguson."

"The guard looked confused, then asked again, "Ferguson?"

"Yes."

"There's no Ferguson here," he said.

"Yes, Steven Ferguson lives in Southern Highlands."

Only at that point, according to the reporter, the guard called the Ferguson home to ask permission to let in their guest.[17]

The ruckus stirred up by Ferguson prompted media questions to three other wealthy black families who live at Southern Highlands, including baseball great Reggie Jackson. Jackson declined to comment, other than to say that Ferguson was a friend. Two other families acknowledged they had also faced some ugly problems in the community, but they didn't want to be identified.

The Southern Highlands story made its way into the *Wall Street Journal Online* on September 18, 2006, in a story called "Trouble in Paradise: Minorities Report Bias in Vacation Areas." Reporter Troy McMullen cited the Ferguson case along with many other cases of apparent discrimination in exclusive communities around the country. One black couple, Philip and Kristina Edington made a bid on a half-million dollar home near the mouth of Oak Creek Canyon, Sedona, Arizona. The bid was accepted. But on the day of closing, the owner suddenly withdrew the property and refused to sell. He took the property off the market. Dr. Edington said he was astonished at how blatant it was.[18]

People like Edington and Ferguson shouldn't be stunned at the treatment they've received. Anyone who closely examines the activities of the Homeowners Association movement could spot major problems. Obviously, not all HOAs are racist and not all HOA members are racist. But the very structure of covenant-controlled "private governments" is problematic. Unless all human nature magically becomes compassionate and fair (not too likely), or unless the Constitution's Bill of Rights is suddenly restored to each and every homeowner in America, bigotry could fester forever. There's too much profit in maintaining the status quo.

## An Insurance and Legal Monolith

The power invested in elected HOA boards is absolute. Most HOA boards are required to buy insurance coverage which indemnifies board members against any and all financial harm should they be taken to court by a homeowner. With more than 300,000 private government compounds scattered across the country, each one paying anywhere from 1,000 to 100,000 dollars a year to insurance companies, the sums of money backing up these compounds are staggering.

An aggrieved homeowner who comes into conflict with his HOA is facing literally billions of dollars of HOA wealth and legal might, all of it aimed at smacking down each and every sign of dissent. It's all about the money. It's always about the money. There are no moral principles at play here, just who gets how much of someone else's cash.

With no personal liability for their behavior, inexperienced board members have every reason to take the most unconscionable actions without fear of redress or backlash. Bias, personal animosity or venal racism is not only encouraged but is almost guaranteed. There is no incentive built into these developers' agreements to create even an appearance of fairness. The system essentially allows every board member or officer of an HOA to claim plausible deniability.

"Harassment-at-will" are the marching orders. Since HOA Boards aren't bound to acknowledge the Constitutional rights of private property owners, annoying little impediments like "equal protection" and "due process" are so much chaff to blow away before a board takes its next action. A targeted homeowner can complain *ad nauseum* that other homeowners aren't similarly required to have conforming fences, or obey parking laws or paint requirements. HOA boards have a free hand to wield the law and the lawsuits arbitrarily. They can essentially remove anyone they choose from the neighborhood. It's not hard to understand how some HOA board members can become drunk with power. But it's difficult to explain why such "government gulags," as they're called by some detractors, continue to exist.

This brings us full circle to old Roy Smith, the kicked-around Gilpin County gold miner and homeowner: despite his personal communication problems, he won an interesting legal battle against his adversaries. He got the chance to be heard in a court of law because of an advantage not shared by others in parallel situations. Roy Smith did not live in a Homeowners Association.

He was not under the control of a board of directors which could flout the Constitution's Bill of Rights, chewing up and spitting out every protection guaranteed by our nation's founders. Roy Smith lived in the free world, where government institutions are obligated to shepherd the very rules that James Madison posited and penned two centuries ago. Had Roy Smith lived inside one of the "private government compounds" that are spreading across the country's landscape, one wonders if his case might have had a different ending.

Tens of millions of homeowners across America have surrendered their access to the kind of justice afforded Smith, and the courts have repeatedly ruled against them in favor of the HOA. "You should have known what you were buying into," many a homeowner has been told. And at a stunning rate the "law of the land" is becoming the law of the HOA. HOA board members, sometimes unappointed, sometimes unelected, have usurped the role of traditional government. They collect untold millions in "taxes" and sometimes award multi-million dollar contracts to friends and family, even to themselves. They foreclose on and evict homeowners with impunity. Many personally profit by seizing those foreclosed homes on the auction block and selling them for a premium. And no one is looking. No one is monitoring. No one is even curious.

# 9

# Cowboys, Crooks and Bad, Bad Men

*If you burn your neighbor's house down, it*
*doesn't make your house look any better.*

—Lou Holtz

"**H**is kid is a faggot! His wife is a Jew!"

The Willowbrook Homeowners Association intended for me to remember that little bit of ugliness for all of my life. I will, of course. That commentary was actually a legal strategy devised by Willowbrook leaders after they initiated their land-grab lawsuit against me in 2003. I've since learned it's a strategy not infrequently used by trial lawyers in many other cases.

While I have no illusions about my own case being ground zero in the national battle for property rights, the Willowbrook strategy demonstrated an interesting point. Across the country there is an end-game moral and political struggle going on between two factions: those who believe the nation's founders felt it important to set aside certain individual rights for each man, woman and child, and those who are trying to neutralize those rights forever.

HOA lawyers across the country have repeatedly demonstrated they will use the most bizarre, the most extreme, the most unethical means necessary to stifle any homeowner who tries to take a stand against the movement. There are billions of dollars in potential legal fees involved. "Truth" is not a factor in this struggle; it's merely a speed bump in the race to "redistribute wealth." Only by dramatic national resistance will the fading Constitutional rights of private property owners be reclaimed.

## HOA Folk Song: "Your Land Is My Land, Your Land Is Our Land"

Most of the baggage from the Willowbrook lawsuits and my countersuit is unnecessary to recount, but some parts are nevertheless entertaining. Other parts might be instructive to folks who've found themselves in the crosshairs of an abusive HOA. A personal website I published after the last trial includes much of the appalling testimony and interrogation.[1] The website lists names, addresses and some of the more vulgar details of Willowbrook's attempted land grab. Since I most likely won't live for the next 100 years, I've registered and paid to keep my website alive for the next century, should the World Wide Web or the promised subsequent "grid" actually last that long.

Willowbrook is a community of about 200 homes nestled in the Rocky Mountain foothills as they begin their dramatic rise from the Denver plains into the "high country." The community has a casual feel, unlike the regimented beige barracks that now cover the landscape in other parts of the state. Each house sits on a plot of land that ranges anywhere from an acre to 13 acres. In other words, there's room for people to spread out and be creative with their home construction and their personal lives. But Willowbrook's covenants mirror the stiff-necked covenants used by 300,000 other Homeowners Associations across the country, and attorneys advise the few members who show up for monthly board meetings that the rules must always be enforced strictly. Stray one iota outside the path of absolute enforcement, and a property owner is likely to end up in court facing a small mob of hostile fellow homeowners.

The Willowbrook Homeowners Association is infamous in Colorado for its decades-long battles to stop any development within miles of its entrance. Once Willowbrook got its own boundaries established, leaders of the Association did their best to ensure this community was the only one permitted in the area. Most of those battles have been lost by Willowbrook, but the community has gained a reputation for stridency, meanness, and for arbitrarily costing nearby property owners massive amounts of money in legal expenses.

Willowbrook was one of the first Homeowners Associations in the country to force a homeowner to remove his American flag. The flag case, as memory serves, didn't actually end up in a lawsuit. The "offending family," though, was ordered to remove its flag and flagpole under the threat of being publicly humiliated, fined and sued for tens of thousands of dollars. Had they tried to fight the HOA, they could very likely have lost their home.

I was probably one of the despicable few who actually felt pride whenever I drove into Willowbrook in the 1980s and saw my neighbor's flag knitting the breezes. More than pride, I wondered about the family who lived there. They had built an attractive, gravel drive to their front door. On the white pole in the center of their yard they raised that flag each day. I recall the emotion I felt driving into my little community; that little heart-pop as I saw the colors rippling against the azure-blue Colorado sky. In my mind, this family wasn't flying the flag for themselves, they were flying it for me. Their flag didn't impact my property values a whit. Families of former military people are probably like that, though. We're trained to feel that heart-thump more than others. I had always meant to knock at their door and ask this neighbor's personal story, and why flying the flag was important to them. The fact that I never did is a failure on my part. I am poorer for having missed the opportunity of meeting them.

The Willowbrook family who put up the flagpole was obviously patriotic. But they were unprepared for the community rage that followed. They were eventually "persuaded" to get rid of the flag and take down the offending pole. Their patriotism was an offense against the community standard, an apparent violation of the HOA covenants they had signed when they first bought their home.

A thousand miles away and a half century earlier my own Grandpa used to raise such a flag next to the gravel drive in front of his own house. His tiny white cottage backed up against the great Civil War trenches from the 1864 siege of Petersburg. The infamous "Battle of the Crater" happened not too far from his home. Thousands of Americans lost their lives in those trenches fighting for either the North or the South. My grandfather was a city attorney in Petersburg and his sentiments were probably southern, but the flag he flew was the American. The red, white and blue colors were meant to unify the races, not to divide them.

Back then, such patriotic observances weren't violations of HOA covenants. Flag-fliers weren't even considered community eccentrics. They just marked another forum where the love of country could occasionally be expressed. Those who've lost loved ones on foreign battlefields sometime have trouble articulating the upwelling of all those personal feelings. It suffices just to put up the flag.

Willowbrook's history was periodically marked by other aggressions, including an unofficial campaign against the only black family to have ever moved into our neighborhood. Actually, this case must have proved a quandary for Willowbrook leaders since only one member of the couple was black. The wife was white. Her skin color was politically correct for the neighborhood but his was several shades on the wrong side of the color chart.

Not only was he black, he sometimes wore his hair in corn-rows. That was audacious. The fact that he was a professor at a local college was immaterial. But there's no question he was occasionally dogged by community rage.

I may have been born a stupid white man, but I just didn't see how the presence of this gentleman lowered the value of my home. In my mind the guy was great. He was smart, he was adversarial, he was the kind of man I'd treasure as a member of my own family. But apparently he, too, was the subject of community shunning.

Where people learn this kind of vitriol has always been a mystery to me. Do they get it in their mothers' milk? I'm not even a bleeding heart liberal, just an average, conservative white guy who still thinks somebody named Jesus popped up in our common history to save us from each others' rancor. As a reporter, though, I've seen bigotry boil up on occasion among people who would be far better served by acting as neighbors.

My black acquaintance actually called me one day in my capacity as a local television reporter. He complained of horrible treatment he'd received at the hands of certain Willowbrook leaders. Obviously, my built-in conflict-of-interest prevented me from exploring his case on the air. Some of the treatment of this man, I had even witnessed myself. It actually happened during one of the first Willowbrook Homeowners Association meetings I ever attended. He was sitting a couple of rows in front of me and he stood up to comment about some neighborhood controversy, the details of which have long since escaped my memory. This black gentleman was no slouch. He was articulate and calm. I do remember my confusion when another Willowbrook home-owner hissed, "Sit down, you don't belong here." Perhaps I was naïve, or a little dumbfounded at the outburst. I said nothing to her, when I could have said something. Again, my loss.

## The Adverse Possession Gambit

Later I learned from this gentleman that he was once accosted on his own property by a member of what he called "the neighborhood Nazis." He related to me that the president of the Willowbrook Homeowners Association had threatened to use the "adverse possession" gambit to condemn a portion of his nicely-groomed corner lot for a horse-riding trail. He told me that riders from the local stable had indeed occasionally cut the corner across his lawn and that he had moved in some big boulders to try to discourage them.

The threat, my friend claimed, was just the last in a series of obnoxious actions this particular HOA officer had taken to make his life difficult. I counseled him that I had faced some similar strains in the past and told him that his claims of racism might be misplaced, or at the least overstated.

Still, he said he had found a novel way of dealing with the white bully from the association. During that confrontation my friend grabbed the HOA president by his shirt collar, pulled him up nose-to-nose and said, "Don't mess with a brother, man, just don't ever mess with no brother." That was the last our neighborhood ever heard of the horse-riding trail across this man's manicured lawn.

Willowbrook apparently liked the theory of adverse possession, though. The phrase could be hauled out and used with abandon against any homeowner who had to be kept in line. Since HOA boards are not bound by restrictions of the U.S Constitution's Bill of Rights, and because many homes in and around Willowbrook had problems with inaccurate 19th century land surveys, the threat of adverse possession could be flung like a cow-pie at any homeowner who community leaders felt they needed to purge. It was a central theme in their lawsuit in the now infamous "Lucas Faggot Case" filed against my family in 2003. More on that in a moment.

In 1986, I was in the process of building my new home in Willowbrook when I first felt the acidity of HOA relations. Much younger, and much more naïve then, I knew absolutely nothing about the politics of Homeowners Associations. The Willowbrook covenants filled dozens of pages of mind-numbing rules and regulations controlling architecture, gardening, television antennas, house colors, roof shingles, how many hours trash cans could be left outside on trash day. It seemed like virtually every aspect of human behavior was controlled in some way or another. The same kinds of regulations are mirrored in several hundred thousand other covenant-controlled communities across North America. Like many other new property buyers across the country, the stack of CC&Rs was handed to me for the first time during our real estate closing. Obviously, there was no time to read them during the hour that we were signing the final documents. The Realtor told us, "Ah, they're nothing. Just some rules to make sure you ask permission before adding an extra room. No big deal."

Having lived in complete harmony with neighbors in three previous neighborhoods, I figured I could be just as good a neighbor as anyone else. My wife and I signed all the appropriate paperwork, closed on the property, and some time later submitted our architectural plan to the neighborhood committee. There were a few rough spots, rejections, and re-submittals, but nothing terribly out of the ordinary.

Midway through that year of construction, though, my wife began suffering some odd health problems. Her energy vanished, her limbs seemed weak. She kept silent about most of her symptoms, but one day she mentioned that she'd had a sudden loss of vision in one eye. Neither of us had ever heard the term "optic neuritis."

A few weeks later, sitting in the office of a local neurologist, the physician told us that an optic neuritis is generally indicative of only one ailment. And we heard his diagnosis of multiple sclerosis. He was understanding and sympathetic, of course, but his words were terrifying. His voice seemed to fade into background noise as we heard things like "wheelchair," "paralysis," and "coping."

The memory of my young wife's reaction will be with me forever. She turned and mouthed silently to me: "I'm sorry, Ward. I'm so sorry." She didn't actually say the words out loud; she just looked at me and said them with her lips. She was in tears, Dr. John Ryan was in tears and I suppose I was, as well. My memory of those first few moments is still like the searing heat of a cattle brand. The doctor was as encouraging as one would expect, but the only comments that really stood out were the ones that told us of the changes and challenges we probably faced. As the parents of two young boys, we were scared. There was a mountain of emotional debris through which to sift.

One thing the doctor told us, "All current research indicates that MS seems to be aggravated by stress. Avoid stress as much as you can." He encouraged us to visit the University of Colorado Medical Center and enroll in biofeedback, stress management classes, and progressive relaxation therapy. In our depression and desperation, we signed up for every program and course we could find.

## Culture Shock for the Handicapped

A number of days after that diagnosis, some impulse led me to call the long-time president of our local Homeowners Association. Perhaps I was trying to solicit some personal encouragement, or find a sympathetic ear in a confusing time. One of my questions was how to go about incorporating some kind of future wheelchair access to our new home. Up to this point, I had not even met this man, but he was well-known in the community as the "self-appointed Mayor of Willowbrook." He was also a man of no small means, having worked as a Martin Marietta rocket engineer in one of the initial designs for the Viking spacecraft to Mars.

I told him in detail of my wife's diagnosis and that at some point we might have to come up with a wheelchair ramp of some sort to get her up the front steps. I recognized that any changes to the house exterior would have to be approved by the architectural control committee. But I'll never forget his response:

Gee, that's too bad. You'll just have to move downtown.

I wasn't quite sure what I was hearing. Our new home was still under construction. Any wheelchair accommodation could have been easily incorporated into the design of the new house and would be totally invisible to neighbors. After all, it was a rural home. I was completely baffled and asked him for clarification.

"We will never approve architectural changes for a wheelchair," he said. "This neighborhood was not designed for people who need 'accommodations.' It was never designed for 'gimps'."

I was speechless, but he poured it on, "I'm sorry to say this, but regular people kind of lose their appetite around gimps."

As streetwise as I thought I was, I had never heard the term, *gimps*. After the call ended, I went for a dictionary. "Gimp: A limp, or limping gait. A person who limps. To walk with a limp." I could scarcely believe I was actually looking up such a word. My wife didn't even have any visible symptoms and this man's words seemed inapplicable to our family's situation.

News reporters and their families tend not to be offended by stereotypical comments or crude insults. In our daily lives we circulate through all strata of society, we meet everyone, shake hands, walk through hospitals, housing projects, nursing homes, prisons, governor's mansions, we meet murderers, gang members, officials from the White House, and generally make time for people from every walk of life. We hear all sorts of language, from sexism to racism. Vulgarities and crudities are just part of the things one hears while living life in the public eye. We hear them, and tolerate them. It's all OK. But this one had a little bit of a sting. I passionately loved my wife. She was a beautiful, gentle, gracious lady. We hadn't even moved into our new home yet, but according to the Willowbrook Homeowners Association "gimps" like her weren't an accepted part of the community.

I don't think I ever spoke to anyone about the "gimp" conversation. Laws protecting the handicapped had not yet seen the light of day in the 1980s, and it was a reasonable assumption at the time that a handicapped person would just have to be relocated. Although the conversation with the HOA president shocked and confused me, I concluded that I'd have to start looking for another place to build a home, one that didn't have such despotic rules. In one of the bizarre twists that makes life interesting I didn't find such a property. The property found me.

## The Wild Wild West

It happened during a Saturday morning hike with the kids a few weeks after my wife's diagnosis and the Willowbrook "gimp" conversation. While walking around the neighborhood perimeter road, I saw an older gentleman emerge from his house and begin waving at me. I had never met this man, but knew him by reputation. He was supposedly a crotchety, ill-tempered farmer whose was long known as the neighborhood nemesis. He was constantly in the Willowbrook newsletter as someone the HOA was either suing or threatening to sue. His acreage was completely outside the boundaries of Willowbrook, and it was pretty well-known that there was some kind of decades-old feud going on between him and the Willowbrook Homeowners Association. He was often blamed for rising legal costs to the community, even though it was

Willowbrook which initiated all of the lawsuits. It brought to mind the old 19ᵗʰ Century feud between the Hatfields and the McCoys in the hills of West Virginia and Kentucky.

The man motioned for me to come across the fence and talk to him.

The "crotchety old man" seemed like a nice enough fellow. He actually looked quite dignified with his glasses and close-cropped gray hair. We shook hands, he asked about my boys, he told me he had two of his own. I learned he had spent his career as a dentist, and was now doing work with the Denver Bone Bank, an organization that worked with patients undergoing reconstructive surgery or bone grafts.

His name, he said, was Bill Cody.

The name immediately intrigued me. As a youngster I had read several books about a man with the same name, "Buffalo Bill Cody." The historic Bill Cody was a 19ᵗʰ Century soldier who'd become a cowboy and big game hunter. During construction of the Kansas Pacific Railroad, he picked up the name "Buffalo Bill" because of the huge quantities of buffalo meat he had supplied for workers laying the rails. In the late 1800s he became one of the best-known celebrities in the world with a traveling show known as the Buffalo Bill Wild West Expedition. His show featured such things as Indian villages, choreographed Indian attacks on stagecoaches, and rifle shooting demonstrations by the internationally famous sharpshooter Annie Oakley. He was probably the most well-known name in Colorado history. In fact, Buffalo Bill Cody's grave and monument now sits on a hillside not too many miles from the entrance to Willowbrook.

I was fascinated and asked if Dr. Bill Cody was any relation to Buffalo Bill Cody.

"He was my great uncle. I'm his grand-nephew." For me, it was a stunning moment. And I had just shaken hands with one of the great man's kin.

A rare early picture of Buffalo Bill Cody.
—Courtesy of National Cowboy and
Western Heritage Museum, Oklahoma

Dr. Cody explained to me that the acreage he now owned next to Willowbrook sat right on the century-old stagecoach road that used to connect the city of Denver to the historic 19th Century mining and gambling towns of Leadville and South Park. Every famous cowboy, explorer, pioneer, gambler or prostitute at one time or another had traveled up and down this road. The land had been parceled off over the years to various property owners.

But here I stood on the very crossroads of the old west. I could reach out and touch the actual ground where Butch Cassidy, the Sundance Kid, William Bonney, Calamity Jane, Doc Holiday, Wyatt Earp and others had traveled. At one time or another, they all got off the train in Denver. When they headed west to the mountain gambling towns, they each walked or rode over this hallowed piece of ground.

For a kid who used to watch every cowboy movie the army post matinees had to offer, it was a thrill beyond words to be this close to an icon of the American West. Dr. Cody wasn't terribly forthcoming with the old cowboy stories, but the few he told weren't wasted on me. He was a gift, right in my own backyard.

Cody's greater obsession, though, was his massive contempt for the Willowbrook Homeowners Association and especially the HOA official with whom I'd recently spoken.

"A complete liar, that man is the biggest liar I ever met," Cody spouted. "If his lips are moving, it's a lie," he said. "That man has a major problem with the truth." To my knowledge, I hadn't yet been lied to or lied about by this HOA leader. My one and only contact with him at this point was the phone conversation about my "gimp wife." I let Cody's outburst pass.

Cody told me he once lived in Willowbrook and in fact was one of the original members. In the neighborhood's early days he had even served as the board president, but he'd become disgusted with the politics and moved to this property just outside the HOA. It seemed that he and the HOA had feuded over their property lines ever since. The association had sued him multiple times for one misstep or another.

*The Cody-Willowbrook Feud.* Somehow the phrase didn't have the same cachet as the *Hatfields and McCoys*. But from what I was learning, it was almost as vicious and precedent-setting. Like the Hatfields, it had even been marked at one time by gunfire. Cody told me about the time an adjacent Willowbrook homeowner had cranked off a couple of shotgun rounds at him and his two dogs. One of the shots, he said, came awfully close.

We chatted for perhaps half an hour about his experiences with the association. Suddenly, he said to me, "Why don't you buy my property and get out of Willowbrook?" It caught me completely by surprise.

There was no way in the world I could afford to buy Cody's hillside. His asking price was impossibly high. The history of the place intrigued me, though. And the thought of having an alternate place to build a future home had tremendous appeal at this point. But money-wise, I was just scraping by.

## The Deed Is Done

Over the next few months, though, Cody taught me how real estate deals are done: someone in the relationship, usually the buyer, just has to stretch and dream. At his encouragement, I doubled my hours at work, dreamt more dreams, and began to make the biggest financial stretch of my life. In my mind, it was the only way out of the Willowbrook gimp dilemma. The Cody land wasn't under the control of the HOA. A house designed with future wheelchair access would be easy to do, and I could solve both Willowbrook's problem and mine by getting my wife out of the neighborhood. I learned to my chagrin, though, the Willowbrook machine was just getting started.

Within months of my purchase of Cody's property, I began hearing of the existence of wild rumors about me, my family, my two young sons. Some of the rumors were vulgar. Most were laughable. There were lurid stories about wild parties either my wife or I had supposedly attended, hideous conversations I had supposedly had with others, people I had reportedly deceived at one time or another. Being a news anchor on a nationally high-profile television station, one becomes accustomed to becoming grist for local tongue waggers and trash mongers. But this one for some reason was in overdrive.

It became obvious that certain local leaders were furious with my purchase of the Cody land. The property, it seems, was intensely coveted by the Homeowners Association as some kind of a barrier against any future development bordering their neighborhood.

Curiously, they had never tried to buy the land themselves, but their strategy was increasingly clear.

Community leaders had repeatedly discussed various ways of forcing Cody off his land. If they incorporated the Willowbrook community as a "city", they could then seize his land in an eminent domain action. They discussed filing for adverse possession and denying him access to water. They even secretly scoped out the property for evidence of various endangered species like the famed Prebles Meadow Jumping Mouse and the Tansy Ragwort. Sadly for them, I think, they discovered that the endangered Prebles Mouse actually spends its time eating the endangered Tansy Ragwort. Ah well, life finds a way to survive.

Anyway, there apparently wasn't an idea left unproposed. My purchase of the property threw a monkey wrench into their plans against Dr. Cody, and all the venom originally aimed at him during his years of ownership was now directed at me.

For the first time I began researching county property records to see what other surprises might be in store. One document rattled me; the letter from Willowbrook President James Carahalios.

The 1995 letter was quietly filed with the county Open Space division and was wildly deceptive. Prior to 1994, all surrounding properties were privately owned and fenced off. There was no Open Space land anywhere nearby. Open Space had never even declared an interest in the Cody land. Willowbrook officials, though, were obviously maneuvering to hit me

> **"We have always used this property as an access for our hikes into Jefferson County Open Space."**
> **—James Carahalios, Willowbrook HOA**

with a future adverse possession land grab. Before they could do so, however, they had to do some radical rewriting of history. There was that annoying little 18-year-rule with which they had to contend. The document quietly filed with Open Space gave me early warning of their mindset.

Within a couple of months of that letter, dozens, even scores of Willowbrook residents began streaming across my property line. The ancient barbed wire fence, which had been in place for more than a century, was repeatedly cut down. The grassland which had been pristine and untouched for decades was suddenly marked by human footpaths. There was little doubt in my mind that some sort of organized campaign was underway.

By design, the Willowbrook HOA attempts to establish an adverse possession path across the author's property. "No Trespassing" signs were torn down almost daily, even though no path through this property had ever existed except for the few weeks prior to the HOA's attempt to seize the property.
—photo by author

Adverse possession actions are one of the most vicious forms of land confiscation on the books. By claiming to have "used" the land for 18 years, Willowbrook leaders could have simply reached out and snatched my property. If I didn't take an aggressive stance to block the trespassing, the HOA could have claimed my land as its own and the courts would have simply changed the names on the deed.

The threat had to be dealt with as forcefully as possible. Willowbrook knew how to do land grabs like this. And I was just learning how they intended to do it. Willowbrook had obviously declared a full scale war on me, and I was at wit's end.

Another property owner on the north side of Willowbrook told me her family had ended up losing a nearly identical battle years earlier. She said:

> My grandmother lost 18 acres that way. They just reached out and took it. We've had that land in our family for more than a hundred years, and my granddad had put up some fences to pen in his cattle. They just snatched a big chunk of land outside the pen because they claimed they'd been using it for a walking trail. I never, ever saw anyone walking on any kind of trail. There was not even a hint of a trail. But we still lost the land. I just don't understand how they have the conscience to do that. It was just theft.

## Block It or Lose It

*"Block the trespass, or lose the property,"* an attorney told me. There were alternate ways to try to protect the land from an adverse possession seizure, but some HOAs and their lawyers are experts at the kind of deception it takes to subvert private property rights. *"Block the trespass."* Those were my marching orders. *"Block the trespass."*

I patched the holes in the historic fence along my property line. I posted a half-dozen new "No Trespassing" signs. In all the years I had either watched or owned this property, the fence and signs had never been touched. Under the new paradigm, each fence repair lasted less than a week.

One day I telephoned HOA president James Carahalios and asked him if there was any way I could establish a more positive relationship with the neighborhood. In an old reporter's habit, I tape recorded the phone call, an effort to better document the weird kinds of things that were happening. His answer was unsettling:

You bought the property, now it's your problem.

Over a period of months, I made multiple trips to the county zoning department. I read every Bruce and Ely book on easement law that I could find. Lawyer after lawyer gave me the same advice, but none offered any solutions other than filing a series of separate legal actions against each individual trespasser. On a rural piece of acreage like this, taking such advice was impossible. In almost every case I researched, filing any kind of lawsuit against an HOA land-grab ended up being the losing strategy.

## The Land War Begins

In some desperation, I began looking for any other landowners across the country who had actually succeeded in beating back organized land-grabs. As my story file grew, it became increasingly apparent that the act of snatching someone else's property was not a rare phenomenon. It was going on all over. In fact, property-grabs were foundational to the development of the old west. The most common theme seemed to be that almost all landowners faced with a snatch, eventually lost their property. There were some scattered success stories of landowners who had actually stopped a land-grab, and many of them shared a fascinating theme.

"Don't mess with a brother, man! Don't ever mess with no brother!" Incredibly, the physical nose-to-nose confrontation my black neighbor once had with his Willowbrook tormentor was the one method that seemed to have some efficacy. The wisdom he had previously shared with me was that "HOA leaders can be cowards. They're only comfortable when they have a crowd behind them. Take that knowledge and use it!" His strategy, obviously, was to create the neighborhood buzz: "That man's crazy! Don't mess with him!"

I wasn't really comfortable with his form of aggression, thinking that if a white guy like me pulled a parallel stunt, this particular HOA would make sure I was hog-tied and ankle-shackled in the backseat of the nearest Sheriff's car. But my research, aside from keeping me entertained at night, turned up some wacky land battles involving property owners around the country. The various battles began hinting at something which looked like it could actually be a pretty good strategy.

## Turning the Tables

In a rural area of Oregon about twenty miles west of Portland, landowner Bruce Campbell purchased and re-located to his 10 acre property a scrapped Boeing 727 airliner which he said he was going to convert into a permanent home. It cost Campbell about 100,000 dollars to buy the retired airliner and move it to his land six miles south of Hillsboro. To this day, the airliner sits on his property at 15270 SW Holly Hill Road near the town of Laurel, and no Homeowners Association has tried to establish itself within viewing distance. In fact, there are several 727 owners across the country who've converted scrapped airliners into homes. Not a single one has faced property grabs by neighbors. For some reason, HOAs seem to give them a wide berth.[2]

Wandering further afield, I discovered Lucas, Kansas, where more than a century ago landowner S.P. Dinsmoor must have faced some kind of a neighborhood beef. He began construction of a so-called "Garden of Eden" on his property right in the middle of town. Everything on his land is built with cement, the statues, the trees, the bushes, the mausoleum, cement people seated on cement benches. The square city block is one of the world's greatest eyesores. Its audacity is breathtaking. And it remains, more than a century later.[3]

Bruce Campbell, a Beaverton, Oregon landowner attempted to stop people from trespassing across his property. He succeeded with the installation of a Boeing 727 which he is now converting into his home. The lady standing on the wing with Campbell is Anja Grossman, a friend of the photographer.

—photo courtesy of Ingo Doienberg

The origin of some property disputes is forever lost to history, but oftentimes amazing monuments last for what must seem to neighbors to be an eternity. "Salvation Mountain" is the name given to a concrete mountain built near Niland, California, by crusader Leonard Knight. The three-story-high cement mountain has been criticized by neighbors, condemned by local officials, and rebuked by environmentalists who've tried to get it listed as a toxic waste dump and Superfund cleanup site. But it has been adored by open-mouthed passers-by since the mid 1980s. Why Knight decided to build it is a mystery. Many community eyesores have a way of becoming institutionalized as tourist attractions. Like the Garden of Eden in Lucas, Kansas, Salvation Mountain took on a life of its own. For more than twenty years, Knight has been winning battles and beating back adversaries.

This acre of concrete rises above the desert near California's Great Salton Sea. Environmentalists have tried for decades to have it torn down. In the meantime, Christian groups from around the world have gathered there for inspirational concerts, sermons and stories about the founder. Detractors call it one of the worst eyesores in history. But it's a major tourist destination in the desert of Southern California. Even California Senator Barbara Boxer has called it a "national treasure." *www.SalvationMountain.us*

—photo by RW Sims

## The Magic of Brassieres

Disputes over property rights aren't just found in this country. A friend of mine in New Zealand who was familiar with my own struggles told me of a sheep farmer in his homeland who found a unique way of confounding the establishment. John Lee of the town of Wanaka had some sort of a disagreement with local officials. When several hundred ladies' brassieres suddenly appeared on the fence that separated his sheep ranch from the main highway into town, he refused to take them down. Each weekend, more and more brassieres of all different sizes, shapes and colors appeared. The road past his sheep ranch became a regional, and then a world-wide sensation as hundreds of local women stopped to remove their bras and knot them to the fence. It became almost a religious pilgrimage as women from a local college made their way to Lee's fence, doffed their bras and tied the ceremonial knot. As word of Lee's dispute with town officials spread, contributions of brassieres began arriving from all over the world. White, pink, red, beige, purple, Lee's sheep fence was just as spectacular as one could imagine.

Brassiere fence in New Zealand. No one really knows what led to the "disagreement" between sheep rancher Stephen Lee and the town of Wanaka. But the fence has almost become a "coming of age" moment where ladies from a nearby college strip and tie their bras to Lee's fence.
—photo courtesy of Picture Nation, Great Britain

Town officials went berserk. They repeatedly ordered Lee to remove the undies. Lee absolutely denied his fence was an eye-sore. He just smiled and spoke of the tremendous inspiration the thousands of bras provided him.

"Bras are like magic to me. I've loved them for all of my life," he told reporters.[4] Many men across the world would have to wholeheartedly agree. The thought of all those young women who took such a magnificent step to help a man in need just makes one's eyes water. Photographs of New Zealand's bra fence have made their way across the World Wide Web, preserved for all time.

## Tit for Tat…Flip What?

Back on this side of the world, several neighborhood boobs decided to harass a Riverton, Utah, landowner who was trying to build a dream home on his property, which is traversed by a city sewer line. Darren Wood sought all the appropriate permits and carefully designed his construction plan to accommodate the pipe. His house plan was "politically correct" for the neighborhood. His planned choice of colors was "correct." But Wood says to avoid the pipe, it was necessary for him to build his home about 18 inches higher than code. Wood proposed bringing in extra fill dirt to raise the ground level by the needed amount. His plan was approved.

The neighbors would have none of it. They demanded the city give the plans new consideration. The city of Riverton then ordered Wood to get new soil tests, thereby costing Wood four months and three thousand dollars. Again his construction plan was approved and the work resumed.

Neighbors began to micro-manage his construction, checking on lot permits, soil preparations, re-examining surveys, inspecting retaining walls, essentially pulling every trick in the book to stop or delay the project. Finally, midway through construction, they complained about the "illegal" extra 18 inches of elevation. Riverton officials ordered Wood to lower the peak of his roof, costing him an additional twenty-five thousand dollars.

But as the house was finished, Wood played the ultimate "tit for tat." He designed a huge vent cover across the side of his house facing his most aggressive antagonists, homeowners Mark Easton and Stan Torgersen. The vent was shaped like a saguaro cactus, the kind found growing throughout the desert southwest. This cactus had four trunks, one of the middle ones slightly taller than the others. From an artistic standpoint, it actually was quite pretty, and attracted attention from news media around the world.[5]

"It's not a cactus," neighbor Torgersen told reporters. "Any objective person would see that it's a human hand with a raised middle finger. He's flipping us the bird."

After months of harrassment by neighbors, homebuilder Darren Wood added this attic vent to the side of his house. "It's just an art deco cactus," said Wood.
—photo courtesy of Darren Wood

"No, I'm not," said Wood. "It's art-deco. I guess it's all in the eye of the beholder."[6] In terms of depressed home resale values, each of Wood's tormentors ended up losing far more than they cost him. Wood is now in complete control of his neighbors' property values. By simply removing the artistic cactus, Wood's house will maintain its true value. But as long as he lives in that neighborhood, with or without the cactus, the homes of his rivals will be hard to sell. His neighbors have only one possible option. They have to be very nice to him.

Darren Wood's Utah home, incidentally, is in the 11700 block of South Whatta View Place. You just can't make these things up.

## The Redneck Solution

Utah seems to have its share of landowners willing to put up a spirited fight to protect a piece of property. Another such warrior is Rhett Davis, a farmer in the community of Hooper. His farm has been in the family for generations. As urban sprawl began spreading westward from South Ogden, brand new housing developments with their draconian HOA rules pressed against his farm from all sides. One development of half-million dollar homes was built right on the edge of the Davis farm. Despite the fact that he'd been there for decades, the homeowners wanted him gone. "Too many flies, the manure stinks, he cuts his hay too late into the evening, too much dust," they whined to county officials. Various health and environmental agencies were called.

Davis responded by erecting what he called his "Redneck Stonehenge," a barrier of old demolition derby cars buried nose-first in the ground. His story made headlines across the country.[7] Whenever reporters tried to get comments from complaining neighbors, they were mysteriously hard to reach.

The Stonehenge theme has actually provided inspiration to many an embattled property owner. In Alliance, Nebraska, a property owner created "Carhenge," a unique series of nose-in-the-ground cars that garnered quite of bit of interest over the years, as a tourist attraction.[8] It replicates the famous Stonehenge in the County of Wiltshire, England, where crowds of wanna-be Druids strip off their clothing during the equinox and greet the sunrise, "skyclad." That idea had some appeal for me. A well-publicized semi-annual gathering of 1500 overweight naked people dancing on my land would certainly have an impact on nearby HOA property values. I would welcome them with open arms, of course, each March and September.

Carhenge is a tourist destination for many visitors to Nebraska. Local government has tried to get it removed. Meanwhile, thousands of tourists visit the spot each year.

—photo by Becky Chapman

In Santa Fe, New Mexico, it was RefrigeratorHenge that was constructed by a creative land owner. Although the photos were hilarious, I wondered if such a structure on my own property would have enough visual impact to thwart a trespassing assault. But in case after case, property owners who had beaten back attempted land seizures generally succeeded because they created some sort of visual show of protest. The more outrageously spectacular, the greater was their chance of victory.

Although the various tactics were fun to read about, most were far too extreme for my liking. I was a public figure. I did volunteer work for several charities. I was on the board of the Alzheimer's Association. My wife did work for a rape-crisis center. I was a spokesman for an organization which encouraged people to rescue abandoned dogs. I made speeches and appearances for groups which promoted medical research on Multiple Sclerosis. Negative publicity could kill my TV news anchoring and civic career. Still, I was obsessed with stopping Willowbrook's ongoing efforts to take my land. One of the zoning officials with whom I frequently spoke was supportive, and even disgusted at some of the tactics used over the years by the Willowbrook HOA.

"You're dealing with some very powerful people, my friend," she told me on one of my visits to the county courthouse. "You really don't have much of a chance against them unless you take some pretty aggressive action." That, obviously, was no news flash to me.

Refrigerator Henge, or Fridge Henge or HengeFridge, as it's variously been called, started out as a two week protest against a nearby nuclear weapons plant. But because local authorities first granted permits, then tore the project down, then permitted it, then tore it down, it gave Fridgehenge a life of its own. The two week demonstration turned into a 12 year demonstration.

—Courtesy of The Santa Fe New Mexican

"You have to block the trespass, or you'll lose your land." That one, I had also figured out. I told her I had repeatedly tried to block the Willowbrook trespassing. At that point she suggested that a certain combination of Colorado state laws might provide a possible solution to my problem.

## It's a School Bus, Stupid!

"As long as a motor vehicle is 25 years or older," she told me, "thereby rendering it a 'classic,' and as long as the vehicle can be licensed in some way (licensed, not necessarily roadworthy), you can park it anywhere on your property. There are no setbacks from the property line. And there is no limit to the number of such vehicles a *collector* could legally own."

I was mystified as to what she was saying. Not being my mother's brightest child, it took me a while to process her suggestion.

"School buses, dimwit!" she finally told me. "It's kind of difficult to trespass through a school bus. If you park enough legally licensed, operable, classic school buses against the fence line, won't your neighbors decide that you're serious about blocking the trespassing? There's nothing they can do to get them removed."

Old school buses? Legal? Stunning, absolutely stunning, I thought. Memories of Ken Kesey, the Merry Pranksters, the psychedelic Magic Bus Trip, *One Flew Over The Cuckoo's Nest*, Hunter S. Thompson, and Ringo Starr. My 1967 experiences in the Haight Ashbury "Summer of Love" weren't totally wasted.

I now knew how to fight back. The idea was simply brilliant. And so Colorado.

As soon as I started looking, I discovered there were ancient school buses for sale everywhere. They were cheap, they were often in amazingly good shape, and they could be licensed under a Colorado state law that allows classic vehicles to be purchased for eventual conversion into recreation vehicles. In fact, I discovered there's an entire American subculture which converts, lives in, and even travels in converted classic school buses. They actually publish a monthly magazine on the subject. They show up at festivals like Burning Man, Sturgis and Daytona Beach.

"God bless my zoning department!" I thought to myself. "God bless each and every one!"

I began running across other like-minded people who had discovered the wonders of using school buses as a form of political expression. One land owner in Wilsonville, Oregon, found he could ease his property boundary frustration against a neighbor by creating a "fence" made up of 11 yellow school buses buried nose-first in the ground, separating his property from the county road.

On a trip to the Pacific Northwest, I made it a point to personally visit this angry gentleman and find out what kind of rage drove him to this end-game strategy. It was visually spectacular, enough to get the attention of the Oregon newspapers. I admired his hubris. It was the kind of aggressive creativity that apparently has a special place in the hearts of Oregonians. It was beginning to win my heart as well.

Back at home, I bought the first two buses I found, historic classics that had actually been driven on some famous routes, and had possibly even transported the children of some of Colorado's more infamous scalawags. One was an ancient white RTD "PeopleMover," the other was a gleaming yellow 1973 48-passenger school bus. They looked spectacular posed against my glistening green hillside. They were both licensed and in perfect driving condition.

I drove the buses right down to the fence line where Willowbrook had planned its land seizure gambit. With care I parked them right across the trespass paths on my property.

Wilsonville, Oregon. A property owner uses school buses in an effort to get control of his nemesis across the street. One half mile of upended school buses. Truly, a sight to behold.

—photograph by author

The author gets his first look at a "protest bus." It was placed across a trespass path to stop an attempted adverse possession by the adjacent Homeowner Association. The trespassing stopped.

—photograph by author

Shock and awe.

The HOA went apoplectic.

But the trespassing stopped. It was a beautiful thing.

## Hell Hath No Fury like an HOA Scorned

One of my greatest miscalculations in life, though, was figuring that Willowbrook would meekly ask for some kind of peace agreement to make the school buses go away. I needed nothing more than an apology and an acknowledgement that they knew I owned the property and that the HOA would give up all further confiscation attempts. Alas, I discovered that Homeowners Associations don't apologize. And they never give up an opportunity to snatch someone else's property. I also discovered how deep the fury runs in a scorned HOA.

During the 1998-1999 time period while I was building my new "gimp-accessible home" outside the Willowbrook boundaries, there were multiple times when hundreds of nails were tossed onto my driveway. Windows in my house were broken. Late one night a prominent Willowbrook leader, well-known to my family for her distinctive and sarcastic voice, called my home and said "You'd better watch that pretty little Dalmatian of yours, or it'll get poisoned." Four days later, my wife's sweet Dalmatian dog, Chelsea, was overcome with convulsions, vomiting and unable to use her back legs. Our veterinarian told us, "This doesn't look like an accident."

In one astonishing episode, January of 1999, an early morning arson fire was set on my front porch. There were repeated telephone death threats answered by several family members. On yet another occasion, four members of the community paid a 5 a.m. visit to my home and painted several swastikas on my home and driveway. My wife happened to be up early that morning and recognized one of them through the shade. Before she could awaken me, the damage was done, and they were gone.

As I opened the door I saw the words, "Willowbrook Association" painted in foot high letters across the porch.

Things seemed to settle down a few months later as we moved out of the neighborhood and into our new "gimp-accessible" home just outside the Willowbrook boundaries. We got settled in, and over the next year or so we even had some nice visits and meals with a few of our former neighbors. The past is past, we thought. Again, that was a huge miscalculation.

## Up Your Road

One day a letter arrived in the mail from the newly-elected president of the Willowbrook Association, a fellow I didn't know. In his missive, he claimed that the longtime access road to my new property encroached over the Willowbrook boundary line. He didn't know whether it was a few inches or a few feet, but he said the HOA planned to change the location of its boundary fence into the middle of my driveway. In a return letter I asked to discuss the matter over lunch.

John Glenn was unlike his famous astronaut namesake. He seemed to me a peculiar, smallish, unimpressive man with almost bird-like features. I didn't know his religion, but his bald spot reminded me of a yarmulke. He had made his personal fortune with an inventive business. He collected large volumes of used rags which he shipped in bulk to the Far East, where the rags were re-processed and made into entirely new products. He apparently didn't have any competitors, and it was a fascinating commercial niche which made him enough money to buy a fine-looking house among Willowbrook's millionaires.

As the newly-elected Willowbrook president, he was un-imposing, inarticulate. At lunch, he hemmed and hawed so much, it took a while to figure out exactly what he was asking of me. He eventually told me about the supposed encroachment of my driveway. He claimed a survey had proven the encroachment. (Later, I discovered there was no such survey.) Although my rural driveway paralleled the county road, and was located exactly on the historic stagecoach road, Glenn said the HOA was prepared to sue me unless my road was completely removed and rebuilt in a different location. However, he proposed what he called "such a deal." Willowbrook would offer me a "license" to travel on my own road if I agreed to remove the visually offensive school buses. I argued that giving me a license was not the same thing as giving me an easement and that Willowbrook could rescind a license at will.

I pointedly asked Glenn if he would ever sign the kind of license agreement he was offering me. In what appeared to be his single moment of candor during that lunch, he replied "No." Since this particular Association is notorious for being "tricky" in its dealings with others, I figured it was probably best not to do business with them. We were amicable and even shook hands, but we parted ways.

## The Fence Also Rises

A year and a half passed with not much noise being made. Probably most of the noise came from me as I continued trying to turn around "Brookies" who still tried on occasion to sneak around the buses to trespass across my property.

One day while returning from my day job, I nearly ran over a man who was standing in the middle of my gravel driveway, ramming fence posts into the ground. He had already hammered in about a hundred yards of fencing that went smack down the center of my road. My attorney would have been proud of how calm I stayed as I got out of my car to talk to the fence builder. The fellow was enormously embarrassed, but he told me what his mission was.

"Willowbrook occasionally hires me to put in fencing. They just told me to move the Willowbrook fence over here onto your road."

"How much did they pay you to do this?" I asked. "John Glenn said he'd pay me 1500 bucks."

"You know the fence isn't legal, don't you?"

The poor fellow had undoubtedly been told to expect some trouble from me. He just shrugged and turned back to his work. He was an innocent workman caught in the middle of a neighborhood pissing match. I went back to the house, got a couple of cold soda pops from the fridge and took them back to him. He accepted the sodas. No more was said, and he resumed his job of hammering in the stakes.

Somehow, five members of the Willowbrook Homeowner Association board thought it would be a good idea to plant a fence right in the middle of the author's road, a road they never owned, a road they never controlled, a road they had no access to. A judge ordered the HOA to remove the fence.

—photograph by author

The next night as the fence job was completed, my attorney joined me on my property, probably to see how much I was exaggerating. He found out I wasn't.

"They can't do that," he said. "That's a tort. You have to take out the fence. You and your tenants use this road. It's your only access. The fence is dangerous, that's absolutely wrong. You have to take it out." As we stood there on the fenced-off road, a half dozen "Brookies" drove by, hooting, hollering and laughing.

Sunday morning, June 1, 2003, I followed through on my attorney's instructions. One of my tenants and I took his pickup truck and began ripping out the couple hundred yards of fencing. My tenant was a big, burly construction foreman named Randy, an obviously intimidating guy, the kind who didn't take guff from anyone. As we worked in the hot Spring sun to remove the fence, John Glenn and about a dozen of Willowbrook's finest citizens gathered on their side of the fence in one of the most bizarre confrontations I had ever witnessed. For 45 amazing minutes, they screamed threats, insults, some of the most vulgar, most slanderous things imaginable, first working me over, then going after my increasingly agitated tenant. Willowbrook president John Glenn took videos as did a couple of the other Brookies. Still another snapped photos.

"In 20 years of doing construction work, I've never heard this kind of thing. I can't believe what assholes they are," Randy told me at one point.

"Just don't say a word," I told him. "If you say anything, we lose."

To his credit, my tenant kept his cool in the hot sun and we continued our job, ripping out the fence posts and wire, clearing our road of the obstruction, ignoring the threats and hysterical rantings of the mob of neighbors. At one point during the confrontation, Willowbrook president John Glenn even put in a 911 call to the Sheriff's office.

"Ward Lucas is tearing out Willowbrook's fence," he told the emergency operator.

A few minutes later a deputy responded to the scene, saw what was going on, and beat a hasty retreat. It was obviously a civil matter. A few days later, true-to-form, Willowbrook sued.

Over three years, the case wound its way through the courts and eventually ended up in three-day trial in front of a District Court Judge. Willowbrook officials were stunned by his decision. The HOA would be allowed to claim possession of a few inches of my land, but I would be granted a permanent easement over that identical property. In other words, the judge essentially ruled that Willowbrook could pay taxes on the disputed two-foot wide strip of land, but control of the property was given to me.

One intriguing side note is that a prominent Willowbrook resident, (a lawyer, board officer and chief provocateur), trumpeted in the HOA newsletter that Willowbrook had actually won the case. Lawyers, of course, say what they will. But the judge's order was what it was. And it was a thunderbolt to the hearts of some people who had tried to confiscate a strip of land they had never controlled, claimed, nor accessed.

Willowbrook tried to get the order reversed. The motion was denied. It tried to get the order modified, and was again denied. The HOA then asked the court to allow it to plant trees between my property and its million dollar homes. That was also denied. It was the cleverest "split-the-baby" decision from a judge I've ever seen.

A wiser man would have stopped right there, relished the victory and shut up. But my ego told me that I should deal a final blow while this giant was on its knees, and I went forward with a counter-claim for harassment, conspiracy, libel, slander, and outrageous conduct. I felt there was plenty of evidence. Over the years, my family and my tenants had been put through some pretty rough experiences by prominent "Brookies." Arson, swastikas, death threats, nails, dog poisoning, incidents so outlandish and incredible that they can only be recounted here because they've been sworn to under oath by multiple witnesses.

The Willowbrook campaign didn't moderate, either. Both my tenants had their own frustrations during this time. Randy's five-year-old daughter was repeatedly blocked from getting onto a public school bus at the demand of Willowbrook Homeowners Association president John Glenn (admitted so under oath).

A few months before our trial in Jefferson County, there was an astonishing moment when another officer of the Willowbrook Board pulled a handgun and threatened to kill this little girl's father (testified to under oath).

It didn't stop there, either. Fireworks were repeatedly shot over my tenants' homes during an incredibly dangerous multi-year drought. A single spark could have ignited a firestorm. Day after day we faced the incoming fireworks missiles apparently fired by the "lady with the voice" (she admitted so under oath).

These actions didn't take place in an inner-city, mobster-ridden crime zone, they happened among ritzy million dollar homes where the *crème de la crème* of Colorado society live, celebrities, dentists, doctors, business owners, professional people. As bizarre as each story sounds, it is all on the public record and was sworn to under oath by multiple witnesses.

Horrific, almost beyond comprehension.

## Filthy Tricks Win Cases

Still, Willowbrook wasn't finished with us. HOA attorneys seemed especially interested in exploring our feelings about the swastikas which had been painted on our home. When they quizzed my family about whether we are Jewish, it was one of the truly *voila!* moments of our twenty year long ordeal. For the first time the true personal character of the people we were up against was coming out.

The HOA attorneys really should have pressed their interrogation further. Had they really been on their toes, they might even have forced me to confess to having several Jewish friends and co-workers. Pushed further, I might even have admitted attending a few *bar mitzvahs* and a *bris.* At the latter ceremony, I even met and shook hands with my first *mohel.* How damaging would that admission have been? Lucas is friendly with Jews? Lucas has some friends who are Negroes? Incredible as it seems, nothing is beyond the reach of an obsessed Homeowners Association fighting to impose its will over others.

I recalled that a few years earlier a prominent Willowbrook leader had used an ugly slur toward one of my sons, calling him "Jew boy." Bits and pieces of this community's mindset almost began to make a warped kind of sense to me.

After all these years, my wife's multiple sclerosis had left her increasingly disabled, mentally and physically. Since she was one of the named complainants in our countersuit, she was compelled by Willowbrook's attorney to testify. In court, while grilling this poor brain-damaged lady, Willowbrook asked, "Isn't it true, Mrs. Lucas, that your youngest son is a homosexual?"

As a reporter I've covered many court cases over the years and I've seen vulgar tactics used by a wide array of trial lawyers. But this strategy by Willowbrook was as fundamentally evil as any I've ever witnessed.

Since I'm sometimes considered a public figure in Colorado, and since I've spent a career as a professional whistle-blower in the local news media, Willowbrook apparently thought lurid allegations about a 31-year-old member of my family might embarrass me into surrendering my land to the association. They never figured that a white non-Hebrew like me might actually have some *chutzpah*. Had I "taken names and kicked *toches*" from early on, I might have saved myself a little grief. But as mean-spirited as my HOA was, it's not unique among Home-owners Associations across the country.

It happens in criminal cases, it happens in civil cases. Rather than being allowed access to all facts, many juries are left to wade through a mystifying jumble of legal tactics that usually have little to do with the search for truth. Even jurors who are perfectly capable of rendering fair decisions based on real facts are placed in the odd position of trying to administer justice by assessing opposing circus acts.

**Lawyers frequently say that they owe their clients "the best possible defense." Sadly, that means no court case can really be an honest search for truth, because in case after case the best possible defense is a blatant fabrication. Working in a vacuum of excluded or "irrelevant" evidence, defense attorneys construct monumental lies to excuse or rationalize a client's misbehavior.**

In short, most legal cases, civil and criminal, are about showman-ship. When attorneys on one side or another are hired to put on a performance, juries are often swayed more by the show than the facts. In such a legal system, trusting one's life or life savings to the hands of a jury is a crap shoot. Defenders of the justice system often claim, "We get it right more times than not, don't we?" That's exactly the atmosphere in which professional gamblers make fortunes. If a legal system is based on administering justice "more times than not," then flipping a coin should be an almost equally adequate way of meting out justice.

The critic is often asked "What country has a better legal system than ours?" which still begs the point. Just because the American system is less corrupt than others, doesn't mean that the system routinely offers justice for all.

The OJ Simpson case showed the world that infamous murderers are far better off hiring clowns and jugglers for attorneys. The 2006 Duke Lacrosse scandal showed that even a professional prosecutor can be disbarred for "dishonesty, fraud, deceit and misrepresentation."[9] The dismissal of an extremely sensitive public corruption case against a U.S. Senator from Alaska, based on the fact that the misconduct of federal prosecutors was even worse that the Senator's, is astounding and contemptible.[10] And a Pennsylvania judicial corruption case, in which a sitting judge took millions of dollars in kickbacks in exchange for sending hundreds of children to private detention centers, shows that personal moral decay runs from the very top of the legal system to the very bottom.[11]

> Trial lawyers repeatedly prove that American justice is not much more than a carnival game, in which tactics trump honesty.

Supreme Court Justice Stephen Breyer famously quipped during one important case, "May the best lawyer win." Though previous judges have made the same lame attempt at humor (*Caterpillar Inc. v. Deere & Co.*[12]), the quip was horrendously callous to those whose lives and fortunes were at stake.

## Fundamental Legal Reform—Long Overdue

Attorney, lecturer and author Philip K. Howard has painstakingly laid out a case for fundamental reform of the American legal system. In his two books, *The Collapse of the Common Good*, and *Life Without Lawyers*, Howard argues that the legal system desperately needs a massive ethics overhaul. He notes that the proportionate number of lawyers in the workforce doubled between 1970 and 2000:

> Our founders were concerned about oppressive laws—they added the Bill of Rights precisely to prevent abuses of state power, even through duly enacted laws. Freedom—by definition, the absence of restraint—can be encroached upon from many sides. Freedom can be destroyed by tyrants, by lawlessness—and by too much law.[13]

Although Howard doesn't identify Homeowners Associations as a source of increased litigation and threats of litigation in society, he does note that a paradigm shift in lawsuits began in the early 1960s. By coincidence, that was the same time period the HOA movement gained traction, mainly as a way of keeping Negroes out of white neighborhoods.

While this writer makes no claim that the entire legal system is corrupt, if corruption exists at all, then the profession is fundamentally flawed and in desperate need of reform. How can any citizen juror trust a system where a mere coin-flip could be considered fair? In which court case can a litigant presume that all attorneys involved are being honest? In which county and state can a juror believe he or she can truly make a fair decision based on facts, not farce?

## Tainting a Jury

In the case of my own family, Willowbrook's allegations of homosexuality and Jewishness as a trial tactic in what was really was no more than a garden-variety land-grab, were designed only to contaminate a typical white conservative, Republican jury. The courtroom trick worked. The jury ruled against our damage claim. But in one of life's unintended consequences, the hatred of an entire community was memorialized in court records, in community gossip, and finally in this book which is now the official published history of the Willowbrook Homeowners Association.

Like "Nigger Roy" of Russell Gulch, some things are on-the-record forever.

# 10
# Expose Yourself

*If you want to annoy your neighbors,*
*tell the truth about them.*

—Pietro Aretino

The preceding chapters should provide some interesting starting points for any homeowner looking for ways to fight back against an abusive Homeowners Association. Speak out. Name names; cite times, dates, addresses, supply as much personal information about your own predicament as you can. Put your story in the most public forum possible. Write blogs. Publish a book. Hiding one's shame and embarrassment at having to be involved in a neighborhood squabble is probably the worst possible strategy for stopping a rogue HOA. Not only is your inaction harming you and your fellow property owners, it does massive damage to all those who come behind.

If you have special access to "ink," going public might cause even the more vicious neighborhood elements to heed Mark Twain's old wisdom: "Never pick a fight with someone who buys ink by the barrel." Someone who regularly writes for a newspaper, a magazine, a newscast is trained to translate neighborhood bitchiness into the kind of news copy that can turn a neighborhood upside down.

> **Silence condones bad behavior—Speak up and act. If you don't, you're giving your "OK" to the excess and abuse by your HOA.**

The news media are supposed to be the "Fourth Estate," the mystical so-called fourth branch of government, the great watchdogs over the establishment. When government rots, even at the lowest local level, no one is better equipped to describe that decay to the populace than the wordsmith at the local newspaper. When wronged by government, take notes and get ready to publish. Your guardian angel is the First Amendment to the U.S. Constitution.

Publicity has an amazing way of stifling bad behavior at least temporarily. In May of 2009 the president of a Dallas HOA threatened to tow the car of a fellow resident, unless he removed or covered up some military stickers and decals on the rear window of his vehicle. Frank Larison is a disabled veteran, a former member of the U.S. Marines. The letter he received from HOA president Darenda Hardy said the military decals on his car were "advertising," which violated the covenants of the Woodlands Creek II on the Creek Homeowners Association. Hardy's letter also threatened Larison with a fine of $50 each time he parked his car in the neighborhood.

Larison pushed back, saying he was a proud veteran of the military and had no intention of complying. He also spoke with the news media, which showed up en masse. Stories in newspapers and on TV newscasts around the country lambasted the HOA, whose president amazingly could not be located for comment. The story made it to the networks, making the military-bashing HOA look more and more ridiculous. When finally reached, HOA president Hardy said she had been fishing in Tyler, Texas, waiting for the controversy to die down. It didn't. Her absence and the public's ongoing anger guaranteed the controversy would have a long shelf-life.

"This has all been blown out of proportion," Hardy told the media. "We haven't had a ruckus like this since I've lived here. It's B.S., that's what it is."[1]

Frank Larison, of Dallas, Texas, is a retired Marine and a Vietnam veteran. But when his Homeowner Association told him he was not allowed to have the military stickers on his car, Larison contacted local and national news media. Among those infuriated by the HOA's actions was Texas Congressman Ted Poe who took to the floor of the House to admonish the HOA. After a barrage of phone calls from around the country, the HOA backed down.
—photograph by Rodney Gray, producer of the documentary, "The HOAX"

B.S. or not, the uproar continued to reverberate through the news cycles. The five member board of directors of the Woodlands II on the Creek HOA voted unanimously to drop the demand against Larison. While the proud Marine won the skirmish, the enemy's retreat may have just been strategic. The HOA's anti-decal rule is still on the books. As long as Larison lives in his townhome, he'll collect the dirty looks, the backstabbing and rumors that invariably swirl around a homeowner who goes belly to belly against an HOA.

Once the public is no longer looking, though, the moment another rogue board member is elected, Larison will undoubtedly face harassment on some new and unexpected front. As a member of the Marines, Larison probably learned long ago that terrorism has no rules or timetables.

Shunning by neighbors will probably be the least of Larison's future troubles. But now, at least, he knows the secret to battling future HOA problems.

## The Internet—the New "Ink"

A changing paradigm of the 21ˢᵗ Century is the Internet. It's the new medium, the ink of a new age, and bloggers are now occupying a space where much of traditional mainstream journalism has collapsed under the weight of its own bias and incompetence. Bloggers have the time and luxury to follow a story like the Marine decal controversy in excruciating and excoriating detail. An honest and credible blogger who works hard to develop his or her own Internet following can actually step into the same role once occupied by local newspaper reporters. Bloggers have enormous power to reach large numbers of people to oppose and expose government wrongdoing, including wrongdoing by the *de facto* governments of Homeowners Associations. Internet exposure of HOA misdeeds reaches millions of Internet users through such websites as *AHRC.com*, and *YouTube.com*.

> Civic terrorism, the kind exhibited in many Homeowners Associations, also works without rules. Once an "undesirable" homeowner is pointed out to the crowd, that person will always carry a target on his back.

Even though the traditional news media continue to decay in the Internet age, there's still a chance of the peoples' voice getting through. America was founded on the ability of the common folk to communicate, congregate and agitate. When used properly, the exercise of those freedoms can do a lot of good in battling government and legal injustice.

## The All-Seeing Eye

Yet another societal shift is that high quality video cameras, once the exclusive domain of TV news reporting teams, are now everywhere. Nearly every home these days has at least one video camera. Every cell phone, every iPhone, every Blackberry, every purse and belt buckle carries one of the most powerful anti-corruption tools since George Orwell wrote of a society where an all-seeing camera constituted the eye of "Big Brother." While Orwell was precognizant, he apparently didn't envision that the all-seeing eye would actually end up in the hands of the common man.

Most courts have come to recognize the value and importance of videotaped evidence. More and more states are mandating that government bodies be required to keep video logs of all public hearings. Cameras can occasionally be disruptive, but their greater good is that they are unblinking witnesses. They tend to encourage more moderate civic behavior and wiser decision making.

If Homeowners Association boards *were required by law* to keep and publish in a public forum video logs of all official and semi-official meetings, bad behavior by elected officers could actually be reduced. Nothing destroys property values faster than a toxic board of directors. But nothing destroys toxic boards of directors faster than publicity.

The presence of cameras generates hives on the hides of many public officials, and as such some government bodies still prohibit them. Video cameras continue to be banned in Federal Courts. As a result, there is still occasional chicanery in those high-ceilinged rooms where Judges and Justices routinely make idiotic decisions and invent laws never approved by any legislature. But let the people witness what actually goes on in such courtrooms, and the level of true justice might improve. Let voters witness the kinds of tactics used by opposing lawyers, and they may begin insisting on long-needed legal reforms.

## Is the Streit Path Crooked?

Public exposure is a common thread that seems to be woven through most stories in which HOA wrongdoing has been exposed and corrected. A fascinating ongoing case-in-point in a Dallas, Texas condominium complex shows what the power of the media can accomplish. The story was done by FOX News journalist, Becky Oliver.[2]

"Homeowner's Hell" it was headlined. In early 2009, Oliver reported on the strange goings-on in the Casa Blanca Condominiums in North Dallas. The complex consists of 120 privately owned apartment units. A year earlier, the HOA board had begun notifying owners that it was going to be making "emergency repairs" on the complex to the tune of $270,000. Each owner would be assessed $3,294 due within 30 days. The charges were apparently assessed after a "special HOA board election" in January of 2008. A number of homeowners claimed they never got notice of any such election.

In the fall of 2008, the HOA began foreclosing on homeowners who had failed to pay the surprise assessments. Additionally, the board began telling all owners that each unit was required to have "matching appliances that are aesthetically pleasing, walls... painted without cracks or bubbles, countertops without cracks or bubbles and shower tiles... that are clean." Owners of these private homes were required to allow the HOA access to do inspections of the interior of each residence. Homeowners who refused to do so could be fined $200 per day plus interest.

Recalcitrant owners discovered they owed thousands, even tens of thousands of dollars in outstanding fines and fees. Home-owners began dumping their properties at "panic rates," and the number of foreclosures increased as owners simply walked away.

Some owners bitterly complained that construction work was started on apartment units immediately above their own. Roofs were replaced, balconies were added. Water began leaking into walls from improperly installed roof tiles. Wallboard cracked, floors sagged.

More inquisitive residents of the Casa Blanca Condominiums discovered the new construction was being performed without any city permits or inspections. The HOA board president was Texas resident Scott Streit. Homeowners claimed Streit and various members of his family had begun buying up a number of properties at Casa Blanca in 2007. Ultimately, Streit's family members ended up owning more than 30 units in the complex. Streit and his wife were "elected" as officers on the HOA board. When another board member suddenly resigned, the board appointed Streit's son as a replacement, giving the family a majority of votes on the five-member board.

Lawsuits against Streit were filed by several of the home-owners. In a subsequent videotaped deposition, Scott Streit was questioned about how he ended up as HOA president and whether a Homeowners Association meeting was ever called as required by the HOA by-laws. According to Oliver's investiga-tion, Streit testified that his election as president of the Association was held without any meeting of the homeowners.

"Why didn't you have an election as required in the by-laws?" asked Stephen Khoury, an attorney for three of the homeowners.

"Brevity" was Streit's videotaped reply.

"That means you wanted to do it quickly?"

"Correct," said Streit.

Fox News reporter Oliver said over a 14 month period, five different property managers were hired by the HOA to collect dues and assess fines against homeowners. Public records showed the last property manager was registered at the address of a 6000 square foot private home, owned by Scott Streit.

Publicity about the controversy caused Dallas zoning inspectors to investigate repairs and modifications underway at the complex. They found enough building violations to immediately shut the project down.

The Casa Blanca story will take years to play out. Attorneys on all sides will end up being paid millions of dollars. Homeowners who thought they'd found a peaceful place to invest in their retirement homes are now consigned to a lifetime of paying legal fees and correcting construction defects.

Oliver quotes one homeowner, Russell Hoff, as saying: "It's been hell. You don't even want to come home." His lawsuit against the Streit family will ultimately cost him a fortune, possibly even his home. It's a sad story, but not an uncommon one.[3] But at least with media exposure, this story is finally all on the record.

## Bonehead Boards Can Cost Big Bucks

A case in California shows that each and every member of a Homeowners Association could ultimately pay a high price for a bone-headed decision made by its own board. This one involved a civil judgment against 330 members of a Homeowners Association sixty miles east of Los Angeles.

Richard and Leslie Fredericks had an easement which allowed them to use a back road to and from their home in Riverside County. In 1991, the nearby Santa Rosa Cove Homeowners Association built an automatic electric gate across the Fredericks' easement. The Fredericks couple agreed to the installation as long as their access was protected. In 2001, the gate broke. The HOA refused to repair it.

The couple continued to access the gate manually, until they discovered that the HOA had chained and padlocked it. The family protested being shut off from their property, but the HOA's response was to order its security guards to block the Fredericks family from using the easement. The Fredericks took the last option that was open to them. They sued.

In the summer of 2008, a Riverside County jury ruled in favor of the Fredericks, awarding them 1.6 million dollars in compensatory damages and 400,000 dollars in punitive damages.

"We were locked out of our property for four years," Richard Fredericks told reporters. "(This lawsuit) was an incredible waste of resources." Most members of the homeowners association were unaware of the lawsuit, and had no idea they could potentially be on the hook for millions of dollars worth of legal expenses, fines and penalties.

Attorney David Peters of the Peters and Freedman law firm said the verdict was the result of a "runaway jury." He told reporter Mariecar Mendoza of *The Desert Sun Newspaper,* "The jury turned this into their O.J. Simpson moment, their day in the sun." He predicted the judge would "get real" and substantially reduce the verdict.[4]

The Peters and Freedman law firm represents a network of about 700 Homeowners Associations in Southern California. It has been involved in a number of controversial foreclosures against individual homeowners. Several years ago, its activities would have been completely beyond the view of HOA members. But because of adverse publicity, especially on the Internet, the public has growing knowledge of the dangers of living in HOAs represented by this network. The law firm has waged a lengthy war against its critics, including an effort to shut down a well-known anti-HOA website which has amassed and published a huge database of stories of homeowners who've lost their homes to foreclosure. (More on this law firm in a moment.)

## *Privatopia*—Buyer Beware

An interesting conflict involving the HOA movement is actually beginning to take shape within the legal community. Early shots were fired by political science and law professor Evan McKenzie in his 1994 landmark book, *Privatopia*. His extensively researched book notes with some alarm the transition of Constitutional government into "private governments" run by the boards of Homeowners Associations. He also notes the history of racial segregation as a motivating factor in the rise of the private government movement. *Privatopia* is probably the groundbreaking work exposing the desiccation of the Constitution by private HOA developers. His newest 2011 book, *Beyond Privatopia: Rethinking Residential Private Government* has also gotten rave reviews. Both books are widely discussed by bloggers who comment on the national HOA mess.

As more websites begin to include the publication of readers' comments, there's an unmistakable rising tide of public anger toward HOAs. Too many people have been lied to, or hurt by the institution. Too many homes have been arbitrarily snatched away from homeowners who got a month or two behind in their dues. Readers who comment on such stories often refer to HOAs as "fascist dictatorships" which revel in their power to cause pain to fellow members.

## Tyrannies, Parasites and HOAs

As institutions, tyrannies of any kind are impressive things to watch. They generally form in the vacuum created by an absence of free thought and speech.

Without intentionally trying to gin up an awkward metaphor here, tyrannies have some of the same characteristics as parasites. As a general rule, parasites can't live long on their own. They must, of necessity, feed and grow on a host organism. If a parasite is moderately passive, it can survive for lengthy periods of time. A parasite that turns virulent, though, has the potential of killing its host and ultimately dying, itself, as a result. That's usually a bad evolutionary strategy for the parasite.

Tyrannies, likewise, come about in the vacuum of human apathy. A tyranny that convinces people of its benevolence can often survive indefinitely. But even a benevolent tyranny has the capability of at some point turning mean and destroying its host, and thus, itself.

Another interesting weakness of parasites (and tyrannies) is that they seem to have an intense aversion to light. In fact, bright light is a well-known curative agent for many types of infection. Intense light reduces the ability of parasites, viruses and mold spores to reproduce and spread. Tyrannies, too, have trouble surviving exposure and public scrutiny. The metaphor, though a bit overworked here, is beyond any counter-argument.

"Sunlight is said to be the best disinfectant," said Supreme Court Justice Louis Brandeis, "and electric light the best police-man."[5] The wonder of transparency in bringing about justice is one of the most well-established principles in American jurisprudence.

## The Internet: The Fifth Estate?

Internet bloggers have become the new Fifth Estate, according to William H. Dutton, professor of Internet Studies at the University of Oxford. He argues that the blogging community is not just an extension of the traditional media (the Fourth Estate), but rather a unique new community of "networked individuals" who are now holding the other four estates accountable for their actions and inactions.[6] The rising chorus of bloggers exposing abuses by the HOA movement may ultimately prove Dr. Dutton to be amazingly precognizant.

Nobody defends more homeowners against abusive Home-owners Associations than the previously mentioned Arizona attorney, Clint Goodman. When asked by this author, "What's the one thing that could be done to control rogue HOA boards?" his response was "News talk, blogs, links, links, links." An obvious fan of the use of the First Amendment on the Internet, Goodman believes that abusive Homeowners Associations have been getting away with murder. And the mainstream news media haven't paid enough attention. His suggestion is that perhaps only the Internet community can spread the kind of intense light that can actually ameliorate the problem. Goodman would agree that the new "Fifth Estate" is a powerful tool to control HOA excesses.

## Dam that Free Speech!

Organizations which try to shed light on the more draconian actions taken by out-of-control HOAs are popping up on the Internet all the time. One of the original ones calls itself the *American Homeowners Resource Center (AHRC.com)*. It was started by a couple who continue to set new standards for anti-HOA stridency. Elizabeth McMahon and her husband first ran afoul of their own HOA in San Clemente, California, in the 1980s. They battled and won after their Palacio del Mar HOA tried to lien their home over a five dollar late-payment fee.

The McMahons fought back when the HOA tried to stop them from planting roses in front of their home. They have been called "extreme" by their neighbors, but Elizabeth McMahon's voice has gotten the attention not only of the HOA movement, but of prominent California officials as well. She has even ended up being appointed to a state legislative committee created to comment on HOA affairs.[7]

The McMahons' major contribution to Free Speech may be the creation of a vast database of anti-HOA news stories and editorials from across the country. Many of their articles cite news coverage of lawyers and judges who've been indicted for racketeering, bribery, mail fraud or perjury.[8] They have amassed hundreds, possibly even thousands of articles on a website that attracts a huge number of page visits by computer users around the world. In a time when the nation's newspapers were going through a cataclysmic collapse in readership, *AHRC.com* was a torrent of HOA news. Stories that were probably too hot to touch by an increasingly paranoid mainstream media were memorialized on the *AHRC's* website. McMahon's reportage would never be mistaken for "fair-and-balanced" or always accurate, but the compiled information is not available elsewhere. There is no better library on the Web for someone doing raw research on rogue HOAs.

With the number of hits the *AHRC* site gets, up to three million a month by their own estimate, the McMahons could probably make themselves very wealthy. But they accept no advertising. Their dedication and their anger are unmistakable, though. Their rage at the Homeowners Association movement is evident from the kinds of articles assembled. A growing number of writers across the country contribute editorials and news stories for publication.

The *AHRC* Internet campaign is often over-the-top, attacking virtually every aspect of the HOA movement and its phalanx of lawyers. One of McMahon's favorite targets is the Peters and Freedman law firm, mentioned previously. Lawyers for the firm have foreclosed on many homes in that state after winning paltry judgments for seemingly petty violations of HOA covenants.

The McMahons are obvious burrs under the saddles of the cowboys at the P & F law firm. In 2008, Peters and Freedman sued the couple and won a judgment on behalf of itself and the Palacio del Mar Homeowners Association. In articles written immediately after the court loss, supporters of McMahon claimed that the law firm was trying to shut down free speech by seizing control of the *AHRC* domain name. (Interesting, that this was the same trial tactic used by the Church of Scientology to try to silence its critic, Lawrence Wollersheim!) The trial court in the McMahon case actually did order the *AHRC.com* website surrendered at one point, but the order was later stayed by the California Court of Appeals.[9]

The McMahons argued that their website is a public library and a resource for thousands of people across the country, and that since it receives no income, it's not an asset that can or should be seized. The *AHRC* site is right at home, of course, among a wild cacophony of sometimes undisciplined bloggers, pajama-clad editorialists, and a legion of formerly-employed mainstream journalists. If Elizabeth McMahon eventually loses her website domain name to Peters and Freedman, the site and its contents will probably be "mirrored" by angry anti-HOA forces across the country, too many for the law firm to fight.

Free Speech is a lot like water: it has a way of seeping past most obstacles. Water, like Speech, can be dammed (or damned), but like waters rising behind a dike, the pressure of unreleased information keeps building until it eventually forces its way out. The new "Fifth Estate" is making that happen.

## Other Important Anti-HOA Websites

Another interesting repository of HOA war-stories is a website called *TheNationalHomeownersAdvocateGroup.com*.[10] Much like the *AHRC*, this site recounts many news stories of non-judicial foreclosures of the homes of people who innocently violated the covenants of Homeowners Associations in Texas. And like other websites across the country, it demonstrates a new "Free Speech" platform that must be frustrating for trial lawyers and HOA boards alike. When the legal establishment tries to profit from the confiscations of private property from homeowners, the World Wide Web provides a cheap and powerful way for aggrieved owners and their sympathizers to fight back.

Yet another strident group has emerged to fight the wave of punitive home foreclosures in Florida. It's called *Cyber Citizens for Justice (ccfj.net)* run by Jan Bergemann, who describes himself as a "retired chef from Germany." He was appalled by what he saw in the American HOA movement. Bergemann does have a good sense of humor, though. In one of the rare moments of comedy in the fight against the HOA foreclosure racket, his *CCFJ* website is accompanied by a cleverly-written, well-performed country music song called "One Way Ticket to Hell" by H.D. Flagle.[11] With the humor, the music, and the book resources it includes, *Cyber Citizens for Justice* could potentially become the national leader-of-record in the fight to restore constitutional rights to frustrated inductees to the private government movement. Flagle's mother suffered from HOA abuse in her home in the Southwest, and that's what prompted his song. He told this author that he has donated his song and the lyrics to the nation's anti-HOA forces, royalty free. So, here's a sample:

Well! I finally bought "My Dream Home:"
　　To enjoy retirement life.
I've made new friends and buddies
　　Lots of parties for my wife.
It seemed that life was perfect,
　　All my neighbors felt the same,
Then along came "Death by CCRs
　　Life's over, I'm fair game.

Those petty rules and regulations,
　　It's enough to make you cry.
They're full of woes, no pink flamingos
　　Someone tell us why?
Slick managers and lawyers
　　Slither close but they won't tell
Why our dream home should remind us
　　Of a one-way ticket to Hell.

There are more verses, and the song is destined to become a classic. The link is in this book's endnotes. Free. If you support the cause.[12]

In Arizona the most vocal opponent of Homeowners Associations is George Staropoli. He's been using the Internet to "joust with windmills" since the last decade when he first ran afoul of his own HOA. With alarm, he has pleaded before the Arizona State Legislature for legal reform. In scores of articles and letters, and from various websites, he rages against the HOA movement; he claims that Americans have sacrificed all their rights by buying their way into covenant-controlled "private governments." Staropoli may not have won many arguments against the massive legal cash brigade that currently backs up the HOA movement, but his knowledge is sophisticated and his voice is one of a growing number on the Internet warning about the downside of HOA membership.[13]

As new anti-HOA websites pop up, perhaps one of the best and most concise for newly abused homeowners is called *TheHOAPrimer.org*.[14] It's a well-organized look at the HOA movement, its lawyers, and the treacherous footing the average homeowner is on when buying into a "private government" compound. The website, written by Dorian MacDougall, while he was a resident of Vestavia Hills, Alabama, is a "primer" in every sense of the word, going into the history of HOAs, the dangers they pose, the people who've lost their homes to arbitrary and punitive foreclosures. In twenty simple steps, the website steers the victims of rogue HOAs through all the obstacles, threats and possible solutions.

## The FBI to the Rescue

In Nevada, which has been slammed by some of the meanest, most unethical HOAs in the country, there's a massive FBI investigation into racketeering by HOA boards. HOAs there have two thorns in their sides, two civilian organizations fighting back against HOA corruption. One is Las Vegas TV Station, WTNV, which runs a regular feature called *The HOA Hall of Shame*. Emmy Award winning reporter Darcy Spears confronts and embarrasses miscreant Homeowners Association officers with some regularity. And again, not least, is the almost superhuman efforts of Jonathan Friedrich, who publishes updates on HOA wrongdoing from the web domain name, *HOACorruption.com*.

Finally, while some homeowners' rights advocates will sadly be overlooked in this section, no writer could rightly overlook perhaps the nation's most articulate, most prolific, and most well thought out defender of the individual homeowner, *Los Angeles Times* columnist and blogger Donie Vanitzian. With co-columnist Stephen Glassman, Vanitzian lays out a case for complete over-haul of the Homeowners Association movement. Their 2002 self-published book, *Villa Appalling! Destroying the Myth of Affordable Community Living*, is an anti-HOA classic. It crafts a critique of the nightmare into which 70 million Americans have moved. With the sweet subtlety of a jackhammer and the gentle finesse of a steamroller, Vanitzian and Glassman crush the false logic used by homeowners who think they're protecting property values by seeking shelter in Common Interest Developments or Homeowners Associations.

Vanitzian has plenty of experience in the area. She's a commercial property manager in California; she has a Juris Doctorate, and is a UCLA Extension Professor of a course on living in Common Interest Communities. As an arbitrator and a journalist, she has seen HOA life at its ugliest, its most bizarre. Glassman is an attorney. Both live in deed-restricted communities and each has spent time serving as members of their respective boards.

In a May 31, 2009 *Los Angeles Times* column, a dismayed California homeowner complained to Glassman and Vanitzian about a case in which homeowners had no idea their board had initiated a massive lawsuit, lost a massive judgment and failed to negotiate a settlement with the HOA's insurance company. This HOA had suddenly notified homeowners that each member was going to be assessed a five-figure sum to pay for the judgment and the legal fees. The homeowner writing the letter to Vanitzian whined that members of the HOA who want to sell and move out have now discovered it's nearly impossible to sell a home there. In the 2009 economic crisis, where many homeowners were already slashing home prices as much as 50 percent, HOA members also facing the huge legal obligation were doubly damned.

Glassman and Vanitzian were appropriately sympathetic:

Unfortunately, there appears to be little alternative...also unfortunate is that the board was not obligated to ask title-holders whether they wanted to file a lawsuit, although... loyalty would dictate such a courtesy.

Associations borrow money for a variety of purposes, including the payment of judgments against them. Those judgments will always remain in force...as associations are unable to file for bankruptcy protection to discharge such debts. That your homeowners association board finally chose to include titleholders in the decision making is only because it was required to do so, not because the board thought it was desirable.[15]

Breathtaking. Several hundred homeowners in a tiny California enclave had no idea their elected board members were litigating a case so idiotic and abusive, that it led to millions of dollars in legal fees and judgments which will hang over the heads of each and every member of that association forever. For many of those member homeowners, their lives won't be long enough to pay off all the debts.

So, there you have it. An HOA board can basically do anything it wants. If it screws up, board members have no responsibility or liability. Board members are insured against misfeasance and malpractice. The residents of the community not only paid for their board members' insurance, they now have to absorb the financial fallout. They also have to pay for any special assessments the board has come up with while the homeowners were still members. Not even a bankruptcy declaration can allow homeowners to escape all the debts that were incurred on each homeowner's behalf.

- It doesn't matter that the homeowners will ultimately band together and impeach the board.
- It doesn't matter that those board members may try to flee the community in shame.
- It doesn't matter that the vast majority of the homeowners in that association were completely innocent, and unaware of the arrogant posturing by the rogue board members they elected.

Each and every homeowner is forever indebted, in the most negative sense of the word. Vanitzian claims that some low-income elderly in California are being hit with assessments of hundreds of thousands, in some cases even a million dollars and more in special assessments to pay for property damage or unnecessary legal fees generated by board excesses and frivolous lawsuits. For a 95 year old owner of a 150,000 dollar property to suddenly be hit with a million dollar assessment is beyond astonishing. It's abuse. It's raw abuse, on a par with the billion dollar ponzi scam of Bernard Madoff. In California, though, an indebted homeowner cannot declare himself broke and walk away from such a lawsuit. That judgment follows a defendant forever, even if that defendant had no idea his elected HOA board was pursuing such frivolous litigation. But again, the word is getting out.

As mentioned earlier, the only thing that gives writers like Becky Oliver, Stephen Glassman and Donie Vanitzian the freedom to document the kinds of nightmares they see is a Constitutional provision our forefathers thought deserved the first spot in the Bill of Rights. As ethical journalists Glassman and Vanitzian have probably sacrificed their right to comment on what goes on inside their own Homeowners Associations. But on the outside they have amazing freedom under the Constitution to alert home-owners to the periodic ugliness that threatens every American family's finances and psychological well-being.

## Public Figures, Public Corruption

While the First Amendment's protection of free speech is under assault in many arenas, about the only power to fight back against an abusive HOA lies in the use of an oft-cited (even abused) court case called *New York Times vs. Sullivan*, 1964. The decision is mandatory reading for any reporter or blogger trying to expose wrongdoing by a public figure. The Supreme Court essentially ruled that to win a libel suit, a public figure has to prove that the reporter or news organization had "actual malice" against the subject of a report.

The definition of "actual malice" is important. It means that the reporter knew, or had to have known, that the allegations he was making were false and that he was acting in reckless disregard for the truth or falsity of the allegations. Unless that burden of proof is overcome, a libel/defamation claim by a public figure is destined to fail.[16]

*New York Times vs. Sullivan* was not just a decision that protected news agencies against libel suits by public figures, it was also an important historical turning point in the struggle for civil rights. In the early 1960s many newspapers in the South were facing a barrage of lawsuits for exposing discrimination against blacks. The chilling effect was obvious, as newspapers began backing away from coverage of civil rights cases for fear of losing major civil judgments.

The Sullivan lawsuit arose over a paid advertisement in the *New York Times* headlined "Heed their Rising Voices." It spoke of "thousands of Southern Negro students... engaged in widespread non-violent demonstrations in positive affirmation of the right to live in human dignity as guaranteed by the U.S. Constitution and the Bill of Rights."[17]

L. B. Sullivan, an elected Commissioner in Montgomery, Alabama, claimed in his lawsuit against the *Times* that he was libeled by factual errors in the ad. The Alabama courts awarded him a half million dollars. But the U.S. Supreme Court overturned the lower decisions, ruling that despite the factual errors, the newspaper had not libeled Sullivan because he was a public figure and as such, had a higher burden of proof. It acknowledged the importance of allowing the media to examine and expose public corruption without fear of litigation. In the years since, the decision has been cited by countless news organizations as a foundational defense against libel/defamation suits by public figures trying to suppress the publication of negative news articles.

Unfortunately, every good court case has its downside, and this one has been frequently twisted to defend indefensible behavior. Many a celebrity or public figure, for example, has cursed *New York Times* vs. Sullivan, and many a celebrity rag has taken advantage of the court decision to shatter the reputation of a completely innocent public figure.

In my own case (an unnecessary fight over the location of a fence line) the Willowbrook Homeowners Association tried to use *New York Times vs. Sullivan* in a novel way: it argued that because I was a public figure, i.e. a prominent television news anchorman, it had the right to safely publish or disseminate such things as "He beats his wife, that's how she got MS," "He's a criminal who can't get regular work," "He's a liar" and other such nonsense. Willowbrook officials also felt comfortable using the "His wife is a Jew; his son is a homosexual" strategy in court. The judge in the Willowbrook case, though, ruled that for the purposes of this specific lawsuit, I was just a regular homeowner in the Willowbrook Homeowners Association, and not a public figure.

The irony in the Willowbrook case is this: *each and every elected officer of a Homeowners Association actually is a public figure.* He or she really can be reported on by a news agency or blogger. Each board officer has voluntarily campaigned for election to public office. His behavior is absolutely a subject of ongoing and important public interest. Each HOA officer has a fiduciary duty to the community. His or her actions, corrupt or non-corrupt, have an impact on the entire HOA membership. As long as a reporter believes the information about a board member is true, he is free to publish details of that officer's behavior.

Reporting on the conduct of a misbehaving HOA officer is just as important as reporting on the wrongdoing of a Congressman, Senator, or President. If the hackneyed phrase by former House Speaker Tip O'Neill is accurate, "All politics are local politics," then the lowest rung of government is just as worthy of media scrutiny as the highest. Every reporter, even one who monitors the behavior of lowly HOA politicians, has the ability and obligation to make a difference; to publish the kind of information that guides public servants away from corrupt or unjust behavior.

Although it seems a brutal leap, Senator John Edwards' 2008 campaign for President of the United States was partially derailed by his poorly-hidden affair with a woman who was not the cancer-stricken wife he had paraded publicly for the news media during his campaign. Similarly, Colorado Senator Gary Hart could easily have become President of the United States in 1988, except for a brazen challenge to members of the news media who were questioning his ethics and morality. Those reporters discovered Hart's extra-marital liaisons with a young lady on a small yacht named "Monkey Business" (again, you can't make these things up).

Although this author makes no judgment on the ethical or moral lapses of either Senator, it must be pointed out that all government officials, high and low, can be held to the same standards. Is a high government official more corrupt when he makes the same missteps as a low government official? Does a bottom-rung government official get a moral/ethical pass simply because he's a lowly Homeowners Association officer and not a Senator? If a piddling, little HOA president was involved in an illicit relationship with another board member, a supplier, an attorney, or anyone else doing business with the HOA, is there any reason that an HOA official's actions shouldn't be just as reportable to the public?

That collapse of morals has legally been used to report on the private lives of the rich and famous. It has absolutely as much political import when applied to the officers of Homeowners Associations. Let the floodgates burst loose. From a Constitutional standpoint, there is really no difference between the high and the mighty and the lowly and loose.

If those board members hold any power over other home-owners, their most private affairs have an impact on the community good. It's a pretty fair assumption that most HOA board officers have never thoroughly looked at their own vulnerability during an intensive ethics investigation.

> **A person who campaigns for election to the local HOA board is a public official in every sense of the warning memorialized in *New York Times* vs. Sullivan. If a common board official has a little shnootzie on the side, the neighborhood gadfly can rightly raise questions about that official's honesty, ethics, morals and fitness for office. Filch a dollar from the community budget, steer a contract toward a buddy, have sex with a fellow homeowner's spouse, an HOA official can and should be pilloried in the press for the same kinds of ethical breaches as the high and mighty.**

## One Downside of Going Public

The story of SueAnn Demerle, a 67 year old widow in the upscale Treyburn neighborhood of Dunham, North Carolina, first broke on in the *Herald-Sun* and on *WTVD*, the ABC News Affiliate in Raleigh-Durham. As wrenching as the story seemed, it's not unheard of among Homeowners Associations, and it's not even one of the most egregious. She lives not far from Interstate 40, which bisects the state from the Atlantic beaches to the Great Smoky Mountains. In 2002, Demmerle's husband died. She was left with the couple's home. A few years later, Demmerle discovered she had cancer. As her bills piled up, she fell behind on her Homeowners Association dues.

"I didn't consider HOA dues first on the list," she told *WTVD* reporter Fred Shropshire.[18]

Demmerle began receiving a series of threatening letters from the HOA, citing her unpaid bills, rising interest charges, legal bills and the threat of losing her home to foreclosure. At one point her dues and delinquency fees climbed to more than $6,700.

In 2008, the HOA foreclosed on Demmerle's upscale home and it was sold at the county auction to the lowest bidder. According to news media accounts, there was only one bidder for the half million dollar home: it was the Treyburn Homeowners Association, itself. Demmerle's lawyer told reporters he was appalled at the situation, including the fact that none of the ailing woman's neighbors stepped in to help.

Here's a woman who's lost her husband; is fighting cancer; misses HOA dues payments because of the cost of her cancer treatment. The HOA accelerates demands, adding legal fees and interest. She lost her half million dollar home to the Treyburn HOA. Can anyone be blamed for thinking that there's something rotten in North Carolina?

There was another interesting part of Demmerle's story: her pro bono attorney said he was having difficulty finding out the exact amount that the Treyburn HOA claimed she owed. Markham B. Gunter of the Gunter & Flowers Law firm represented Treyburn. In an email to Demmerle's attorney, Markham Gunter said, "Part of the reason her fees were growing was the attention the case has garnered in *The Herald-Sun*."[19] In other words, because a newspaper reporter was covering the case, Demmerle was being assessed additional fees. There's just no way to read Gunter's quote and have any degree of faith in the fairness of the American legal system.

## Tyranny by the Majority

In a twist of history that would spin our nation's forefathers in their graves, the current crop of Homeowners Associations or Common Interest Developments (CIDs) are exactly the kinds of tyrannical democracies Americans were warned 240 years ago to avoid. The Federalist Papers were foundational in encouraging the country to adopt the U.S. Constitution. In Papers 9 and 10, Hamilton and Madison warned that any future creation of "a democracy" would suppress the rights of minority factions. On the other hand, they argued that spreading government power over a series of constitutionally established bodies would tend to thwart corruption, bribery and other great "misdeeds of office."

The very thought of a "democracy" was enormously troubling to them. "A tyranny of the majority," Alexis de Tocqueville had described it. "The majority rules" meant that a minority, no matter how substantial, had no representation and no rights. Democracies don't recognize the fact that unalienable rights flow from God to Man. In a democracy, all rights come from the good will of the majority. History, of course, has shown that majorities are rarely of good will and almost never wish for the common good of the groups they outnumber. It's doubtful that a true American Democracy would ever have allowed the great civil rights revolution to overturn historic racial injustices.

One can only imagine what James Madison or Alexander Hamilton would have thought of the modern Homeowners Association movement. The individual HOA member has no basic rights. He has no right to argue that an arbitrary change in rules is made to target and remove a single homeowner. He has no chance to argue the unfairness of a decision to seize any individual's property. No decision or whim of an HOA majority can be declared unconstitutional because each homeowner, as a pre-condition to home ownership, has signed away all access to equal justice. And there is no court of last resort. In a private association the democratic majority is the grantor of all rights and as such can arbitrarily rescind them at will.

A civilian court cannot suddenly bestow human rights in a case where all members of a private association have voluntarily signed them away.

Aggrieved homeowners, in many cases, will never even see a judge before their homes are sold on the auction block. As impossible as it is to believe, one need only research the literature to find cases across the country where HOA law firms have enriched themselves in just such a manner.

There's no purer democracy than a Homeowners Association. If pure democracy is a desirable goal, then the HOA Movement has achieved it, and many homeowners are now discovering its pitfalls. But our forefathers didn't want pure democracy; they argued against it. They must have known how future generations of Americans would try to pervert the limitations they tried to establish over "democratic" government.

**More than 70 million Americans have moved into such communities composed of home-owners who have little if any knowledge that *their own neighbors and the HOA's law firm* have the power to arbitrarily confiscate private property almost at will.**

When Benjamin Franklin emerged from the Constitutional Convention in 1787, he was asked by one of those waiting outside, "So what kind of government have you given us?"

"A Republic, Madam. If you can keep it," he said.

We have gotten ourselves into a pickle, as they say.

# 11

# "Cai! Cai! Cai!"

*"The Birds"*
—Alfred Hitchcock (1963)

Unsuspecting homeowners targeted by rogue HOA boards often discover their Homeowners Associations and lawyers are affiliated with the Community Associations Institute, or C.A.I. Originally conceived as an organization that "educates" communities, in 1992, C.A.I. changed its original mission and re-invented itself as a lobbying and referral group benefitting lawyers and trade groups that work for HOAs. The C.A.I. has subsequently become one of the most powerful lobbying groups in the country. Statistics posted on a C.A.I. website show the wallop this organization is capable of delivering:

> The estimated real estate value of all homes in community associations approaches $4 trillion, approximately 20 percent of the value of all U.S. residential real estate. The total annual operating revenue for community associations in the U.S. is $41 billion. Community Association boards also maintain investment accounts of more than $35 billion for the long-term maintenance and replacement of commonly held property.[1]

What's not disclosed in C.A.I.'s official statistics is the potentially tens of thousands, even hundreds of thousands of HOA trial lawyers and law firms who either pay dues to the organization, or who are on the receiving end of trial work referred by the C.A.I. or its members and associates. The massive potential wealth of the organization ensures that it can fund intensive lobbying campaigns in every corner of the country.

> In state after state, legislative efforts to control the more rabid actions of the HOA movement have been repeatedly shot down after lobbying by C.A.I. affiliated lawyers.

To see them in action, one need only attend a session of any State Legislature when a bill impacting Homeowners Associations is under discussion. The lawyers are ever-present, hovering over the desks of individual legislators, battling any attempt to enumerate rights for homeowners against arbitrary or non-judicial foreclosures of homes.

## C.A.I. Lawyers: Milkin' the Cow

C.A.I. affiliated lawyers, despite their protestations, will claim to the death that they only handle serious cases where homeowners' rights are in the balance, but their record shows otherwise. They're trial lawyers who make no money unless they are litigating. It's no wonder that HOA boards are instructed to aggressively litigate every homeowner's aberration and error. It's a cash machine for lawyers. They'd be crazy to try to fix a system that literally pours money into their pockets. You will never see an HOA lawyer standing in the front lines of a protest demanding legal reforms.

A stunning example of the naked power of well-connected HOA lawyers was on display in the California Legislature in the Fall of 2008 when a Legislative committee began a multi-year effort to overhaul the state's ability to control rogue Homeowners Associations.

By way of background, California Homeowners Associations are regulated by a 1986 state law known as the Davis-Stirling

Act, named after Assembly members Gray Davis and Lawrence W. Stirling. Stirling is listed as the author, but he acknowledges in interviews that he knew absolutely nothing about land use issues when he introduced the bill in the 1985 Assembly.[2] The bill was actually written by his acquaintance and friend, law school professor Katherine Rosenberry.

The law did a number of things: it forced Homeowners Associations to be more accountable about their financial activities, it immunized board members against lawsuits by homeowners, but above all, the Davis-Stirling Act was a bald-faced end run around Proposition 13, the 1978 California taxpayer revolt against government bodies arbitrarily raising property taxes on besieged homeowners. Although Homeowners Associations are considered by many to be nothing more or less than *de facto* governments, under Davis-Stirling they are not considered government entities and as such, are immune from the restrictions mandated by Proposition 13.

> **A California HOA can arbitrarily raise "taxes" on members anytime it wants as long as the additional revenues are considered "dues."**

Various courts have upheld the Davis-Stirling argument. One appeals court found that Homeowner Associations:

> …function almost as a second municipal government, regulating many aspects of… daily lives…. one clearly sees the association as a quasi-government entity paralleling in almost every case the powers, duties, and responsibilities of a municipal government. As a "mini-government," the association provides to its members, in almost every case, utility services, road maintenance, street and common area lighting, and refuse removal. In many cases, it also provides security services and various forms of communication within the community.

There is, moreover, a clear analogy to the municipal police and public safety functions.[3]

Yet in this same ruling the court found that California Homeowners Associations have the right to a jury trial in disputes with their developers. Another court handed down a similar opinion with the comment that the Constitutional right to a jury trial (involving developers and the HOA) was so fundamental that it cannot be "frittered away." The judge further said that in lawsuits between developers and Homeowners Associations, the right to a jury trial is so important that it must be "zealously guarded."[4]

For some readers, the previous paragraph might have caused more head-spinning than that famous movie scene from *The Exorcist*. The twisted logic is beyond rational explanation. A Homeowners Association (a *de facto* government) has a Constitutional right to a jury trial. On the other hand, individual homeowners in a dispute with an HOA do not have the right to a jury trial! Why should jury access be so zealously guarded on behalf of Homeowners Associations, yet so callously denied to some hapless homeowner when he's about to lose his home or life savings?

One might be tempted at this point to answer, "Follow the money." The Homeowners Association movement isn't about the zealous guarding of Constitutional rights. It's about putting all power and money in the hands of the HOA.

## The Fox in Charge of the Henhouse?

In any event, with such wild swings in the courts, the California Legislature decided that the Davis-Stirling Act should probably be overhauled. The Legislature's Law Revision Committee (CLRC) went to work setting up hearings. Obviously the profound implications of any such overhaul meant bringing together some good legal minds, so a committee of 25 attorneys was assembled to advise the Committee on how to improve the law.

Who were these lawyers? According to members of a home-owners watchdog group, *CCHAL (CalHomeLaw.org)*, each of the 25 was a "member of the HOA industry." That meant these twenty-five lawyers represented Homeowners Associations, not homeowners. In other words, they were C.A.I. lawyers. Their very income depended upon their ability to file lawsuits, fines and foreclosures against individual homeowners, and now they were being asked to guard the henhouse.

The C.A.I. connections were discovered by Norma Walker and Carole Hochstatter, two California women who became political activists after being burned by their own Homeowners Associations. These two courageous women began questioning the legislative committee about whether even a single lawyer on the advisory committee had ever represented an individual homeowner against an HOA. The answers were, as expected, embarrassing to the state.[5] Both women were affiliated with *CCHAL (CalHomeLaw.org)*. The organization has waged an aggressive war for homeowners rights in California. Despite their activism, though, Davis-Stirling continues to lean heavily against home-owners in favor of the lawsuit industry.

## The Sharing of HOA Wealth with C.A.I.

Despite the almost incomprehensible financial impact that C.A.I. has on the lives of millions of homeowners, it flies way under the radar. Far more people know about the CIA than the C.A.I., and its existence is thus more secretive than any spy agency. Yet behind those initials, many lawyers and law firms enjoy almost total employment. To better understand the kinds of profits reaped from the turmoil in HOA neighborhoods, consider a recent California study that said 75 percent of that state's HOAs are involved in litigation against homeowners at any one time.[6] There's no way of knowing if that study is applicable to the entire nation, but assume for the sake of argument that the figure accurately portrays the current state of American neighborhoods at war. Being overly conservative, let's also assume that there is only one ongoing lawsuit in each of those impacted neighborhoods per year. Again, being conservative, assume that each side in each lawsuit employs two lawyers, or four for each court case.

Finally, consider that there are 300,000 Homeowners Associations in the United States. Rough math shows that lawsuits inside the HOA movement provide significant employment for 900,000 lawyers per year. Multiply that figure times the thousands or even hundreds of thousands of dollars that are wasted in abusive HOA lawsuits, and one can begin to understand why the Community Associations Institute fights so hard to protect the ongoing transfer of wealth from homeowners to trial lawyers.

No matter how one tries to slice or dice the above math, a lot of money is changing hands in situations where no goods or gross domestic product are produced. Lawyers often feign embarrassment at the more blatant abuses of the legal system, but they never decline to deposit a check from a beaten up citizen who's lost his life savings to an abusive lawsuit.

## Where are the Checks and Balances?

A white collar crime investigator who spent a career with a well-known federal agency once told this reporter, "Any dollar spent on goods or services not rendered is a dollar that's inflationary." Although that federal official has since passed away, his wisdom did not. Whether it's money removed from the economy by swindlers like the infamous ponzi scheme mastermind Bernie

Madoff, or it's money taken from a retired couple's nest egg by HOA lawyers in an excessive or abusive lawsuit, the tragedy is massive and national in scope. Stories of the removal of the life savings from hard-working Americans can be wrenching. No neighborhood is served by a reputation for being litigious, but the lawsuit industry cannot allow its HOA clients to do otherwise.

Law Professor Paula Franzese, in her no-holds-barred critique of the Homeowners Association movement, writes of HOA or CIC/CID members who've faced significant fines or judgments because of such accusations as a tenant being guilty of nothing more than messiness. She notes that community rules have been devised to compel "poorly dressed guests" to ride in service elevators. The wearing of "flip flops" in common areas has been prohibited by some HOAs. Pets, if allowed at all, are supposed to "look nice." They cannot weigh over a certain number of pounds. Certain kinds of cooking, in a wok for example, are prohibited because they could produce less than "desirable" aromas in the neighborhood. In her 2005 paper written for *The Urban Lawyer*, Franzese asked:

> What is going on? We have entered the golden age of privatized "government for the nice." A significant lure of the common interest community is in the desire to live in a "nice environment." Residents equate "niceness" with cleanliness, orderliness, image, the preservation of property values... these desires... have yielded, in numerous instances, to the litigious realities that excessive regulation and aggressive enforcement... can inspire... transforming the relevant inquiry of "how is my neighbor doing?" to the far less desirable "what is my neighbor doing?" Sadly, government for the nice has produced governance by the not-so-nice, as the "nice

police." Those who depart from governing strictures can and have been punished severely, subjected to hefty fines, costly litigation, and even foreclosure. Incentives to litigate are built into existing systems, since most associations are authorized to tax residents to finance lawsuits.[7]

Franzese also writes that there are no meaningful checks and balances on the authority of Homeowners Associations and that bad judgment abounds:

A North Carolina resident, fined $75 a day because his dog exceeded governing weight limitations, was forced to declare bankruptcy when the cumulative assessment totaled $11,000. A Texas resident whose brain tumor caused him to fall behind on $600 in dues was sued, generating $4,600 in legal fees. The association foreclosed on his home. A California couple returned from vacation and found that their association had cut down their very expensive pine trees in response to a neighbor's complaint that the trees violated a covenant preventing foliage from obstructing views - no matter that the association had approved the trees in the first place. That is not nice.[8]

Franzese notes the story of an 89 year old resident of a Homeowners Association who was fined for having an unauthorized "social gathering" when he was joined on his front lawn by two friends who stopped to chat.[9] Franzese predicted a "budding national backlash" against the increasing numbers of such stories.

In the Twin Rivers New Jersey Supreme Court Case, the AARP wrote a Friends-of-the-Court brief saying the organization was deeply concerned that the rights of homeowners were being lost to Homeowners Associations. It included what it termed a "scathing report" on HOAs in 2002 by Edward R. Hannaman, a regulator with the New Jersey Department of Community Affairs. Hannaman reported on the frustration of many complainants about the undemocratic life in a number of associations:

> Problems presented by complainants run the gamut from the frivolous (flower restrictions and lawn watering), to the tragically cruel (denial of a medically necessary air conditioner or mechanical window device for the handicapped), to the bizarre (president having all dog owners walk dogs on one owner's property), air conditioners approved only for use from September to March.... In a disturbing number of instances, those owners with board positions use their influence to punish other owners with whom they disagree.... Complaints have disclosed the following acts committed by incumbent boards: leaving opponents' names off the ballots...by mistake; citing some trivial "violation" against opponents to make them ineligible to run; losing nominating petitions; counting ballots in secret—either by the board or their spouses...[10]

When a homeowner moves into a Common Interest Development or a Homeowners Association, it's generally to seek the kind of peace and solitude that seems to be guaranteed by the rights enumerated in the Constitution. "Quiet enjoyment of property" is a longed-for goal. But the boards which control HOAs are completely beyond the controls or limitations of the U.S. Constitution. As private non-profit corporations they are not bound to respect such concepts as "quiet enjoyment." In fact, they often violate "quiet enjoyment" just to get rid of what they arbitrarily deem to be "neighborhood undesirables." It's diabolically clever: just do whatever it takes to make an unwanted member miserable and he or she will move on. It's insidious, *and legal.*

## Jacking the Stats

Heavy-handed actions by HOA boards against individual members are far from unusual in American suburbia. The Community Associations Institute claims the majority of HOA members are satisfied with life in these so-called "private government compounds." To back up its stance, the C.A.I. even contracted with the Zogby polling organization to query 709 homeowners.[11] Indeed, the C.A.I. found the polling results it expected. Only one in seven homeowners surveyed by Zogby rated the HOA experience as a negative one, and the C.A.I. quotes its own survey often.

Not surprisingly, other surveys of homeowners' attitudes have turned up feelings diametrically opposed to the C.A.I. findings. One private study cited by *Los Angeles Times* blogger Kathy Price-Robinson polled 3000 HOA members. It found that two-thirds of those interviewed thought of their HOAs as "annoying or worse." Less than a quarter of those responding had any favorable things to say about their HOAs and even submitted that they planned to avoid living in one in the future. A majority felt "they'd rather live with a sloppy neighbor than deal with an HOA."[12]

Obviously with such a disparity in poll results, one side or the other is "jacking the stats." Since the C.A.I. is essentially a lobbying organization run by trial lawyers to protect trial lawyers some might suspect the C.A.I. report of being self-serving and lacking in credibility. Others may criticize the polling methods in Price-Robinson's report.

## Bullies, Parasites and Lawyers, Oh My!

John Stossel, an award-winning reporter for ABC's 20/20, argues for a legal system in which the loser has to pay the legal expenses of the winning side. He says it's the only way to control litigators who misuse force against the people they needlessly sue. He refers to trial lawyers as:

> …bullies and parasites who enrich themselves through extortion. It's legal extortion, but extortion nonetheless…We ought to avoid using lawyers the way we avoid firing missiles…. Our legal system invites lawyers to act like bullies… America needs judges willing to say no to the lawyer bullies…. Otherwise, the parasites will bully away your money and your choices.[13]

While Stossel's sentiments are probably right on target, the Homeowners Association movement has turned his wisdom on its head. In Homeowners Associations across the country, the odds are massively stacked in favor of HOA lawyers and against the individual homeowner. HOA covenants invariably contain a clause that requires any homeowner involved in litigation with the Association to pay all legal fees for both sides.

Even if an HOA's lawsuit is overreaching and improper, a homeowner who wins such a battle never gets back the attorney's fees that were wasted. His damage is never compensated. This isn't a "loser pays system." It's "loser-pays" on steroids. And the loser is always the homeowner. It's a guarantee of full employment for lawyers and it has taken legal bullying to unprecedented heights.

**An Association which files even the most abusive and frivolous case is almost guaranteed of recouping its expenses. There's no reciprocity, of course. There's no clause that mandates a homeowner be awarded legal costs if the Association loses an abusive or frivolous case.**

Still, this is just the starting point where gaming of the system by HOA lawyers takes the most vicious turn of all. A Homeowners Association which levies a fine or files a lawsuit against a homeowner is not initially covered for its legal expenses by its insurance company. However, if an HOA's actions are so provocative as to invite a counter-suit by the targeted homeowner, the HOA's insurance policy suddenly kicks in. From this point on, it's a free ride for the Association. A targeted homeowner soon learns that he or she now faces the legal and financial might of the entire HOA lawsuit machine. It's not a level playing field. As such, it's absolutely in the interest of the rogue HOA board to be as outrageous as possible in its actions against neighborhood "undesirables." The whole point is to provoke a counter-suit. An out-of-control board desperately wants a targeted homeowner to hit back. In a nutshell, that's what has ruined life in the suburbs for single moms, minorities, the disabled, for anyone who doesn't fit the white-bread, cookie-cutter conformist stereotype so desired by private real estate developers.

## Homeowner Meetings—Neighbors At War

Most of the 300,000 covenant-controlled, deed-restricted neighborhoods in America have annual homeowners meetings. It's an interesting exercise for the casual observer to drop by and eavesdrop on what's going on. The observer is more likely than not to see the seething resentment. Neighbors who in any other situation might actually be acting neighborly are pitted against one another. Yelling matches are common. Something in this picture of life in suburbia is desperately wrong. It's ugly out there.

In a growing number of cases across the country, citizens who thought they were protected by the Constitution's Bill of Rights have discovered to their horror that they have purchased property inside what for all intents and purposes is an "American gulag" where perceived rights are not only disrespected, but openly mocked. Many of the unwary feel they were somehow tricked into making that choice.

Whether by lack of knowledge, lack of understanding, or lack of information provided at the time of sale, homeowners who thought they were simply buying a home discovered they had actually accepted a fundamental change of government. This kind of fascism and social control has never before been a part of American life, so it's understandable how some starry-eyed young home buyer can be left gasping at the stark realities of life in the new neighborhood.

Conventional wisdom might suggest that in suburbia, neighbors would try to be very nice to one another. But HOAs are governed by another paradigm; that there is no "nice." Even in the depths of the 2008-2010 recession, the advice from C.A.I. lawyers to their HOA clients was the same. Whether a non-conforming bumper sticker on a car,[14] the wrong kind of people moving in,[15] or a disabled veteran trying to fly the American flag,[16] the advice was to enforce the covenants and foreclose on miscreants.

No sympathy.

No compassion.

No compromise.

One Dallas company which tracks such things, Foreclosure Listing Services, wrote that during the two year period, 2006 to 2008, home foreclosures filed by HOAs (not mortgage companies, but HOAs) had soared 30 percent in deed-restricted neighborhoods in at least 19 Texas counties.[17] The same trend impacted homeowners across the country.

As this author strays out of "politically correct" territory, it was and continues to be a wet dream for lawyers. This cash machine is always open, and there's no limit to what a lawyer can withdraw. The redistribution of wealth from private homeowners to C.A.I. associated lawyers is as massive as it is incomprehensible.

Enforce those covenants. Make sure to target "undesirables." And that means *sue*.

Sue, baby, sue.

# 12
# Two Plus Two Equals Four

*In the end the Party would announce that two and two made five, and you would have to believe it.*
—George Orwell, *1984*

*If the Führer wants it, two and two makes five.*
· —Hermann Göring

Every book of any societal value seems to have a fulcrum, a tipping point if you will, upon which the entire narrative either survives or collapses on the balance of its cumulative logic. Please note the way we use the word, *balance*. Any critic who says this author failed to balance the pros and cons of HOA membership obviously doesn't yet get it. The multi-billion dollar HOA industry already floods all communication channels with the pabulum that Homeowners Associations are completely benign. They are anything but benign.

The "industry" is the one which writes the books, the manuals; it lobbies the legislatures, controls the dialog, assigns the lawyers, and sues the naysayers. *Neighbors At War*, therefore, *is* the balance. It's one of a very few that tries to show the underbelly of the beast through the eyes of its victims. In a subsequent chapter we'll explore some possible solutions that could ease some of the insanity surrounding the HOA movement. But this chapter has a *special purpose*. It's a final attempt to drive a stake in the beast, to blast a few last holes *in the single biggest myth about your*

*Homeowners Association; that the reason for its existence is to preserve property values.*

The original comfort food offered by your Realtor was reseassuring. You knew in your heart that your choice was the right one. Your home wouldn't lose value, and that rubric was shouted up and down the street, by neighbors, friends, your mortgage company. After all, your lender was so anxious to do business with you that you may have even been offered a 100 percent or 125 percent loan to value mortgage.

Then the 2008-2010 economic meltdown slashed the throats of all those mellifluous, honeyed voices. As home prices dropped 20, 30 and even 60 percent in many areas of the country, covenant-controlled neighborhoods suddenly became about as attractive as a three-day-old case of hemorrhagic fever. From California, Nevada, Texas and Florida, on north to the Carolinas and Maine, and back west across the great states of Michigan, Colorado, Idaho and Washington, if you owned an HOA home, what happened? In some areas, an under-water home couldn't be unloaded at any price. Neighborhood covenants locked the homeowner into finan-cial disaster. Those who'd bought into the "two plus two equals five" logic must have felt they'd been betrayed by some mysterious new math. But short of hand-wringing and moaning about lost retirement savings and ruined lives, is there any deeper truth yet to be uncovered? Perhaps there is. And it's based on seven of the most profound words ever uttered by any philosopher:

"WeeWillow Heights is such a wonderful place to live," they hypnotically intoned. "We have a special way of life here, one we want to maintain. By enforcing the covenants and keeping out the wrong kind of people, our property values will always be protected and your investment is safe."

That government is best which governs least.

That quote, alternately attributed to Thomas Paine, Thomas Jefferson and later even to Henry David Thoreau, should be memorized by every school child. At every grade level, youngsters should have that pounded like a jackhammer into their fragile little psyches. Sadly, one of the most important politically foundational statements ever uttered will never be heard by most American schoolboys and girls. It's simply not taught. Most teachers, administrators and school boards who control our nation's education system don't believe it anyway, and it probably would be anathema for them to see it required in the curricula.

As for the quote, Thoreau used it to show his anger over slavery. He saw the southern governments as a tyrannical hand which would eventually drag the entire country into a costly civil war, one that neither side was capable of winning. Paine and Jefferson both knew that the newly formed United States would remain free only as long as government was kept out of the daily business of the citizenry. Freedom, they felt, was inversely proportional to the size of government. History shows that all three men were right.

## Less Is Better

Regardless of the origin of the quote, the concept that *less is better* was the overriding thought as the U.S. Constitution was conceived, articulated, drafted, debated, published and defended. The Constitution was as simple as it was unique.

That one belief, that *less is better* had never before been uttered during the founding of a Constitutional government. It was so revolutionary that it inflamed the sensibilities of Czars and Princes, Kings and Queens, tyrants and despots as they watched the awkward founding of our Republic. Across the Old

World they watched and mocked, and waited for our new creation to collapse on the naiveté of its founders. But it didn't. The fledgling Republic thrived, and grew, and strove mightily to overcome its early mistakes. After the sacrifice of 620,000 American lives, it even overthrew its greatest historical embarrassment: the failure to forbid slavery.

> —No other document in the history of mankind summoned up such a desire by its citizens to be free.
> —No other document so explicitly compiled the precise powers that a government was never supposed to use against its people.

## The Rise of Progressivism

Sadly, the message from our founders was savaged in the 20th Century. A new movement materialized, one destined to change America forever. Beginning with people like John Dewey and Woodrow Wilson, and with the help of a flood of college professors imported from supposedly more enlightened universities in Europe, American students began learning about a different kind of Utopia. True justice, it was argued, was not a product of the system established by our freedom-obsessed forefathers; it could only be brought about when all citizens became cogs in a giant social wheel, serving a ruling class of professional politicians.

Average folks were generally believed to be too stupid to govern themselves; they needed a government babysitter regulating and steering all aspects of their lives. The answer was *Progressivism*, a word unknown to most Americans. But under the changed paradigm, massive new social programs were created by a growing bureaucracy. A progressive income tax was created that leaned heavily on the well-to-do. Huge numbers of citizens (and non-citizens!) began to rely on a promised monthly stipend from the government. The nation's elite were no longer the inventors, innovators and builders of business. The boy heroes in Horatio Alger novels were demonized; advertising geniuses like Conrad Hilton became the "greedy rich."

Through annual deficit spending, government began piling up staggering amounts of debt. Succumbing to the logic of economist John Maynard Keynes, politicians in both major political parties argued that government intervention and "public investment" (code words for higher taxes) were capable of creating jobs. National debt, it was thought, wasn't real debt because we actually owed that money to ourselves.

In the unprecedented tragedy of World War II, the massive amount of debt at one point exceeded the amount of Gross Domestic Product. That trend was reversed for a few short decades following 1945. Spending was controlled and the debt brought down. During that time period innovation exploded. A national ethic of patriotism and exceptionalism seemed again to become the norm.

Sadly, it wasn't to last. Gnawing away at the timbers of the nation's foundational framework, the old termites of Progressivism continued their work. As the 21st Century approached, the men and women once feted as "the Greatest Generation" were railed against on campuses across the nation. American exceptionalism, once the single overriding philosophy that hovered over the founders as they drafted and ratified the Bill of Rights, became a subject of doubt and derision.

The size and intrusiveness of the federal government continued to grow until the national debt once again exceeded the amount of the nation's entire gross domestic product. And for the first time in history, the average salary for a public employee exceeded that of the average private sector worker. Even though unemployment in the 2008-2010 meltdown soared to ten percent (unofficial counts put the practical rate at closer to twenty percent), job loss and underemployment was almost entirely in the private sector. In fact, one of the safest jobs in America was behind a government desk; any government desk, anywhere.

A new kind of economic bubble began gaining size. Fear was rampant, creating a bubble so large that its eventual collapse could fundamentally change the social and political structure of the entire world and potentially lead to the collapse of American Constitutional government. The debt generated in the first 12 years of the 21$^{st}$ Century reached the point where no reasonable economist could envision any kind of resolution, outside of massive regime-killing inflation.

So, why discuss Progressivism in a screed about the Home-owners Association movement? It's simply this: they so perfectly complement each other. Progressivism is exactly what its name implies; it grows. It progresses. It believes in constant government spending to right all of society's perceived wrongs. Progressivism cannot allow the Constitution (even with all its Amendments) to be considered a perfect document. Progressivism is all about the creation of rules, rules so complex that they can't be compre-hended much less followed. Progressivism out of necessity is continuously reinforced by the constantly expanding litigation industry. Thus, tort reform of any kind simply cannot be tolerated.

It's all about "change," whatever context that word may take. It envisions a fully homogenized future Utopia once all of its "change" is implemented. All wealth is equally distributed and the proof is in the perfect conformity of all lives, jobs and residences.

## The HOA Movement—Utopia

So, too, the modern Homeowners Association Movement is Utopian, constantly growing as more and more Americans make the unwitting and sometimes unwilling move into island neighborhoods where unwanted races, religions, disabilities and non-conformity are quietly screened out. Their existence is useful as a tool for traditional government to rid itself of low-level spending without the complication of having to respect annoying property and personal rights. And the HOA system does what traditional government cannot; it can arbitrarily and capriciously harass, fine, sue or foreclose with stunning speed, unimpeded by any limits of the Constitution. As such, the movement will fight to the death any and all attempts at tort reform.

HOAs cannot exist without a growing litigation industry. Homeowners Associations, too, demand homogeneity and again, the complete conformity of all housing is a not-too-subtle demonstration that incomes are being distributed evenly. Any display of one's wealth or individuality would be considered a vulgarity, and as such, these neighborhoods are a fulfillment of the promise of Progressivism.

**Once all Americans are governed by HOAs then the U.S. Constitution will be largely superfluous.**

Ayn Rand, the anti-Progressive author of such revolutionary works as *Atlas Shrugged*, *The Fountainhead* and *We The Living* once wrote:

> There's no way to rule innocent men. The only power any government has is the power to crack down on criminals. Well, when there aren't enough criminals, one makes them. One declares so many things to be a crime that it becomes impossible for men to live without breaking laws.[1]

The entire Declaration of Independence *and* the U.S. Constitution can fit into about 16 pages of a shirt pocket handbook. But the Covenants, Conditions and Restrictions of a typical Homeowners Association can fill up to 120 full-sized pages of unintelligible fine print.

In a nutshell, you now have the single biggest reason why your HOA does not protect your property values. Progressivism is the exact antithesis of the right to own property and as it continues amassing its huge debts, it uses the perceived value of private property rights as exploitable and expendable collateral. Since Progressivism is so antithetical to property value, that value has essentially been unknowingly transferred out of the hands of the private individual into the hands of the Collective. All it takes for homeowners to realize how ephemeral their property values are is for any garden variety financial or real estate bubble to come along. Instead of that bubble being absorbed into the usually mild cycles of a free market economy, property values are trashed.

> The Constitution acknowledges that every citizen possesses God-given rights which protect him against government. The CC&Rs of the WeeWillow Heights HOA don't even acknowledge that a homeowner has any rights at all. The community as a whole has rights, but not any individual person.

In places like Las Vegas and Southern Florida where the HOA movement dominates the landscape, people who thought they were private property owners in 2007 suddenly discovered they owned almost nothing of value in 2010. Millions of people had uncritically placed all their rights and property values on the sacrificial altar of Progressivism. And hundreds of billions of dollars in property value simply vanished. No one could tell where.

Think about it: Why should housing prices drop so precipitously, when the population increases every year? Eighty to ninety percent of the population is still working. They pay for housing in some way, through either rent or mortgage payments.

There's no equation that can account for the contradiction. But sixty to seventy million Americans can at least say that they've now experienced the promise of Utopia. Was it worth it? Is it worth it?

Harsh? Too abstruse to be credible? OK, in exchange for this author hypothetically accepting that criticism, permit me to be a little more specific about why your HOA fails to protect property values. Remember that any expense or obligation against your new dream house in WeeWillow Heights has little or no effect on its net value. Its mortgage, for example, is a liability that cannot possibly raise the value of a property. A plumbing bill does nothing to raise your value, nor do the annual property taxes. It's the same thing with monthly HOA dues.

## Hidden Costs: the Dark Shadow over Your Home's Value

With that in mind, let's take a close look at some of the hidden costs of being a dues paying member of WeeWillow Heights. Despite occasional periods of legal quiescence, your new HOA has been known to file a lawsuit or two when homeowners failed to keep their lawns green or when some schmo parked the wrong kind of vehicle in his driveway. Those lawsuits, of course, are financed by the dues paid by all members. Your share of those legal fees is a financial obligation that lowers the net value of your home. Your one comforting thought, though, is that you appreciate neighborhood conformity and you're confident you'll never be sued.

But let's dig deeper. There are some admittedly negligent homeowners in WeeWillow Heights, the kind who fail to keep up to date on their own HOA dues. Those people might merely have overlooked the overdue bill, or perhaps they're struggling with a job loss and simply can't afford to pay at the moment.

Since you and all other dues-paying members have to make up for their shortcomings, your net value falls respectively. But again, those are really negligible losses.

Let's grow our analysis, here; your HOA is known to use local debt collection agencies to harass and collect from those negligent non-dues paying homeowners. These collection agencies are historically very good. They have complete access to your credit reports, your personal banking information, often your passwords, and a massive amount of extremely private information about you, your family, your phone records, who you call, who calls you, your personal relationships and your most intimate habits. The WeeWillow HOA board has signed a contract which allows the debt collector to grab his own fees and reimbursements first; the attorney's expenses second, the interest and penalties third. Finally, the HOA get its past due bills reimbursed.

A late paying property owner can rack up thousands, sometimes tens of thousands of dollars in collection and legal fees before a single penny is applied to his HOA debt. That means the original debt and penalties keep climbing while the homeowner is trying to pay down his bill. It's a marvelous cycle that keeps money flowing to lawyers and collectors, and if the HOA is lucky, it gets reimbursed at the end of the line. Several State Legislatures are considering restricting that practice, including California, Nevada and others. But CAI lawyers are out in force, lobbying passionately against any change in the status quo.

The bottom line, though, is that every hint of strife in your new neighborhood lowers the net value of your property. If you have an aggressive HOA, coupled with an aggressive litigation/collections arm—your home value can spiral down. Why? Because buzz happens—if word gets out, prospective buyers will have little interest in buying into your neighborhood.

If, for any reason, you are contemplating moving into a deed-restricted HOA community, the wise advice would be to investigate whether the neighborhood has a history of litigation. But wait! As we've repeatedly demonstrated, even the mildest, gentlest HOA can turn rogue in a single election. It's a perpetual "buyer beware" market. And what does that do to protect property values?

Still on the subject of unpaid HOA dues, let's examine a very real situation reported by *CalHomeLaw.org*, the California HOA watchdog. It seems like many responsible homeowners allow their HOAs to withdraw monthly dues payments from their checking accounts. Automatic checking withdrawals take the headache out of making sure dues are always paid on time. But if a Homeowners Association changes property managers (as often happens), the new company may not legally be able to continue automatic withdrawals. Suddenly, it appears like your dues are unpaid. At this point you get hit with 10,000 or 15,000 dollars in legal bills, interest, penalties and a debt collector who has little respect for credit and collections law. From CCHAL's (*CalHomeLaw.org*) own website:

> CCHAL has gotten COUNTLESS complaints about this (and we're HOPING that this isn't yet another predatory business practice...[2]

When you first moved to WeeWillow, you told yourself you would never be sued; that you live in a nice, neighborly community. Now you're the scofflaw. What does that do for your net property values?

## Homeowner Beware:
## What's in Your Board's Background?

Moving closer to total cynicism, let's take a wider and wilder look at your HOA board's history. There are sporadic times when some egomaniacal neighborhood nutcase gets himself elected and the WeeWillow Heights board votes 3-2 to file a retaliatory lawsuit or two. As documented repeatedly in *Neighbors At War*, it happens daily, even hourly, from the East Coast to the West. Suddenly, your WeeWillow Heights address has some real financial risk associated with it. You might think you're following every single regulation in the CC&Rs. But remember that eight inch wide oil stain in your driveway? It doesn't matter that it pre-existed your purchase by a decade or two; that crotchety new Nazi with the swing vote on the board says you're being sued for not removing it.

> **At the very least, anyone who buys into an HOA should set aside a monthly reserve fund to pay for possible future legal bills. A lawsuit instigated by a single vindictive board member can ultimately cost you many times the net value of your home.**

You might not have known it at the time, but your legal exposure was there before you ever signed your loan papers. It should have been calculated into the purchase price of your home.

Even though the odds say you probably will never actually be sued, the odds are high that some other nearby neighbor *will* be sued. And the legal fees from that lawsuit will be charged off to all the other homeowners, including you. Every home in the HOA is now less attractive to potential buyers. You've lost net value.

## 78 Cents? Seventy-Eight Cents?!?!?!?

Do frivolous, insane lawsuits really happen in the world of Homeowners Associations? Or is that just a myth; an exaggeration by an overwrought author? Well, let's examine the real life case of a Florida woman named Cheryl McKenna.

A single mother struggling to raise a son, McKenna thought she'd found heaven when she moved into the upscale West

Boca neighborhood of Camino Real Village. In August of 2002, her Homeowners Association determined that she had underpaid her dues and it filed a lawsuit to seize her home. Her underpayment on the original bill was 78 cents. Because of the shortfall, Camino Real Village immediately attached attorney's bills to her overdue notice. Late fees on the 78 cents soared to more than 5,500 dollars. Unless she paid all the attorneys' fees and fines, McKenna was destined to lose her home.

"Having this foreclosure hanging over my head has been a nightmare," McKenna told reporter Ral Abbady of *The Sun Sentinel*.[3]

Any number of people involved in the McKenna case could have ended it by simply donating 78 cents worth of pocket change to the lady's cause. But the case chugged on, legal bills on both sides rising with each billable hour.

On July 21, 2004, the McKenna case ended up before the 4th District Court of Appeals in West Palm Beach. The judge ruled that the Camino Real Village Homeowners Association had not followed its own bylaws when it foreclosed on McKenna's home two years earlier. The HOA, according to the ruling, had not allowed the 30-day grace period to expire on the 78 cent shortfall before filing its lien against McKenna.

The president of the Camino Real Village HOA, Robert Blake, refused to give details to reporters but he claimed that board officials had tried to work out a payment arrangement with McKenna. Still, the thought of an HOA trying to foreclose on a homeowner's property over 78 cents is breathtaking.

Sadly, it's not a rare event. In Homeowners Associations across the country, many HOAs are continuously embroiled in litigation. In one survey in California, more than 75 percent of all Homeowners Associations were found to be involved in at least one lawsuit at any one time. In any one of those lawsuits, a large verdict on behalf of a homeowner against an HOA could potentially result in massive financial losses for members of an association who weren't even aware they were parties in a lawsuit.

## "Gonna Take a Hyperbolic Journey, Hyperbolic Journey Home" (apologies to Doris Day)

You've finally built your dream home, your McMansion in the suburbs. You didn't know at the time that your community center and pool desperately needed to be repaired or replaced. Your HOA board has voted on the matter and it'll cost at least $400,000, with each homeowner assessed his pro-rata share. Your share of the special assessment is $4,000.

Ah, and another surprise; the nearby municipality has been planning for some time to put in a sewer system and remove all septic tanks in the area. Hooking up to the city sewer line isn't cheap. But at this point you really have no option. Since the HOA Board voted to obligate all member homeowners to join the city sewer network, you're stuck. Each homeowner will be assessed $30,000 to pay for the hookup. You have to do it. You've got thirty days to come up with the money. How's the heartburn?

But can it actually get worse? Lordy, Lordy, let us count the ways. Your Realtor forgot to tell you about a pending community "situation." A couple of houses in WeeWillow Heights sit near a well-tended nine hole golf course, a lovely place, really. You never actually planned on playing there, though perhaps it might have been fun to take some lessons. But about six months ago, a visitor to the course hit a slice that went through a resident's picture window and hit her grandson in the eye. Yes, the lad suffered serious eye damage from the splintered glass and no one knows who smacked the wayward ball. The HOA's insurance company has denied liability since the HOA had previously neglected a warning to erect a net to catch those predictably errant golf balls.

The homeowner won a judgment against the Association for four million dollars for its negligence. You didn't even know such a lawsuit had ever been filed and your house is almost a mile away from the course. But yes, your share of the judgment will be approximately $40,000.

All things considered, you and your neighbors might have actually gotten off easy. The jury was extremely sympathetic and the boy's trial lawyer had originally asked for a judgment of ten times as much.

But didn't your HOA Board recently ask all the neighbors to pay for an insurance policy to protect it from such lawsuits? Yes, it did. *But the money you and your neighbors spent for extra insurance was actually for a policy that protects only the board members against liability.* You, Bunky, are now in a category called "practicing naked." And there isn't an insurance company in the world that'll protect you against intentional negligence by your HOA.

Worse? Worse? Didn't we use that word before? If so, forgive the repetition. But with all these special assessments and hidden fees being aimed at the heart of your personal wealth, could you really foresee the kinds of charges which could someday bring you to the point where you might start thinking about such things as bankruptcy? It's been tried. And previous HOA members in several jurisdictions have found that homeowners cannot discharge debts from judgments incurred while being a member of a Homeowners Association. Fly to Singapore, and they'll still find a way to ding you. You will get to know the word, "lien" very well. But it won't be a cuddly relationship.

Let's go in a completely different direction, here. You're working on your PhD in human sexuality, but your spouse just caught you in a moment of, shall we say, *accouplement* with someone other than her in your locked university office. You forgot your spouse had a key, and your phony excuse about wanting to do some after-hours research just didn't fly. Anyway, the two of you have decided to split the sheets, or at least take some time to let the dust settle.

To make ends meet, the two of you decide you'll just rent out the WeeWillow house while you both separate for awhile and work on mending your relationship. You find the perfect tenant, sign the one-year lease, and withdraw from the Friday Night Fights. But a few months later, a process server locates you and hands you papers. WeeWillow is suing you because it forbids an owner from subletting his house.

What? You checked the CC&Rs to make sure you were going by the book. There's not a single word forbidding you from leasing your home to a tenant. But you see, the covenants you signed said you would not set up a "home business" in your house. By renting it out, you're operating a home business. The phrase "neighborhood Nazi" is frequently overused in Home-owners Association squabbles, but as you look at that 3-2 vote on the board, the phrase seems more and more applicable.

Finally, one last word on lawsuits; many an HOA has lost its insurance coverage after filing an idiotic or frivolous lawsuit. No company wants to insure an HOA whose Board Members have a reputation for being terminally stupid. And those companies have occasionally withdrawn coverage to limit their risk. That leaves those HOAs on the edge of a cliff with the homeowner expected to pick up the tab for the next bad decision. Again, any guesses as to how all of this affects your net property value?

## New Neighborhoods and the Real Estate Bubble

Here's a giant controversy for those tragic folks who bought into brand new housing developments right before the real estate bubble burst. Many paid a small fortune for their homes. The builder went bankrupt, leaving half the homes unbuilt or unsold. Now the bank has taken over the project and is motivated to rid itself of those properties. The best solution: sell them at half price. Those who bought $600,000 homes thought they were going to be living in a community of $600,000 homes. Now, the newcomers will be paying just $300,000. The churning neighborhood dynamics are going to be fascinating to watch. "I got screwed, and you didn't!" is a phrase that will reverberate for generations around that community.

Along the same trajectory, when the real estate bubble popped, the growing number of homeowners not paying their dues meant that typical neighborhood maintenance expenditures could not be made, things like landscaping the common areas and monthly cleaning of the neighborhood pool. Now imagine trying to sell your own home while potential buyers are driving past the overgrown entrance, the empty guard shack, the unpainted and rotting WeeWillow sign. And envision that most embarrassing moment: the tour of the community pool where the untreated water is a toxic, bilious green.

It's also difficult to imagine explaining to your potential buyers that a two or three week bout of intestinal giardia often comes after a dip in that fetid pool. Tell your client it'll all eventually be worked out by your HOA, but don't be surprised if the client's offer for your McMansion is far below the asking price. Again, there goes your net value.

In an upcoming chapter, we'll discuss a huge upsurge in the number of Homeowners Associations which have lost millions of dollars to HOA embezzlers. Replacement of embezzled funds has to come from somewhere. Since true restitution is rarely made by the bad guys, the money comes from you and your neighbors. The potential risk of embezzlement also has to be figured in to the net value of your home.

This next story is almost petty enough to not even rate worth telling, but it's still an amusing insight into the mentality of many in the current HOA movement. A ritzy neighborhood in the suburbs of the movie-obsessed Hollywood has long been known as a place where the film industry is welcome. A film production crew shows up and leases a glamorous home for a two or three day shoot, they're in and out, no damage is done, and the homeowner gets a year's worth of mortgage payments for hosting the film crew. It's a fun pastime seeing the big stars come and go, and the excitement has always been part of the Hollywood scene. But in the Los Feliz Estates Homeowners Association, the five member HOA board has ruled that one couple won't be allowed to lease their house to a crew from *Law & Order: Los Angeles.* The homeowner, Adrine Adreasian, has in effect lost $30,000 in the net value of her home. One board member said, "That's not fair to the other 200 members of the community for one family to reap all that money, while the other neighbors get nothing." Ah, the many wonders of the collective.

**One can understand why more and more home buyers, cash in hand, are asking Realtors to only show them homes that are *not* located within a Homeowners Association.**

In the case of the Andreasian family, it wasn't even a big movie shoot, just two filmmakers inside the-house for a few days, no traffic tie-ups, no big stars, still the promise of a year's mortgage payments covered. But the HOA rule sticks: No more movie shoots in the neighborhood. It's just not fair for one homeowner to get money while others don't.[4]

# 13

# *"De Factos, Ma'am, Just De Factos"*

—Sgt. Joe Friday, *Dragnet* ©1957

In 2008, more than one out of every four homes purchased was accompanied by a real estate deed that mandated membership in a Homeowners Association. Local governments in a growing number of areas require that all developers create deeds by which homeowners are forced to abide by a complex set of CC&Rs (covenants, conditions and restrictions) that supplant services normally supplied by established government.

The massive transition into these controlled-life compounds has largely taken place over the past fifteen years. Tens of millions of Americans are now living inside what are essentially *de facto* governments (governments-in-fact), yet those citizens have no access to many of the basic rights set out in the U.S. Constitution. The C.A.I. and the Homeowners Association Movement are now deeply woven into American life. If a straying homeowner deviates even slightly from the neighborhood rules, he will inevitably be introduced to the "new aristocracy," a small group of career busybodies who monitor and regulate private behavior. This aristocracy is backed up by the huge legal hammer wielded by the nation's trial lawyers.

In schools across the country, American youngsters used to be taught about the struggle of our founding fathers to limit the powers of government by setting aside certain legal protections for every citizen. The birth of the Constitution and the Bill of Rights are heralded as unique in the history of mankind. Although the Magna Carta eight centuries ago began to recognize that a King's power can be limited by the people, the U.S. Constitution created something new, a set of freedoms against government that had never before been enumerated.

In the past, no child could get through the American educational system without at least hearing of these freedoms. In the future, school kids will have to learn a new paradigm: that many Americans once had these rights and with a signature on a real estate contract, gave them away.

> HOAs were invented by private land developers for the sole reason of increasing housing density, thereby maximizing their own profits and limiting losses. But the deed restrictions they created run with the land. They're nearly impossible to eliminate. Human rights are incredibly fragile, even ephemeral. *HOAs are forever.*

Advocates of "private government compounds" are fond of saying that home buyers voluntarily choose to live in covenant-controlled homes. But, in many parts of the country, homes outside of a Homeowners Association are difficult or impossible to find. From Arizona, to Colorado, to Florida, covenant-controlled neighborhoods dominate the landscape. Municipalities, of course, view these developments as a clever way of imposing taxes that don't actually look like taxes and therefore can't be limited in some future taxpayers revolt. But for each new homeowner, a stroke of the pen during a real estate closing essentially does away with a 230 year history of fundamental Constitutional and human rights.

By accepting covenants that allow arbitrary fines and foreclosures for virtually any misdeed or offense against the community, homeowners have set loose upon themselves almost uncontrolled police powers, exactly what the writers of the Constitution tried to prevent.

## The Magic of Corporate Protection

As acknowledged by court after court, citizens have the right to contractually sign away Constitutional rights. The right to "contract" without government interference is deeply embedded within our Constitution.

When a citizen, for example, goes to work for a private corporation, he or she contracts to abide by rules created by the corporation. The corporation may demand all sorts of behavior modification in prospective employees, such as the refusal to allow weapons in the workplace, controls on speech, a demand that speech be politically correct, even the acknowledgement that "private" conversations may not be confidential, but in fact may be monitored and taped. Over the years, most employees have become accustomed to those controls over their public and private behavior.

But the Constitution holds a private home up as being different than a workplace. More than two centuries of law have treated the home as being beyond the reach of the intrusions of government. It's not a place where most people intentionally decide to assign away their rights. Most families have grown up with a longstanding wisdom that "your home is your castle." Private homes, many believe, cannot be arbitrarily entered, searched and inspected by warrantless government snoopers. Sadly, many members of Homeowners Associations have discovered to their chagrin that they were wrong about their right to privacy. HOA board members can *and do* come onto private property for the lamest of reasons.

In California's Laguna Hills Village, homeowners have been ordered to stand by and allow HOA officials to inspect their homes for hoarding. Among things hoarded include "large quantities of books, magazines... and clothing kept in a disorganized manner."

> **Large quantities of books? One can only stand back in amazement at the implications. What defines a large quantity of books? In whose judgment is a collection of books too large? And what infamous historical figures inspected and disciplined those who hoarded books?**

Homeowners Associations in other parts of the country mandate occasional garage inspections. Still others require Social Security Numbers, and copies of drivers' licenses as a condition for residency. The list of privacy invasions is almost endless.

Here's another fascinating wrinkle that drives Constitutionalists crazy: "Bills of Attainder" are a product of English Common Law and were either a Legislative or Parliamentary act, declaring some person or group of persons guilty of a past high crime such as treason. Those citizens who were "tainted" or hit with Bills of Attainder were essentially convicted without trial, and considered without civil rights. Instead of the "tainted" person's property being inherited through will or testament by family members, it was confiscated by the British Crown. America's founding fathers saw Attainder as a massive abuse by Royalty and insisted it be outlawed in the new Constitution.

Indeed, James Madison, in the Federalist Papers, wrote that:

> Bills of attainder... are contrary to the first principles of... sound legislation. The sober people of America.... have seen

with regret and indignation that sudden changes and legislative interferences, in cases affecting personal rights, become jobs in the hands of enterprising and influential speculators, and snares to the more-industrious and less-informed part of the community.[1]

In 1787, when the U.S. Constitution was crafted, it twice out-lawed Bills of Attainder, first for Congress, and secondly for State Legislatures:

No Bill of Attainder or ex post facto Law shall be passed (by Congress).[2]

And again:

"No State shall… pass any Bill of Attainder, or ex post facto Law, or Law impairing the Obligation of Contracts…"[3]

In other words, no government body, federal or state, could confiscate property without due process and without all Constitutional rights being observed, revered and upheld.

But Homeowners Associations are not bound by laws against such irritations as free speech, privacy in one's home, and Bills of Attainder. Since covenant-protected neighborhoods are created and joined by contract, they are not technically an institution of government. Indeed, these private, non-profit corporations are not obligated to respect any part of the Constitution. HOAs are given the power of election, the power to legislate, the power to micromanage behavior, the power to tax, the power to issue permits, the powers to fine and foreclose.

In many ways, they are far more powerful than any government. And they confiscate property on a daily basis, in city after city, where no family member has the ability to raise the specter of attainder. Once your property is gone in a community-ordered confiscation, it's tainted; your family members can never get it back. Ever. Your heirs have been forever stripped of their rights of inheritance. In addition, private corporations don't have to obtain search warrants or respect religious choices.

The growth of the HOA movement suggests an interesting question: at some point, will private government compounds be so woven into the landscape that the judicial system may have no choice but to finally declare them all to be governments-in-fact? As millions more homeowners move into covenant-controlled compounds each year, the tipping point will have to be reached sometime. At least one higher court in New Jersey once declared that HOAs are in fact a level of government, and are therefore obligated to acknowledge that homeowners in these compounds are indeed covered by the Constitution. Since that decision was overturned by the New Jersey Supreme Court (Twin Rivers), the matter is still in dispute. In the meantime, thousands more Americans have lost their homes in what can only be described as one of the most blatant kinds of thefts imaginable, one never envisioned in the Constitution. One can only imagine the confusion that will erupt if and when all HOAs are either legislatively or judicially dissolved.

Seton Hall Professor Paula Franzese notes in her 2007 paper, *The Costs of Privatizing Communities*, that:

> Private Homeowners Associations should be treated as quasi-government because they are. Homeowners Associations extensively regulate land-use and home occupancy, and collect fees from homeowners that are the equivalent of taxes. Increasingly, they maintain streets, provide curbside collection, provide their own security forces and operate water and sewer services.[4]

Yet the controversy has remained largely invisible. Franzese argues that it's off the political radar screen and not yet the subject of vigorous public debate. Her papers could ultimately be another major step in the beginning of such a discussion.

But there's a far more ominous tipping point to plug into this equation. What if the Judiciary or Legislative branches never do make an affirmative decision that Homeowners Associations are indeed *de facto* governments? What if the HOA Movement is gradually allowed to become America's predominant form of governance? At least as far as home ownership is concerned, the entire nation will have made a completely passive transition into *de facto Marxist/communism*. A majority of the voters, even the landed, the privileged, will have silently accepted the concept that our Constitution as a "living document," has outlived its usefulness. It won't be dissolved in some future Constitutional Convention; it will simply have passed into irrelevancy.

Sometimes the HOA movement, itself, seems conflicted over the implications of *"de facto* government" vs. rule by extra-Constitutional assumptions.

In the spring of 2009, Florida Homeowners Associations threw their weight behind a bill to mandate that all lenders which had foreclosed on HOA homes pay the monthly dues on behalf of displaced owners. At a time when the mortgage industry was desperately trying to stay afloat, in a year when financial pain impacted nearly every family and corporation in America, the HOA movement demanded that the Florida Legislature force already stressed mortgage companies to pay billions of dollars in past HOA dues. More than 374,000 homes were in some stage of foreclosure, meaning 11 percent of all Florida home loans were in default.[5]

A May 29th editorial in the TCPalm newspaper whined "THUMBS DOWN: Lawmakers side against homeowner associations on scofflaws":

ANOTHER BLOW TO HOMES: Among the worthwhile bills that went nowhere at the 2009 Legislature was a measure that would have helped homeowner associations collect dues from recalcitrant lenders.

Under current law, banks and other lending institutions holding foreclosed properties only have to pay a small portion of past-due fees. Not surprisingly, 60 percent of communities report that mortgage lenders who have foreclosed homes are ducking monthly maintenance fees or other assessments.

Banks are dragging their feet, and residents are paying for that," said Ken Direktor, a Fort Lauderdale attorney whose firm represents hundreds of communities around Florida.

Unfortunately, the foot-dragging financial institutions had more legislative clout than homeowner associations in Tallahassee—which made Rep. Julio Robaina's House Bill 1347 dead on arrival."Better luck next session."[6]

> **The Homeowners Association Movement wants it both ways; the power of government to enforce dues payments during the bad years. But during the good years they want their own unsupervised bully power back.**

One panicked HOA advocate pleaded with other homeowners to lobby Florida Governor Charlie Crist to call the legislature into emergency session to reconsider its rejection of the bill. The letter writer complained of the growing burden on remaining homeowners to pay for maintaining common areas, insurance and legal fees.[7]

Certainly, Florida neighborhoods felt the excess foreclosures were murdering property values. But again, their actions raise a critical question: are Homeowners Associations *de facto* governments, or not? For years, "private government compounds" have been using their massive legal clout to confiscate homes from members who fell a few hundred dollars behind in monthly dues. In those years, those HOAs didn't want to be considered true governments, because homeowners would be able to defend themselves with such wicked arguments as equal protection, free speech and due process.

In any event the Florida Legislature, as *TCPalm* complained, took the side of "the foot-dragging financial institutions." And Governor Crist ignored the demands to call back the Legislature.

## Changing Governments

Tens of millions of Homeowners Association members have, by signing their real estate contracts, opted to leave the protections of representative Constitutional democracy, and enter into corporations of communities which have a completely different style of democracy. They are democracies run by a privileged elite, elected by the whim of the tyrannical majority, the exact kind of "soft despotism" that De Tocqueville warned Americans to avoid.

Tyrannical majorities have brought us some pretty ugly things over the years, like the institution of slavery. To turn back to them, knowing our history, seems somehow bizarre.

Certainly there's a good place for Homeowners Associations, especially in tight living quarters such as New York's vertical real estate. An entire building can be ruined by a single disruptive or dangerous tenant who creates a public nuisance. But there's an oft-repeated saying in law enforcement academies that goes, "Bad police work makes bad case law." A parallel saying in Association governance might be, "Bad Homeowners Associations make bad neighbors." Bad Homeowners Associations also collapse the public trust. That collapse in trust can take an unlimited number of pathways, including:

- the loss of property values;
- the loss of the sense of community;
- the loss of access to the court system;
- decreased desire to improve a community;
- increased neighbor vs. neighbor hostilities, and most profoundly;
- the loss of belief in the uniqueness and importance of American Constitutional law.

There's no question there's a need for good management of common areas and some HOA boards actually do a pretty good job. The problem is that the institution, itself, is fundamentally flawed. But because of the Internet, for the first time people are paying attention. They're being warned that a single change of board membership, a single vote, puts all homeowners at risk. Unlike the U.S. Constitution there is no built-in system of checks and balances. If an HOA board has the potential of "turning rogue" at any moment, then each and every homeowner is a possible future victim. Outside the HOA environment "victims" have rights. Inside, such rights are non-existent. That knowledge, alone, can pulverize property values.

To entrust one's life savings to the flip of a coin seems risky. Likewise, to invest one's savings into a piece of property where rogue management could pop up at any time seems ludicrous. The promise that HOA property values are historically destined to rise is empty. In fact, when the 2008 housing bubble burst and HOAs across the country discovered their property values diving by double digits each year, many homeowners found they had none of the protections they had expected when they first bought into their communities.

"I like my own HOA," many people will testify. "The board does its best to protect neighborhood property values and it does its best to improve life for all members of the community."

That statement may come from the innocent, but it sounds like one from the ignorant. In an ideal world, we could believe the promises of the HOA Movement. But reality shows there are too many abuses of homeowners and homeowners rights to set aside our suspicions. Many individual board members actually do their absolute best to promote the community interest, and we, of course, revere board members who honestly work to improve the lives of others.

But what are the chances that a community controversy at some point could result in a change of leadership that ends up in a "rogue board," one that has the capacity to begin enforcing the rules to the point that they become petty and dictatorial? The chances are pretty close to 100 percent. Boards change. Boards change for specific political reasons. Boards change to "correct" some perceived community problem. The only thing that never changes *is* change.

A homeowner who denies the reality that a single board election could completely change the character of a neighborhood probably deserves the inevitable result.

Every HOA board is one election away from turning from beneficent to fascist. Only one election.

Just one.

# 14
# Of Guns and Greaseballs

*When tyranny becomes law, rebellion becomes duty.*
—Thomas Jefferson

Frustration between homeowners and aggressive HOA boards sometimes becomes so extreme that it leaves the social and civil arena and makes its way onto the police blotters. One such tragic episode involved a neighborhood in Peoria, Arizona.

Richard J. Glassel and his wife, Susan, bought their retirement home in the Ventana Lakes subdivision in 1994. From the beginning, Glassel apparently had trouble with others –from the developer to his neighbors. A defective air conditioner kept freezing up, but the developer refused repeated requests from Glassel to replace it. Glassel applied to the HOA board to allow him to put up an awning over his patio. His request was rejected, apparently because the awning did not come from a list of approved vendors. At HOA meetings, he protested an apparent double-standard, noting that a board member was able to get a variance to modify her own home with a similar awning.

Neighborhood tensions escalated as Glassel became increasingly agitated with other actions taken against him by the Ventana Lakes board. He had arguments with HOA-hired landscapers who had trimmed shrubbery on his property without his permission. He began picketing the developer's sales offices warning potential homeowners not to buy property there. Finally, Glassel was hit with an injunction, and ordered to pay the association more than one thousand dollars in attorney's fees. He refused.

Glassel's property was foreclosed upon and sold at auction. When the buyer walked into Glassel's former home, he was stunned by the interior damage. Walls had been ripped out, doors were smashed, plumbing was destroyed. In a wild rage after losing his property, Glassel had obviously decided to leave the home in shambles.

But Glassel wasn't done. Whatever mental illness had begun to eat into his brain, whatever aberration or obsession had taken hold of him, whatever anger he felt boiling up against his HOA, his tortured mind apparently decided to settle the score by wreaking additional havoc. On April 19, 2000, Richard Glassel armed himself with several handguns and a rifle and walked into a meeting of the Ventana Lakes Homeowners Association. He opened fire on the board members, killing two of them outright and wounding three others. When one of his weapons jammed, several people in the room overpowered him and held him down until police arrived. Newspapers across the country carried headlines of the tragedy.

Over the next two and a half years, the murder case wound its way through the legal system. Glassel's public defender offered virtually no defense in his trial and Glassel, himself, took little interest, even refusing to appear in court. Glassel's attorney presented no evidence from his bitter dispute with the Ventana Lakes Homeowners Association. In 2003, a jury convicted him of first degree murder. He was sentenced to death.[1] As of this writing, Glassel remains on death row in the Arizona Department of Corrections.

## Death by Foreclosure

Sadly, violence is not rare in neighborhood disputes. Robert Nelms, an elderly resident of the Velda Rose Estates Homeowners Association in Maricopa County, Arizona, was fined ten dollars a day because his boat stuck out a few inches from his carport.

When the HOA filed suit to have his house and possessions sold at auction, he may have been confused about the actions being taken against him by his neighbors. In any event, he had a weapon. And he used it to take his own life.[2] His suicide resolved a major problem for the Velda Rose Estates homeowners. They obviously wouldn't have to deal with him anymore.

In yet another Homeowners Association, a Florida homeowner brandished a gun at two HOA employees. Patrick Dellisanti was upset about overdue condo dues at the apartment where he lived with his 87 year old mother. The man was apparently distraught and confused because the HOA was demanding that he pay a 15 percent late fee on the dues. One of the employees dialed 911, and police officers surrounded the Pompano Beach HOA management office, ordering Dellisanti to come out. As Dellisanti emerged from the building, he took the handgun out of his pocket and held it to his head. The SWAT team saved him the trouble of a suicide and shot him to death. Family members say the violence was tragic and unnecessary.[3]

An even more dramatic foreclosure took place in August, 2010, in the normally peaceful Ogden, North Carolina Planters Walk Homeowners Association. The South is known for its honeysuckle sweetness, its late evening lightning bugs, its willingness to help neighbors in trouble. And the Carolinas have always been known for their soft manners, friendly "Good mawnin's" from the front porch, and "Anything I can do for you folks today?"

But few knew the fires that burned inside the soul of Peter Darius. He was a man of limited mental means, not stupid but born and bred to be a southern gentleman, self sufficient whenever possible. But from the moment he moved into Planters Walk, he didn't receive the reciprocal neighbor-helping-neighbor experiences he'd had in previous neighborhoods. He was 66-years-old and obviously adjusting to some of the challenges that sometimes hit the elderly while they try to cope with deteriorating bodies and increasing mental and memory difficulties.

At any rate, once he moved into his dream home on Planters' Walk, he tried to place his personal touches here and there. He built himself a white picket fence, the kind that often mark country drives and southeastern rural roads. He built a decorative five foot windmill in the back yard. And he built a gazebo and a shed behind the house where he stored some of his equipment.

Peter was always in his garage tinkering with some sort of project or another. Occasionally neighbors would drop in to chat. But then the notices started coming. Peter was in violation of some covenants. The white picket fence had to go. It hadn't been preapproved by the architectural committee. The little windmill; same thing, it was out of place, unapproved and unappreciated by neighbors. They started fining him a hundred dollars a day for his misdeeds. There's no record that anyone tried to talk to him about the different kinds of responsibilities one has in a covenant-controlled community.

Peter paid almost $50,000 dollars in fines as he tried to straighten out the problems. But he was increasingly confused about what offenses he'd committed. His home, worth an estimated $180,000 was foreclosed on and sold at auction to Henry Herring Jr. for about $84,000, less than half its appraised value. But in the early morning hours of August 15, two days before Peter was to be evicted, he walked through his home spreading a flammable liquid on the house, the walls, the carpet, himself. He lit the match. His badly burned body was found among his treasured belongings in his now-scorched and ruined house. "Too bad," said the neighbors. "Peter wasn't 100 percent there. We think the Homeowners Association was too hard on him. Everyone in the neighborhood says they pushed him too hard."[4]

Planters Walk.

Planters Walk, North Carolina.

## "The Right Thing To Do"

The growth of the Internet, though, has led to the publicizing of many cases of abuse of homeowners that would otherwise have escaped notice. One such story even made its way onto the floor of the U.S. Congress.

Addie Polk was 90 years old. Since 1970, she lived with her husband in their house on La Croix Avenue in Akron, Ohio. She lived alone after her husband's death. Addie had always tried to be financially responsible. She took out a $45,000, 30-year loan for 6.35 percent interest from Countrywide Mortgage. It didn't seem like an unreasonable amount at the time. Additionally, she took out an $11,000 line of credit. Countrywide re-sold the loan to Fannie Mae.

The foreclosure notices started coming. Fannie Mae announced it was going to take Addie's home of forty years. At the end of her financial rope, and not really understanding what was happening to her, Addie Polk carefully laid out her car keys, her pocketbook and a life insurance policy on a downstairs table and slowly climbed the stairs to her bedroom. She awkwardly turned a long-barreled handgun toward her own body and aimed. Even as sheriff's deputies were standing on the front porch waiting to evict her, she began pulling the trigger. The first shot failed to kill her. Despite the noise and confusion and a bullet wound in her shoulder, she was intent on keeping her promise to herself, and she fired a second time.

With the two deputies waiting outside, a concerned neighbor who had heard the two shots climbed a ladder to her second story bedroom. He saw her lying on the bed, the gun right beside her. He climbed through the window and discovered that she was bleeding from a chest wound. But she was still alive. Addie Polk had done a poor job of trying to take her own life. Still, she had taken the only action that seemed reasonable to her at the time.

Addie Polk's tragic case made the news wires. Newscasters and columnists across America began telling her story. In debate over the mortgage bailout bill, Ohio Congressman Dennis Kucinich brought up Addie's name on the floor of the House. A few hours later, a humiliated Fannie Mae Mortgage Company (or its bailout remnants) began trying to abate the public relations disaster. As Addie lay in her hospital bed in critical condition, the bankrupt company announced it would dismiss its foreclosure action against the dying woman, and sign over the property to her outright.[5]

"We're going to forgive whatever outstanding balance she had on the loan and give her the house," said Fannie Mae spokesman Brian Faith. "It's the right thing to do."[6]

Sadly, Addie Polk never got to experience "the right thing," whatever that means. Six months later, she died in a nearby nursing home away from the surroundings and memories she loved.[7]

While forgiveness of debts and fear of public relations disasters might be found among failing mortgage giants, those are decidedly not traits of the American Homeowners Association movement. In fact, there is growing realization among HOA board members that they have far more power to foreclose on and confiscate private homes for almost arbitrary reasons than even the mortgage giants.

*Always keep in mind, as private non-profit corporations, HOA boards are beyond the constraints of the U.S. Constitution.* Those boards are backed by a massive insurance industry that employs armies of lawyers and lobbyists who aggressively fight even the slightest attempts at reform. Homeowners who believe otherwise often find that power being used against them like a jackhammer.

## The Embezzlers—HOA Style

But a more troubling trend began making news headlines in the mid-2000s even before the economic crisis poked its head out of Wall Street, and the cabal of Mortgage Bankers was so enthusiastically issuing all those sub-prime, bundled, securitized loans. Americans began hearing about a new wave of embezzling going on in Homeowners Associations all across the country. The bad guys were the very board officers who'd been elected to their positions by friends and neighbors. The sums of money stolen from neighborhood treasuries in many cases were staggering. All this time, while homeowners were being sued for such things as planting the wrong kinds of flowers, putting the wrong kinds of bumper stickers on their cars, having a dog that weighed more than 20 pounds, embezzling board members were busy pocketing money from HOA bank accounts.

How many such cases are there? In a lifetime, one researcher could never locate them all. The vast majority of cases don't make the news headlines, therefore are never picked up by Internet search engines. But here's an interesting experiment: uncork a bottle of wine, make an all-night date with your best friend, Google Search, and try to build a list of all Homeowners Associations that have been hit by embezzling officers or property managers. The list is ever-changing, ever-growing, but it's an interesting exercise to see if you can locate even one-tenth of one percent of the embezzling that's going on. The following compilation came from such an all-nighter by this author. Understand that it's not a complete list; some information was unavailable because news articles or court files carried incomplete details. This was just a one night excursion through the sewage surrounding America's Homeowner Association Movement:

## Short List of HOAs Recently Hit by Embezzling

| Location/Name | Estimated Loss |
| --- | --- |
| Adams County, CO | 761,000 |
| Arizona time share | 766,000 |
| Bakersfield, CA | hundreds of thousands |
| Balch, Nevada City, guilty plea | 100,000 |
| Ballston Spa | 426,000 |
| Baltimore | unknown |
| Bear Valley Springs Assoc | hundreds of thousands |
| Blake, Loislaw citation | 75,000 |
| Bloomfield Woods HOA | unknown |
| Bolingbrook case | 100,000 |
| Briarwood HOA, OK | 9,000 |
| Brookwood Village HOA | unknown |
| Buck Island HOA | 861,000 |
| Business Gazette citation | 140,000 |
| Buxton Properties, FL | 1,000,000 |
| Calabasas, CA | 450,000 |
| Camarillo | 1,000,000 |
| Cambridge Village HOA | unknown |
| Camelot HOA, CA | 18,000 |
| Carolina Beach | 30,000 |
| Carolina Trace | unknown |
| Carlyon Beach HOA | 95,000 |
| Casablanca Isles HOA, FL | 166,000 |
| Chandler | 145,000 |
| Chandler | unknown |
| Charles County HOA | 40,000 |
| Charlotte | 100,000 |
| Coconut Grove | unknown |
| Coronado Foothills | unknown |
| Country Cottage HOA, LA | 20,000 |

| Location/Name | Estimated Loss |
|---|---|
| Coventry Cove HOA | 10,000 |
| Covington Point | 8,200 |
| Darrin case | 65,000 |
| Deshutes Colony HOA | unknown |
| Diamondhead HOA | unknown |
| Dilworth HOA, Rock Hill SC | 14,000 |
| Dupont East HOA | 30,000 |
| Eastview HOA, NC | 38,375 |
| Excellence Community Mgmt | 100,000 |
|    Bluffs Village II HOA | |
|    Glenwood Village Comm Assn | |
|    Montaire Comm Assn | |
|    Tantara Unit Owners Assoc | |
|    Legacy Highlands POA | |
| Fairfax | 24,000 |
| Fegenbush Place Subdivision | 10,000 |
| Fourth Ward HOA | 118,000 |
| Fox Park, Gillette, WY | 400,000 |
| Gander Road, guilty plea | 87,000 |
| Glenmore Community Assoc | 700,000 |
| Green Valley Ranch, CO | 248,415 |
| Gulf Breeze Condo Assn | 114,000 |
| Hasley Hills HOA | 486,219 |
| Hefner Village HOA | 24,495 |
| HighBeam Research citation | 145,000 |
|    HOA unknown | |
| HighBeam Research citation | 2,000,000 |
|    HOA unknown | |
| HighBeam Research citation | 1,500,000 |
|    HOA unknown | |
| Hilton Head | 2,100,000 |
| Hoffman Estates case | 10,000 |

*Neighbors at War!*

| Location/Name | Estimated Loss |
| --- | --- |
| Integrated Property Management | 100,000 |
|   Egrets Walk in Pelican Marsh | |
|   Village Walk | |
|   Pebble Creek | |
|   Middlebrook at Ave Maria | |
|   Regency Reserve | |
| Irvine HOA | 60,000 |
| Jonathan Association, MN | 18,000 |
| Kalispell | 120,000 |
| Kirkwood HOA, NV | 40,000 |
| Koger | 2,000,000 |
| Lake Murray Gardens HOA | 20,000 |
| Lake Placid | 170,000 |
| Lakes HOAs, VA | 60,000 |
| Lexington HOA, OR | unknown |
| Loislaw Fed District Citation | 75,000 |
|   HOA unknown | |
| LoisLaw citation | 75,000 |
|   HOA unknown | |
| Maison Ville Condos, WA | 80,000 |
| Management Van Nuys | 748,564 |
| Masons Passage | 250,000 |
| Melwood Oaks HOA | unknown |
| Mesa | 145,000 |
| Meadow Lake HOA, MT | 122,000 |
| Miles Landing HOA | 93,000 |
| Minieville, VA HOA | 300,000 |
| Mission Hills | 10s of thousands |
| Mitchell, Pensacola | 856,000 |
|   Sailwind Condo Assn of Gulf Breeze | |
|   Sabine Yacht & Racquet Club | |
|   Heron's Forest POA | |

| Location/Name | Estimated Loss |
|---|---|
| Bayview Terrace | |
| Baywind HOA | |
| Montgomery Mgt Assoc | 856,126 |
| Sabine Yacht & Racquet Club | |
| Sailwind Condo Assoc of Gulf Breeze | |
| Heron's Forest POA | |
| Bayview Terrace | |
| Bay Wind HOA | |
| Montgomery Village | 40,000 |
| Multi Vest, OH (many HOAs) | 3,400,000 |
| Newport Beach | 530,000 |
| Nevada City | 100,000 |
| North Woods, WI | 24,000 |
| Buck Island HOA, Kitty Hawk | 800,000 |
| Ocean City | 19,000 |
| Orange County | millions |
| Palatine Countryside, IL | unknown |
| Pajaro Dunes | unknown |
| Parkvale HOA, UT | 100,000 |
| Parma Community, OH | unknown |
| Pembroke Pines HOA | 400,000 |
| Penochle Farms | 1,400,000 |
| Pleasantview HOA | unknown |
| Portico HOA, Cherry Creek, Denver | 308,000 |
| Portland OR, Sheriff's Deputy | unknown |
| Prestige Property Management, FL | 1,200,000 |
| Providence Green HOA | 40,000 |
| Quail Hollow | 162,574 |
| Queen Villas, HOA Inglewood | 134,000 |
| Red Rocks Ranch, CO | 315,0200 |
| Reedy Group Management, AZ | 145,000 |
| Regency Park, Merrillville | 5,000 |

| Location/Name | Estimated Loss |
| --- | --- |
| Remington Park HOA, TX | 115,000 |
| Rock Springs HOA, OR | unknown |
| Sandpiper Village HOA | 86,750 |
| Sanford | 315,000 |
| Santa Ana Oaks HOA | unknown |
| Smoky Mountain | 15,000 |
| Solano Verde Ranches HOA | 400,000 |
| Sonoma jury verdict | 500,000 |
| Spanish Hills HOA, guilty plea | 400,000 |
| Spanish Hills HOA | 100,000 |
| Springfield Place HOA, GA | 11,500 |
| Stow, OH | 100,000 |
| Strickland Farms HOA | 75,000 |
| Summerset Village HOA | 200,000 |
| Timberbend, FL | unknown |
| Tony Tank Creek HOA | 221,000 |
| Vail Point Townhomes, CO | 700,000 |
| Vernon Woods Apartments | 181,000 |
| Village (Business Gazette citation) | 40,000 |
| Via Verde | unknown |
| Villages at Cornwallis, NC | 10,000 |
| Virginia | tens of thousands |
| Virginia | 100,000 |
| Vista Management, Colorado (handles about 40 HOAs) | 700,000 |
| Westridge HOA, West Bend | 11,000 |
| West Lake, OK | 2,000 |
| Westlake Canyon Oaks HOA | unknown |
| Waynesville, Smoky Mountain news | 15,000 |
| Willow Creek HOA, VA | 277,914 |
| Woodbridge Townhomes HOA | 1,292,063 |

## Complete List Will Never Be Tallied

Homeowners' advocates who've been in the business longer than this author will scoff at the above list and call it inadequate, insufficient, incomplete. Those are all valid criticisms. The number of real victims is far more likely in the thousands, or even scores of thousands. In any event, most cases of embezzling are probably covered up, not discussed publicly or not uncovered at all! Homeowners Associations are more skittish and secretive than banks when there's an *internal problem*. They are loathe to talk about how much was lost and how the crime was accomplished.

The victims of these thefts are not rich people, they're just folks who've gotten a little bit ahead in life, put away just enough for a down payment on a nice home. But these folks all have to find a way to make up for the losses through increased dues or special assessments. Some neighborhood greaseball whose job is to open the mail and sort the dues payments is dividing the money into two piles; some for neighborhood maintenance, some for himself. Bookkeeping in Homeowners Associations is notoriously loose. There's little double entry bookkeeping being done here, no "two-signature" checks. But the amounts just keep adding up: a hundred thousand here, a half million there. In short, massive sums seem to be hemorrhaging out of HOA coffers.

Are all HOA boards and board members corrupt? Of course not. But the structure of the typical Homeowners Association gives it all the hallmarks of a ticking time bomb. When investigative reporter Ron Regan of Channel 5 News in Cleveland, Ohio, began looking into HOA embezzlements in his state, he discovered several including a $3.4 million theft which he called "the largest embezzlement in Ohio HOA history. How can it be so easy? Our investigation found absolutely anyone can become a property manager or association officer in Ohio. No license, fingerprints, training, education, bonding, or even a yearly audit is required."[8]

Regan further found that state after state across the country has had the same experience, a high number of embezzlements from HOAs and virtually no oversight of property managers and HOA board officers as they handle millions of dollars.

## Homeowner Members Are Stuck with the Tab

Board members traditionally use the neighborhood treasury to buy insurance coverage to protect themselves from liability. But no insurance pays for the princely sums that are embezzled away by some of these same board officers. No, the innocent homeowners are the ones who have to fork over the money. Of course, HOAs could hire attorneys to pursue collections from the crooks who steal from their neighbors. But then, any attorney would be glad to take that kind of a case, for billable hours, of course. It's a pretty vicious circle in which the innocent home-owner always loses. By the way, the most frequent comment you'll hear from HOA board officers is, "We have no comment!" If nothing else, the CAI lawyers who advise these guys are good.

And consistent.

In almost every case of embezzlement, homeowners have to make up for the money that's been illegally drained out of HOA treasuries. That means dinging each and every home-owner for extra dues or extra assessments. The courts often order restitution by convicted embezzlers, but rarely do the victims ever really recoup their real losses. HOAs, of course, can and do file lawsuits to try to get back their money but history has shown that more often than not they're throwing good money after bad.

The big money, of course, goes to the lawyers, the ones who represent the HOAs as they fight to maintain the status quo.

While the embezzler may or may not get jail time, and while the homeowners strain to refill damaged neighborhood treasuries, seemingly sympathetic lawyers laugh their way to the bank. They'll benefit in another way, of course. Hand-wringing board members will ask their lawyers how it happened and how it can be prevented, and the lawyers, as always on billable hours, will work out various plans for keeping better track of neighborhood funds.

## Kick-Backs: "Right Here in River City!"

But theft from an HOA doesn't have to be as dramatic as embezzlement. One well-worn tactic of HOA chiselers is the old conflict-of-interest scam. It's almost a no-brainer. The HOA needs the grass mowed in the neighborhood's common areas. Bob, the board president, mentions that he knows a guy named Sam who mows grass at the HOA just across the street. He suggests that Sam's fee might be more competitive than other lawn maintenance companies because his equipment and employees are already on site once a week. The board, thinking the idea is a winner, votes for it. The bills come in, they seem reasonable, and Sam is paid on time. But president Bob never mentioned that grass cutter Sam is his brother-in-law. They also never discussed the fact that Sam pads his bill with gasoline, repair costs, down time, extra fees for making sure there are always enough employees to do the work. Sam then overbills the HOA by 500 bucks and kicks back 250 to president Bill for steering the contract his way.

Neat. Tidy. Dishonest as hell and you'd face certain damnation if the neighbors ever found out. But kickbacks are deeply woven into the fabric of Homeowners Associations all over the country. Want to get your landscaping plan approved more quickly? Slip a couple of Ben Franklins to the head of the architectural control committee. Need quick approval for a new roof? You know what to do. As General George Patton once said, "Slick as grease through a goose."

## A Personal Note

Sharing one more bit of full disclosure here, this author has personally witnessed this practice. In fact, in one of the lawsuits against me, it was disclosed that one of my attorneys, before she died, left a memo saying she'd been approached by at least one HOA official who said he could make my homebuilding problems go away for a payment of say, $75,000. The documents and this HOA President's testimony are on the public record forever. This HOA president has since passed away, but I've always wondered if his ice cream melts too fast in his new eternity.

## Collusion and Conspiracy

But let's stitch together a wilder and much more complex gambit. In certain unspecified cities, one law firm, or perhaps even two law firms decide that several HOA home building companies were negligent in the construction of their developments. Homeowners complain of substandard work, leaky foundations, improper drainage flows, defective plumbing and substandard building materials. The law firm, knowing that a class action lawsuit could generate huge verdicts, decides it needs the various HOA boards under its influence to agree to the class action. But some HOA board members are reluctant to tackle litigation which could result in massive legal fees for homeowners.

Matter over? Not by a long shot. The law firm goes into overdrive to get rid of reluctant board members and bring in officers more willing to cast the "correct" vote. Homeowners in the HOA are baffled; they have no idea who these new board members are. The new people running for the board are not even homeowners in the neighborhood. Election ballots appear which cannot be tied to any member of the community. Proxy ballots show up on Election Day which can't be verified but end up being counted in secret by only those board members who support a lawsuit.

The newly constituted boards quickly approve the filing of enormous construction defect lawsuits and builders are subsequently hit with judgments of hundreds of millions of dollars. Attorneys, of course, receive tens of millions for their work in court. But it gets far more complicated from here. The winning law firm arranges to funnel the money to just a few construction defect mitigation firms whose owners are, by weird coincidence, close friends or business partners of the lawyer who set it all up in the first place. Some remediation work gets done, but in many places the construction repairs are superficial and cosmetic.

In the meantime, the plight of the original homeowners never seems to get better, property values don't rise, in fact values go further into the tank as word gets around that certain neighborhoods are toxic because of all the uncorrected defects. Entire neighborhoods become almost unsalable.

The key storyline here: hundreds of millions of dollars are flying around in a Universe where everything is uncountable and unaccountable from the initial board elections, to the lawsuits, to how the remediation firms are selected, to how well their subsequent work solves the initial problems. Any child could conclude that there's something fundamentally wrong, that it's too complex to follow, too complex to be comprehended.

## Hypothetical? Here Comes the Vegas Caper

The date is September 24, 2008. The scene: the West Valley of Las Vegas. Black SUVs with shaded windows begin cruising back and forth in front of a law office on South Rainbow Boulevard. Across West Valley more black cruisers pour into the parking lots of property managers, construction firms, HOA offices and private homes. At a pre-arranged signal, the car doors all open and scores of FBI agents and employees of the U.S. Attorney's Office pour into the streets. Search warrants in hand, they begin knocking on doors. Employees of the law firm and property management offices are told to back off and let the feds start searching and seizing files, computers, phone records. At another location across town, the agents use explosives to blow open the gates of a business owned by a well-known night club figure. It's an unprecedented federal raid against a huge part of the Homeowners Association structure of Nevada.

The investigation had been repeatedly requested by home-owners, who three years earlier complained to the Nevada Real Estate Commission that massive court-ordered settlements weren't reaching them, and that remediation work on their neighborhoods was not being done. They also complained that suspicious things were going on during HOA board elections. Mysterious proxies arrived from other states from people who didn't own homes in Nevada. Candidates who no one had ever heard of were suddenly elected to prominent board positions. Those newly elected *mystery board members* then began steering legal work to one of two Las Vegas law firms.

The FBI reportedly interviewed hundreds of people in more than a hundred Homeowners Associations across the West Valley. One arm of the investigation was focused on longtime Las Vegas businessman Leon Benzer. Among his many businesses were a nightclub, a brand of tequila, and several construction firms, including Silver Lining Construction. He claims to have been involved in more than 300 construction defect remediation cases.

Benzer's relationship with attorney Mark Kulla was also explored by the federal investigators. Kulla had set up several of Benzer's businesses and was also the attorney for the Vistaña. A 19 million dollar Vistaña construction defect lawsuit was handled by Kulla's law firm. Not surprisingly, Benzer's Silver Lining Construction was handed much of the remediation work.

Vistaña and Paradise Spa, two Las Vegas Homeowner Associations raided by the FBI in a massive corruption investigation.

—photos by Jonathan Friedrich

Several board members on the Vistaña HOA board were apparently connected with Benzer, including Steve Wark, a prominent Republican political strategist in Nevada. Despite owning only a one percent interest in a Vistaña condominium, Wark got himself elected as the president of the Vistaña Homeowners Association. He was also a former Benzer business partner. Shortly after the raids, Wark even appeared on Las Vegas television to claim that he knew nothing about collusion, fraud or election rigging. He said he was totally mystified by the raids and he denied he was a target of the FBI investigation.[9]

Another arm of the federal investigation focused on a second of Las Vegas' most prominent construction defect attorneys, an attractive, photogenic, then 48-year-old Nancy Quon. She knew everyone in town from judges, to U.S. attorneys, to police officials. She even hosted her own Las Vegas television show in which she advised members of Homeowners Associations on how to approach and solve the myriad problems that pop up in everyday HOA life. She was a stone cold rock star in three universes: media, legal and social. Her wealth was great. In a word, she was untouchable.

The federal agents, though, were undeterred by Miss Quon's reputation as they seized thousands of documents and began carting them off to be analyzed. Quon's law firm, Quon, Bruce, Christensen, was in an uproar; the public was in an uproar. Radio, television and newspapers did repeated updates on what they thought might be happening in the investigation. In 2009, the law firm found it necessary to dissolve and the partners headed in different directions. One moved to Florida to set up the same kind of business in a state that's been slammed by the housing recession, collapsing neighborhoods and a plethora of construction defect complaints. Nancy Quon remained in Las Vegas to deal with the investigation growing around her.

A grand jury was empanelled to look at possible charges. The jurors couldn't decide if there was a chargeable crime. A second grand jury produced the same outcome. There were rumors of improper communication between investigators and subjects of the investigation, and allegations that certain critical documents in the case might have been destroyed. Suddenly the entire staff of the U.S. attorney's office in Nevada was ousted from the criminal probe, and replaced by a team of federal investigators from the U.S. Justice Department in Washington DC.

At that point, the Las Vegas story took some incredibly bizarre turns. In November of 2010, Quon's unconscious body was pulled out of her burning home. She was revived by paramedics. Investigators immediately arrested Quon's live-in boyfriend, former Las Vegas police officer William Ronald Webb. News reports indicated that Webb had tried to help Quon commit suicide by having her overdose on GHB, a well-known Rave drug which is supposedly undetectable. Police alleged the motive for Quon's suicide was to allow her family to collect on her substantial life insurance policies. Quon and her attorney called the allegations "nonsense." But an undercover tape surfaced which purportedly recorded Webb buying the drug from a police informant while telling him how he intended to use it. Astonishingly, the illegal drug had actually been manufactured in the Las Vegas Police lab. Both Webb and Quon were arrested and hit with a variety of charges including arson, insurance fraud and conspiracy to commit murder.

In the meantime, another Las Vegas police officer, Christopher Van Cleef, whose name had also surfaced in the HOA investigation, suddenly committed suicide. He, too, had been said to be very close to Quon.

As of March, 2011, there was no official word from federal prosecutors, but unofficially indictments were being prepared against more than 50 co-conspirators, including police officers, attorneys, judges, Homeowners Association officials, and Nevada Justice Department officials. Still, after three years of inaction, some openly speculated that the entire federal investigation had collapsed.

All of a sudden, in August of 2011, the FBI investigation began to crack open with a guilty plea by Steve Wark, the famed Nevada Republican strategist. In exchange for a reduced penalty, Wark agreed to testify to his own criminal wrongdoing, his posing as a "straw buyer of a Las Vegas condo," and the rigging of HOA board elections for the purpose of steering construction work to Leon Benzer's Silver Lining Construction Companies. Then other guilty pleas began falling into place, one after another, an office manager, a businessman, and finally a prominent criminal defense lawyer who may ultimately sacrifice his law license for conspiracy to commit mail and wire fraud by rigging HOA boards with phony straw men who had little or no connection to their communities.

By June of 2012, 26 co-conspirators had pleaded guilty, again making this FBI investigation almost unique in the agency's history. Most of those who pleaded guilty to various official corruption charges were lower level figures. But investigators promised that the names of higher level political figures, law enforcement officials, judges and politicians would continue to rock the Las Vegas scandal.

Then the "suicides" began in earnest. Lt. Van Cleef was the first. The second was Robbie Castro, a former board member of the Vistaña HOA.

In November of 2011, one of the indicted suspects, attorney David Amesbury, was found severely beaten on a street behind the gates of his gated community. His pants were down around his ankles. His face was severely beaten, his ribs were broken, and both his kneecaps were crushed.

On March 20, 2012, two more stories shocked the citizens of Las Vegas. Nancy Quon, the multi-millionaire TV star and HOA attorney was discovered dead in her bathtub in her condo above the shops at The District, a high end business and residential mall near the Green Valley Ranch Resort in the town of Henderson.

Police arrived at her home at 1:40 pm after being called by a family member. They refused to discuss whether a suicide note was found.

Federal investigators looking into the vast HOA scandal were among those who showed up at the crime scene. It's believed that federal officials were just days away from indicting twenty more suspects in the HOA scam. The list included at least one attorney, HOA board members, straw buyers and a number of figures in Las Vegas Community Management companies.

The upscale home where Nancy Quon died.

—photo by Jonathan Friedrich

Five days later, police were called again to Henderson, Nevada. This time, attorney David Amesbury's body was found hanging from a rafter in his brother's barn where Amesbury had apparently been hiding out.

The stunning list of "suicides" stymied the federal investigation. At this point, all the suicides are listed as being unconnected with the investigation, which stretches credibility beyond the breaking point.

Unconnected with the Las Vegas FBI investigation was a long time person-of-interest by law enforcement in several states who had not been named in the current investigation. Yet he and his partners had left a trail of destruction in rental real estate developments from New York to Oklahoma City to South Las Vegas Boulevard. They've thrown around tens of millions purchasing various properties, but they seem to have very few satisfied tenants anywhere. New York's *Village Voice* named Massoud Aaron Yashouafar one of the ten worst landlords in the city. In an Oklahoma project, he declared bankruptcy after doing few repairs, raising rents to unconscionable levels and was targeted by a series of lawsuits.

In Las Vegas, Yashouafar purchased the ritzy Las Vegas Sky, billed as "the most desired address on Las Vegas Boulevard." Yashouafar and his associates hold a majority interest in the homeowner association, yet they have not paid their own outstanding dues of more than a million dollars.

A little farther down the road, Yashouafar still owns 75 percent of Paradise Spa. But the luxury development of 384 homes was hit by a devastating series of fires two years ago. The development has a number of elderly couples to whom Yashouafar leased units in a different part of the complex. Some of those homeowners are now having to make double payments, first on their original mortgages, and second to Yashouafar. Yet, repairs on the burned out apartment complex have still not begun.

Growing protests as Nevada citizens became aware of the corruption in their local HOA boards. This protest led to the creation of the website *HOACorruption.com*.

—photo by Heinz Jurisch

People affiliated with Massoud Aaron Yashouafar said the businessman intended on buying a few more apartments in the complex to give himself 80 percent of the units. That would force the existing homeowner association to be turned over to him and he could essentially develop the entire property in any way he wished.

In April 2011, the State Attorney General's office filed a search and seizure warrant for all the financial records of Paradise Spa. Investigators say Insurance companies gave Yashouafar nearly a million dollars to pay for repairs. They say the insurance money was transferred out of Nevada to another business account over which Yashouafar maintains total control.

No Tom Clancy novel could have envisioned so many twists and turns.

After the federal investigators finish their work in Las Vegas, they may have the knowledge and experience to start looking at similar situations in California, Colorado, Texas, Alabama, Florida, Pennsylvania, the Carolinas and any number of other states where HOA law firms are surrounded by construction defect lawsuits, non-judicial foreclosures, allegations of rigged board elections, embezzlements, and favored contractors being funneled money from court-ordered restitution.

Smoke is rising from many communities in the HOA world in America.

There may actually be some fire.

# 15
# The Power to Abuse

*Where an excess of power prevails, property of no sort is*
*duly respected. No man is safe in his opinions,*
*his person, his faculties, or his possessions.*
—James Madison

A recurring theme in *Neighbors At War* involves "rogue boards," out-of-control Homeowner Associations, and abuse of power by the "neighborhood Nazis." Although that last term is overworked in popular discourse, it's an obvious comparison between Adolph Hitler's war crimes and the aggressive tactics used by the modern Homeowners Association Movement to keep neighborhood scofflaws in line. There is no legitimate comparison, of course, between Nazi atrocities and the "covenant enforcement squads" that roam the streets of modern Homeowner Associations. But the term "neighborhood Nazi" is not an invention of this author. It's actually in common use by HOA critics across the country.

Additionally, this author occasionally refers to the HOA movement in America as being "fundamentally flawed." So, what does that that mean? How is a concept, whose stated purpose is to reduce neighborhood strife, "fundamentally flawed?" Surely, the author is straying a little too enthusiastically off-base with this accusation? In anticipation of such criticism, let's begin to delve deeply into two of the most controversial psychology experiments ever conducted.

The studies were done by psychology departments in two prestigious universities in 1961 and 1972. Both experiments were ethical disasters, but even to this day, the studies' conclusions point to some hideous weaknesses in human character. Both experiments have profound implications for any situation where one human being is granted unchecked, unsupervised power over another. Psychology students know the two studies as the Milgram Experiment and the Stanford Prison Experiment.

## Shocking! Just Shocking!

Dr. Stanley Milgram was a Professor of Psychology at Yale University. As a Jewish youngster growing up on the streets of the South Bronx, he often wondered about the cruelty of Nazi guards in the concentration camps of World War II. Like countless millions of others, he had pondered how perfectly intelligent, seemingly average human beings could inflict such gut-wrenching acts of brutality on Jewish prisoners. Were the guards so blinded by ethnic hate that they actually believed they were doing humanity a favor by exterminating an entire race of men, women and children? It's impossible today to comprehend such perversity, or understand how it could have existed during the reign of the National Socialist German Workers' Party. But fifteen years after the end of World War II, Milgram devised an experiment to find out.

Milgram knew that in the Nuremburg trials after World War II, most of the guards and officers accused of horrifying war crimes used the defense that they were "just obeying orders from superior officers, as all soldiers in wartime are required to do." A soldier is never supposed to question orders from a commanding officer. Refusal to obey an order is an act of rebellion tantamount to high treason. In most cases the crime is punishable by death. Film of Nazi guards callously laughing while throwing the bodies of children into mass graves is as nauseating today as it was when it was actually happening. In fact, the acts of Nazi war criminals are still held up as the ultimate act of human sadism.

Dr. Milgram must have thought himself a genius when he devised a psychology experiment to test the bounds of human cruelty. Could the Nazi concentration camp mentality ever happen in America? Could an average person punish or even kill a fellow human being if he felt he was officially directed to do so by some authority figure? Milgram's findings stunned the country. And it made him something of a pariah among his own associates.

Through classified ads run in community papers around Yale University, Milgram solicited the help of a number of volunteers. He wanted average people from age 20 to 50, and offered to pay them four dollars a day to take part in an experiment that would supposedly help people improve their memory.

Participants in the test were "randomly" chosen to be either "teachers" or "learners." The two people were placed in adjoining rooms where they communicated over a microphone. The experiment required that the "teacher" read a set of five words to the "learner," asking him to identify which two words were best paired. Each "learner" was guaranteed of getting a large number of wrong answers.

An administrator, dressed in a white lab coat, at all times stayed in the room with the "teacher." If a "learner" returned a wrong answer, the "teacher" was required to throw a generator switch which administered an electric shock to the "learner." After each wrong answer, the "teacher" was instructed to raise the voltage a notch higher, increasing the pain level to the "learner." "Teachers" were also to deliver a shock if the "learner" remained silent and gave no answer at all.

At the upper end of the voltage scale were switches labeled *extremely painful, XXX pain,* and finally *450 volts-fatal.* If a "teacher" resisted continuing the experiment, the man in the lab coat responded, "The experiment requires you to continue," and "You must continue."

At some point, the "teacher" could hear protests coming from the "learner" in the other room. As more powerful shocks were administered, the "learner" began shouting, crying in pain, pounding on the wall, screaming that he wanted to end the experiment.

Milgram's secret was that the "learner" in the other room was not getting shocked at all. The "learner" was actually an actor playing the part. An audio tape of a man being shocked, screaming in pain, and demanding an end to the experiment was played to convince the "teacher" that his actions really were responsible for the anguish being caused. The real objective of the study was to see how many people would actually deliver a fatal shock just because someone in authority told them they "must continue."

Milgram polled several dozen psychiatrists and psychologists to see if they could predict how many of the volunteers would commit such an act of torture. Most of them calculated the odds at about one percent, the approximate percentage of psychopaths in the general population.

The experiment was replicated many times, eventually covering a thousand people of all ages and occupations. Each time, the results were similar: 65 percent of all people were willing to administer a fatal shock to the subject. In one of the tests, more than 90 percent of the participants were willing to "execute" a fellow human being.

When Stanley Milgram went public with his findings, and revealed that two out of every three people went all the way up to administering the "fatal shock," it outraged the nation. Milgram, himself, was widely criticized in his own academic community.[1]

## Slippery Slope of Evil

A decade after the Milgram Experiment, a psychologist at Stanford University devised an unrelated test to study the interactions of people in a prison population. By grand coincidence, Dr. Philip Zimbardo was a high school classmate of Stanley Milgram. In fact, they were in the same class in 1954 at James Monroe High School in the rough and tumble streets of the South Bronx.

Zimbardo's experiment was also preceded by advertisements for volunteers in a study. Out of 75 volunteers, 24 young people were eventually chosen. They were people who did not seem to have any physical, mental, or psychological problems. Zimbardo told the volunteers that some of them would be selected as "prisoners," and the rest would be elected as "prison guards."

Not many significant instructions were transmitted to the two sides. The prisoners, of course, would wear prison garb complete with inmate numbers. The guards would wear uniforms, carry clubs, and wear mirrored sunglasses which minimized eye-to-eye contact. Guards were just told to keep the prison under control, but they were not to be physically abusive to prisoners. Zimbardo filmed the experiment and sat back to see if anything interesting would develop. It did. But it ultimately forced Zimbardo to cancel the two-week experiment after just six days.

On the Sunday morning when the experiment was to begin, Police in Palo Alto, who were cooperating with Zimbardo, showed up to "arrest" the twelve volunteers. They were hauled out of their homes in full view of neighbors, handcuffed, and then put into the back seats of police cars. Police delivered the "prisoners" to the basement floor of a building on the Stanford campus.

There, the "guards" blindfolded the "prisoners", stripped and de-loused them with a spray of water, and put the prisoners into one of three "cells" which had locking doors and barred windows. Across the hall from the cells was a "hole" where disobedient "prisoners" could be placed for punishment.

The first day, little happened. But on the second day, some of the prisoners began complaining about conditions. The guards responded with verbal abuse of the prisoners. The inmates were forced to clean toilets with their bare hands. They were repeatedly awakened at night and asked to do menial exercises like pushups.

Tension continued to grow between guards and prisoners, apparently as each side began acting out roles they presumed they were playing. As hostilities increased, the abuse of prisoners and their reactions became more bizarre. Prisoners were stripped and mocked because of their genitalia. Vulgar personal insults were hurled at the guards, which in turn made the guards even more abusive. Some prisoners, as a punishment, were forced to go into the "hole," the unlighted isolation cell.

The poisonous atmosphere worsened as the prisoners became increasingly agitated. Some demanded to be released. Dr. Zimbardo, himself, broke all ethical standards by getting personally involved in his own experiment. He assumed the role of "prison warden," counseling some of the more distressed prisoners to remain until the end of the two week test. He advised some of the prisoners to "just keep going," and told them that he would talk to the guards about toning down the abuse. Still, Zimbardo says five of the prisoners had significant emotional breakdowns. At one point, a colleague of his walked into the experiment, observed what was going on, and told Zimbardo, "These are just boys! Your experiment is flawed. You have to discontinue it." Zimbardo says he did, the very next day. But his test made the history books.

Zimbardo acknowledges his errors, but he still frequently lectures on the experiment. He talks of the consequences of giving any group of people unchecked and unsupervised power over others. He says the problem is not that there are some bad people here and there. It's that a large percentage of the populace have the ability to become abusive if just the right circumstances and conditions are in place. Zimbardo notes that all people have the ability to be either evil, or good, and he quotes Aleksandr Solzhenitsyn, from *The Gulag Archipelago:*

> ...the line between good and evil passes... right through every human heart.

In a 2008 lecture before TED, a global non-profit corporation that spotlights experts in all disciplines, Zimbardo addressed the topic, "What makes people go wrong? What makes them turn to evil?" He pointed to a recent scandal, the abuse of Iraqi prisoners in Baghdad's infamous Abu Ghraib prison, and said those American service members who were responsible for the abuse weren't inherently bad people.

Zimbardo said he was not surprised when the 2004 Abu Ghraib scandal erupted. He said it was also no surprise when U.S. officials referred to the scandal as "isolated incidents" and "the result of a few bad apples." Zimbardo, who was hired as an expert defense witness for one of the eleven U.S. servicemen facing prosecution, says the guards were not bad apples, but just a good example of what happens when unsupervised power is given to one group of humans over another. He says the guards were placed into a social situation which was ripe for abuse.

The abusers were Army Reserve Military Police; low level guards working the night shift at cellblock T-1A, the military intelligence cell block where prisoner interrogations were going on. Most of the guards had just arrived at the prison two weeks earlier. It was well known the CIA was not having much success extracting information from the terror suspects. But apparently, the unsupervised guards took it upon themselves to help the efforts along by abusing the prisoners. Upper level officers, at some point, may have looked the other way after becoming aware of some of the abuse. Several were disciplined or demoted. The guards were prosecuted and sent to prison.

Zimbardo points to several social processes that "grease the slippery slope of evil." Among them:

- dehumanization of others,
- recognizing one's own anonymity,
- spreading personal responsibility to more than one's self,
- blind obedience to authority,
- passive tolerance of evil through inaction.[2]

There have been other military scandals that shared the theme of "unsupervised power." One of the most prominent was the My Lai Massacre in Vietnam. American soldiers killed between 300 and 500 Vietnamese, many of them women and children. Again, My Lai was a perfect demonstration of Zimbardo's "slippery slope of evil."

There are also civilian scandals where "unsupervised power" led to horrible consequences for the victims. A recent example was the 2011 travesty involving the Penn State University football program, when a Grand Jury began looking at allegations that assistant coach Jerry Sandusky had sexually assaulted a number of young boys. Other members of the coaching staff and University had either witnessed or were made aware of illegal acts over a fifteen year period, yet they kept silent. In that vacuum, the most horrendous behavior imaginable was allowed to exist over many years. When the scandal finally broke, the reputation of Penn State was scarred forever.

## The Watergate Debacle

A different dynamic was at work during one of the most notorious scandals of the 20th Century. When the now-famous "third rate burglary" at the Watergate Hotel brought down the administration of President Richard Nixon, and led to the conviction and imprisonment of 40 government officials, the perpetrators were quickly brought to justice. Those officials certainly tried to dehumanize others, sought anonymity, spread responsibility to others, claimed blind obedience, and passively tolerated evil through inaction, but it didn't work for them. In fact, it took just fourteen months for the Nixon administration to be deposed.

The fact that the Watergate crimes brought down an entire administration was a credit to the nation's founders, who recognized that evil lies in every human heart. In arguing for the creation of a Bill of Rights, James Madison wrote:

> Wherever the real power in a government lies, there is the danger of oppression… Wherever there is an interest and power to do wrong, wrong will generally be done.[3]

To combat the human instinct to abuse power, the founders created checks and balances over virtually every element of the new American governmental system. Even as President Nixon and his associates tried to hide, destroy and cover up evidence, even as they tried to tar the reputations of their accusers, they faced the wrath of the Senate, the House of Representatives, and the Supreme Court. Despite the fact that 61 percent of the public voted to give Richard Nixon a second term in the White House, his efforts to hang onto power were frustrated at every turn by the Constitution's balance of powers.

Twenty-five years later, President Bill Clinton discovered that he, too, was vulnerable in the perjury/sex scandal that threatened to bring down his own administration. He found that an obscure woman from Arkansas was able to bring him into a deposition and demand honest answers from the highest officer in the land.

## Fundamentally Flawed

So, taking a giant leap back to the fundamental flaw built into the modern Homeowners Association Movement; it is simply that there is a complete lack of checks and balances. Homeowners Associations, in their role as *de facto* governments, can defend themselves against nearly every attempt by home-owners to impose balance in the system. The only way for a homeowner to stop an out-of-control or rogue board is to persuade a super-majority of homeowners to throw a toxic board member out of office. Super majorities are almost impossible to achieve. Indeed, many HOAs require a 100 percent vote to overthrow a bad decision. Irresponsible HOA boards can cause devastating financial consequences to homeowners who have nowhere to turn. Those who try to seek relief in the courts, discover that courts will not accept jurisdiction over the rules created by developers and agreed to by property owners.

This flaw is so deeply woven into the deeds of covenant-restricted neighborhoods that it simply cannot be erased short of a major court decision against the fundamental HOA concept. But seeking justice in the civilian court system can be next to impossible. Even when the U.S. Supreme Court outlawed housing discrimination based on race (in 1948 and 1964), the unintended consequence was decades of ongoing racial discrimination. Who knows what unintended damage might be done by a major court decision against HOA abuse?

**To ensure that the fundamental flaw is a perpetual flaw, each HOA board can buy liability insurance which is then used to batter and beat down any homeowner who demands access to justice.**

Once an HOA is sued, its insurance kicks in and the great mass of wealth and wrath of the insurance industry is brought to bear on the single protestor. In the words of French philosopher Blaise Pascal:

> Justice and power must be brought together, so that whatever is just may be powerful, and whatever is powerful may be just.

The ingenuity that led to creation of the U.S. Constitution has been called "The 5000 Year Leap." It's not a perfect system, of course. But the giant leap that is now carrying mankind from Constitutional Government into Private Government may be the most devastating leap of all. Many citizens are just now beginning to realize "what Man hath wrought."

# 16

# Too Many Snouts,
# Too Many Stallions

*"Woe unto you also, you lawyers, for you place on men's shoulders a burden too great to bear, yet you yourselves won't touch the burden with one of your fingers."*
—Jesus Christ (Luke 11:46)

With the American dream of peaceful home ownership cascading into a pit of legal despotism, is there any real solution to the *Neighbors at War* syndrome? Surprisingly, there are some intriguing ideas floating around that might be challenging to implement, but they could have a profound effect on restoring neighborhoods to a state of peace, quiet enjoyment, and shared responsibility that more truly represent the long-sought American Dream. Most of the proposed solutions have a central theme: *do whatever it takes to get HOA disputes out of the courts.* As Emmy award-winning reporter John Stossel says, "avoid hiring lawyers the way we avoid firing missiles."

The biggest obstacle to that accomplishment, of course, is the lawsuit industry's addiction to its multi-billion dollar, easy money stream. HOA disputes are like crack cocaine to lawyers. As you've seen earlier, C.A.I. lobbyists have a lengthy history of using homeowners' money to try to protect every single tentacle of the self-serving HOA octopus. The mentality is: pretend to be completely benign, but keep the anger stirred, keep the rancor churning. As long as the cauldron is bubbling, neighbors are helpless to turn back the flood of litigation.

A single annoying homeowner can become the metaphoric hole-in-the-dike, and the lawsuit industry works overtime to ensure that no hero is able to plug that hole. And yes, as the author strains for one more bad metaphor here; any good ol' country boy knows that prying hungry snouts from the trough is dangerous. He could get gored. Even more dangerous is standing between a stud stallion and the new mare. Any attempt at changing the paradigm puts the activist at great personal risk.

No reasonable observer can question that homeowner disputes are clogging the courts. While there's no accurate count of the real numbers, it works to say that hundreds of thousands, even millions of HOA members across the country live in constant fear that some overzealous board member will take personal aim at them and retaliate for some past grievance.

Theoretically, positions of power should not be used for personal or retaliatory gain, at least that's the ethical and legal standard that dominates normal elective politics. Personal and business politics exist everywhere. They're rehearsed in the corporate boardroom. They're a fixture at all levels of government. Sadly, the same rule is not recognized in the Homeowners Association Movement. If an HOA member with a deep-seated and unsatisfied power lust gets himself elected to the board, he is literally beyond the control of almost any law or standard of ethics. If you doubt it, ask any HOA to produce its ethics policy. They can't. They are almost non-existent.

Embezzling by board members? It's massive and widespread. Kickbacks from contractors and managers to the board? It's astonishing. Election fraud? Routine and endemic. Something in the air or water is telling the HOA elite that no crime is too low or too high to commit.

## Institutionalized Theft

As mentioned earlier, the one fundamental right that makes a society free is the right of the individual to own property. All other rights are subservient to it. True freedom, really true freedom is inversely proportional to the ease by which a citizen can be separated from his property. Whether by taxes, or government fiat, or by condemnation, or lawsuit, or even by theft by neighborhood association, the amount of one's personal freedom is profoundly connected to the right to own property. As such, any attempt to restrict that right should be approached with the utmost of awe, respect and caution. Sadly, the Homeowners Association Movement, originally touted as a way of protecting property values, has devolved into a mechanism which uses a thousand different tricks to institutionalize theft.

One of many examples of how wildly the HOA movement is slobbering at the trough is a little gem called "private transfer fees." A simplistic explanation is that a PTF is a sum of money, perhaps one percent of the gross sales price on any HOA home that changes hands. That sum, $7500 on a $750,000 home for example, would be paid by each seller to a New York company called Freehold Capitol Partners, a financier of many developers around the country. The mandate to extract that fee from each person who tries to sell a home would be written into the developments' covenants and would be just as unbreakable as any other covenant.

Despite the fact that Freehold Capitol Partners has little or no interest in a development once it's completed, it will receive those transfer fees in perpetuity. Every single sale involving a property in a Homeowners Association will kick back a payment. Freehold Capitol Partners proposes that the hundreds of billions of dollars that'll pour into its coffers will be bundled and securitized on Wall Street. That verbiage should sound vaguely familiar, bringing back echoes of the recent Wall Street chaos and housing meltdown. A number of state legislatures are pondering whether the practice should be outlawed.

## Beware the Shylock

Another form of buck-naked theft-by-HOA is hidden in a recent wave of debt collections aimed at homeowners who fall behind in their HOA dues. The bad economy in the 2008-2011 recession threw huge numbers of homeowners into that category. Increasingly, HOAs find their budgets pinched, so HOA attorneys farm the work out to debt collection companies which are well-known for their ruthlessness.

The collection agencies agree to pick up all those late dues, if board officers sign contracts which prohibit them from having any contact with homeowners who are in collection. The debt collectors then show up on the homeowners' doorsteps and demand the homeowner either immediately vacate the house, or sign a contract to set up a payment plan to "get their dues paid." Homeowners, especially the elderly, have no idea what's in the papers they're signing. Under extreme pressure, they contractually agree to set up payment plans. But in fine print which they discover too late, they learn that they have to pay the debt collectors' fees, the attorneys' fees, and the HOA fines before a single dime is applied to the unpaid HOA dues. In the meantime, the unpaid dues keep soaring, which in turn generates new collections, fines and attorneys' fees.

Grief-stricken homeowners appeal to their HOA boards for mercy or at least a hearing but they're told, "We are contractually forbidden from talking to you." In some states like California, the practice is patently illegal. But does that stop anything? A few minutes of Internet research would suggest, "No. It goes on despite the law."

**A single late payment of one or two hundred dollars can spiral into thousands, sometimes tens of thousands of dollars until the owner's dream home is deftly snatched away and sold on the auction block, sometimes to the very attorneys and debt collectors (or their friends) who initiated the actions in the first place.**

## Is There a Solution? Try "IDIOT!"

If one wanted to stem the growing tide of corruption and abuse in the HOA system, what would be the starting point? How can HOA disputes be kept out of the courts? While this admittedly liberty-minded author takes a satirical crack at suggesting a partial solution, the reader is asked to suspend judgment for a few minutes to test whether such a quirky idea might actually have a chance of working. And since it involves creation of yet another bureaucracy, it's only with trepidation this author tries to separate the hog snouts from the trough and the stallion from the mare.

The proposal: create a positive financial incentive to Homeowners Associations and their members to stay out of court. Reward HOAs for defusing the polarization that produces the *Neighbors At War* syndrome. Establish what we'll call the "Institute to Defuse Intractable and Objectionable Turmoil," or IDIOT for short.

Our new creation will have two branches, on one side, a long-term neighborhood investment club, on the other side will be a judicial arm perhaps supervised by a state HOA Ombudsman.

1. Each homeowner who buys into an HOA will be required to purchase shares in the investment club based on monthly or annual dues.

2. A homeowner who sells a home and moves into another HOA will take his shares with him to his new neighborhood.

3. If any homeowner moves out of the HOA system altogether, he will receive an immediate cash payment amounting to his entire investment plus all interest earned. Any compound interest table will show that over thirty or forty years a monthly or annual investment with a better than average interest rate will yield a sizeable amount. A thousand dollars a year at ten percent will produce a lump sum of more than a half million dollars after four decades of homeownership.

For probably the first time since 1964, homeowners might pay more attention to their surroundings. No more cars on blocks and purple painted houses, not by fiat, but by positive financial inducement.

Ah, but as always there is a catch. The investment trust fund will occasionally be used to mediate a neighborhood dispute where actual damages are caused. Payments from the fund would lower the value of shares in the company, of course. But it would also create enormous social pressure on neighbors to avoid provoking disputes in the first place. HOA boards would face stiff pressure to use diplomacy and caution whenever handing out fines or other discipline for minor violations.

The out-of-control, jack booted, goose-stepping, power-tripping new board member could be quickly pulled off his high horse by other board members who don't want to provoke costly confrontations with homeowners. And the more behaved those board members are, the higher the eventual net return to all homeowners. What's not to love?

## To Make IDIOT Work, Try STUPID

Now for the judicial side of IDIOT. Under the State Ombudsman, a panel of neutral volunteer mediators would be established. They would have to be the wisest, gentlest and fairest negotiators available. The panel would officially be called *"The Stupid Court."* Their job would be to patiently listen to each side in a neighborhood dispute. No lawyers would be allowed to argue for a client, in fact the very presence of a lawyer would disqualify the litigant, unless of course the lawyer, himself, was a party to the case.

This process, again, would be pure from the standpoint of allowing respective *Neighbors At War* to present the raw facts in his or her case. Traditional rules of evidence would not apply. The affair would have the raw informality of a Small Claims Court, and courtroom tricks would be excoriated. Cross examination would be strictly controlled to prevent the kind of legal and verbal trickery for which lawyers are both famed and maligned. As wonderful as Atticus Finch might have been, he and his ilk would be on the outside looking in.

The official ruling from the Stupid Court in each case would be refreshing. The panel of judges would turn to the losing combatant and say something along the lines of:

> We really do understand why you're upset, but if you pursue this case any further, you would officially be stupid. You would spend $600,000 in legal fees to recover a $20,000 loss. If you insist on going forward with your lawsuit, you will have to wear this *Scarlett S* on your shirt and display the same on the front door of your covenant-controlled home. However, we can intercede. Let us help pay for your loss and help you save face in the community. If you just cool off a bit, we

will keep both you and your antagonist from wasting hundreds of thousands of dollars.

The Stupid Court could then order the IDIOT fund to pay out a token amount of money to convince the warring sides to stand down. Since the money would come out of the community's investment pool, there would be intense social pressure not to exaggerate one's damages.

Counseling would then be aggressively provided to each side to help them understand the wisdom of accepting the Stupid Court's advice. Nothing would preclude a litigant, of course, from taking his case to civilian courts outside the HOA system. At least he'd have fair warning that being STUPID and accepting IDIOT reimbursements would be far less traumatic than getting SCREWED, which would surely happen once he left confines of the HOA environment and entered the unregulated jungle of the American tort system.

## The Price of Embezzlement

And some final cleanup matters: since recent years have shown such a massive trend of HOA officers embezzling large sums of money from neighborhood coffers, we don't advocate that embezzling cases be heard by the Stupid Court.

In addition, the amount of money the embezzler confesses to stealing from his or her neighbors should be multiplied four-fold and withdrawn from the embezzler's share of the IDIOT fund.

> The embezzler's crime should be considered an act of rank hatred against neighbors and should be handed over to the regular criminal courts for prosecution.

Said funds would then be reinvested for the sole purpose of further enriching her neighbors, the ones she tried initially to cheat.

With all the chiselers and cheaters popping up over the past few years, their reparations to the IDIOT fund could add up to some spectacular long term investment gains for the more honest homeowners. Such a move might finally stem the tide of those HOA treasurers and presidents who somehow think it's OK to steal someone else's retirement dreams.

One final consideration is that the significantly reduced pressure in infrastructure costs should please public agencies which have been overrun by HOA disputes. Although it would never ever happen, it would be nice to think that the HOA system might be financially rewarded in tax breaks and refunds for its diligence in keeping its members out of court. If the experiment was successful, everyone involved would be winners; everyone, except the lawyers. Yes, the lawyers. They would be significant losers. On second consideration, our thought experiment here couldn't possibly work. There are too many snouts in the trough and the stallion still wants that mare.

## So, Let's Get Real

Turning to the slightly more practical; because of escalating violence, confrontations, and often illegal treatment of homeowners by rogue HOA boards, a number of state Legislatures have tried to nibble away piecemeal at some of the more egregious abuses. A new Colorado law, for example, creates a State HOA Ombudsman who would theoretically be able to mediate disputes. The creation of that office was fought and eventually eviscerated by C.A.I. lobbyists. The Ombudsman's office now exists but the chief executive of the office takes great pains to assure HOA boards around the state that his presence is largely ceremonial. He says he's only there to provide advice and information to sparring neighbors. So far his most controversial demand is that all of the state's 7,000 or so Homeowners Associations obey the new state law by registering and paying a ten dollar fee to help fund his office. The proposal is weak-kneed enough to be comical. Many HOA boards are just ignoring him.

Other states are becoming slightly more aggressive in addressing some of the tactics used by the HOA Movement. California and Nevada, for example, launched proposals in 2011 to make it harder for debt collectors and HOA attorneys to illegally run up the fees on overdue HOA debts, the scandal addressed earlier in this chapter. The proposed legislation would prohibit the use of debt collectors until unpaid HOA dues reach a level of $1,950. Debt collection fees would also be capped. And homeowners would have to be personally warned before their homes could be seized and auctioned.

## Wobbly Knees in Texas

The 2011 Texas Legislature stumbled its way through thirty proposed laws to control its out-of-control HOA industry. For the past decade, Texas lawmakers have fought any attempt at reforming the system. The turning point was a torrent of negative national headlines involving an Army officer whose home was snatched while he was serving a tour of duty, fighting in the war in Iraq.

US Army Captain Michael Clauer was stationed overseas, when he got word that his HOA had foreclosed on his home in Frisco, Texas, because of approximately $977 in late Homeowner Association dues. In his absence, Clauer's wife, May, had allowed what she thought was junk mail to pile up. Hidden in the stack of junk mail were some threats to foreclose on their home because of the late dues. Despite a federal law that prohibits such actions against servicemen on active duty overseas, the Heritage Lakes Homeowners Association grabbed Clauer's $315,000 home and quickly sold it at auction for $3,200 to a firm called Steeplechase Productions. It was rapidly sold again to yet another private party for $135,000.

The entire process was blatantly illegal. But then, Homeowners Associations are "extra-Constitutional" because homeowners officially, albeit unknowingly, sign away their legal rights when they buy into covenant-controlled neighborhoods. After an expensive court battle, the Clauers did end up getting their home back through a "confidential settlement," which in itself is fascinating. A confidential settlement means that the Clauers signed away their First Amendment right to ever talk about how the case was settled. It's yet another demonstration that Constitutional rights can be arbitrarily signed away during the stress of resolving a personal crisis.

But as national headlines criticizing Texas piled up, embarrassed legislators pawed through some thirty proposals to help end some of the rampant HOA abuses. House Bill 1228 created some new prerequisites to foreclosure on homes. It outlawed non-judicial foreclosure, at least allowing a judge to look over a home seizure before it takes place. It mandated that homeowners be allowed to set up alternative payment schedules if they got behind on dues. It also gave homeowners who got into trouble the right to redeem their homes for a certain period after a home was seized. Governor Rick Perry signed the bill into law on June 17, 2011.

Still, nothing in the new law would have prevented the seizure of Captain Michael Clauer's home. Clauer called the new law "insufficient"—the height of understatement. The Clauers eventually moved away from their Heritage Lakes Home to another state. They say they'll never live in a Homeowners Association again. At least, Texas Legislators took a bigger bite out of the scandalous national tragedy than other states have. But Texas lawyers are working overtime to try to find ways around the new law. They'll find some good escape routes, simply because attorneys are good at what they do.

Elsewhere in the country, other service members stationed overseas have had tougher battles to reclaim their HOA-auctioned homes, including U.S. Coast Guardsman Keith A. Johnson, former Military Officer Robert Hall and many others who arrived home from the battlefield to find that lending institutions and Homeowners Associations had seized and rushed their homes to the nearest auction block.

The next good proposal to solve the HOA mess has been hinted at previously. Sadly, the proposal has apparently been derailed by the very organization that generated it.

The proposal is the product of Texas attorney Frank Kahne on behalf of his client, AARP, the American Association for Retired People. AARP has long been watching storm clouds gather on the HOA horizon and at one point it tried to come up with a solution. Since many targets of rogue Homeowners Associations are the elderly, AARP hired Kahne to develop a Homeowners Bill of Rights. Among the elements were:

1. The right to protection against non-judicial foreclosure, including the mandate that the foreclosing party obey all customary real estate laws. Homeowners have the right to establish a repayment plan without incurring additional penalties. Additionally, homeowners would have a 180 day right to redeem before their home was taken.
2. The right to resolve disputes without litigation.
3. The right to fairness in litigation.
4. The right to an Ombudsman for homeowners.[1]

The proposed HOA Bill of Rights is not extreme and essentially reinforces what the U.S. Constitution says about a citizen's rights to own property. A call by this author to David Kahne indicated that the AARP paid for and owns the rights to the exact text of the HOA Bill of Rights. The AARP, however, may be backpedaling away from its product. Despite its presence on many sites on the Internet, the HOA Bill of Rights has not been proposed to any legislative body. And repeated inquiries to AARP by this author have not been answered.

A similar Bill of Rights was proposed by the late sociology professors Lois and Samuel Pratt of North Bergen, New Jersey. It follows a parallel line of thinking, that American homeowners have fundamental rights which should not be supplanted by the modern Homeowners Association Movement. Their work and their articulate critique of the HOA movement are footnoted here.[2]

Longtime homeowner rights activist George Staropoli is perhaps one of the earliest, most vocal and most articulate advocates for a true Homeowners Bill of Rights and a re-statement of those rights guaranteed by the U.S. Constitution. He knows better than most what Americans have lost by buying into the HOA debacle. Each of his speeches, and appearances before various legislative bodies is worth studying.[3] The problem with well-known and vocal activists is that the establishment can find a way to ignore them. No matter how intelligent and honed their arguments, one raised eyebrow on a panel of legislators is enough to completely dismiss the activist from having anything important to contribute to the discussion. It's one of the weaknesses of political discourse because it prevents critically important information from reaching the public.

But Staropoli has long been able to articulate the deficiencies and the pending bombshells contained in the Legislature's denial of the obvious: that the HOA system is badly broken and in desperate need of an overhaul.

Enacting a "Homeowners Bill of Rights" may be problematic in areas, but it's an idea that is long overdue. Abuse happens in a vacuum. Our forefathers 230 years ago reasoned that out. They knew that our republican form of democracy would survive only as long as we recognized the rights of others to exist and be left alone.

While it seems that another Bill of Rights should be superfluous, the above proposals are not. As we've observed continuously throughout this book, tens of millions of homeowners have made an unwitting and sometimes forced leap away from their Constitutional protections. These proposals would essentially say that certain rights are indeed unalienable and cannot be signed away.

Yes, we do have to have the right of contract, but the huge growth and dominance of any system which forces citizens into unwanted contracts amounts to a fundamental change of government that needs constant reevaluation.

In the past forty years, Americans have blindly waltzed over the Contract Clause to create a massive societal tipping point at which Constitutional balance is thrown wildly off-kilter. Whether by knowledge, lack of knowledge, or whether by being forced to sign covenants in a *de facto* government where there were no reasonable housing alternatives, seventy million Americans have surrendered their access to the rights enumerated in the U.S. Constitution. Those seventy million Americans have quietly accepted a brand new form of government. For all intents and purposes, they no longer live in the United States of America. They live in a fascist dictatorship whose more malevolent manifestations have not been fully tested or vetted.

The Homeowners Movement of today has nothing in common with the property ownership statements of Thomas Jefferson, or Charles Paine or James Madison. Our founders would look with horror on the society we have created for ourselves. They would grieve at what we have brought about.

When a majority of all homeowners have given up their Constitutional rights, how can they ever reclaim their country? They can't. The slow slide into an entirely different form of *de facto* government seems strangely like the one our parents and grandparents used to warn us about many decades ago. But we have, indeed, made that slide and there are precious few ways to claw our way back. As the character in the old comic strip, POGO, used to say, "We have met the enemy and he is us."[5]

Our country desperately needs to recognize that a Homeowners Association really is a *de facto* government. In Legislatures across the land, elected officials are right at the cusp of beginning to understand this paradigm shift. If these private governments are determined judicially to be *de facto* governments, then perhaps the battle is not lost and rogue Homeowners Associations will finally be introduced to the restrictions in the Constitution's Bill of

> The puzzle is that a Homeowners Bill of Rights is not a left wing or right wing political issue. It can be comfortably embraced by freedom minded politicians on both sides of the political aisle.[4]

Rights. Unless that happens soon, though, the HOA movement will run wild through the assets of HOA members, grabbing all the equity that is not tied down.

Make no mistake. Your neighbors are not your friends when they discover that your net worth is available for looting. Margaret Thatcher is reputed to have said, "The problem with Socialism is that you eventually run out of other peoples' money."[6]

Sadly, as a nation we're there. A cynic would say that only a massive reordering of Society will ever give us a ghost of a chance of restoring our glorious past. In recent years, we have loosed the looters. And they've now coined the word "redistributivism."

Have we gone too far to recover? Perhaps. But that doesn't mean we give up the fight. Still, one has to ponder the plight of the country boy whose job it is to separate the hog snouts from the trough and the stallion from the mare.

God Bless that kid.

Somebody has to do it.

# 17

# Collectivism, Progressivism and Beige

*America will never be destroyed from the outside. If we falter and lose our freedoms, it will because we destroyed ourselves.*
—Abraham Lincoln

The wind was whistling by my open window that spring morning in 1988 as the green train car rumbled against the tracks on our trip across the Soviet Union. The train wheels were excruciatingly loud; the berth so uncomfortable, that none of us had gotten much sleep the previous night. When dawn broke and we stood at the berth car windows watching the countryside pass by, I saw the deep circles under my co-workers eyes. Mine were just as pronounced I was sure.

The train we had boarded the day before in Tbilisi, Georgia, was obviously of ancient construction. It didn't look safe. Dull paint slapped on plywood exteriors couldn't hide obvious years of wear and tear. Still, we were exhilarated. The experience was too novel for any of us to complain.

For nearly two weeks we had worked at breakneck speed, doing interviews by day, budgeting our dwindling supply of videotape in the evenings, writing all night. For the first time since our arrival our frenetic pace had seemingly crashed to a stop. Despite the perception of movement, we were confined to one spot in one train car on its jolty all night trip to the Black Sea town of Sochi. Sleep was impossible.

Our two Soviet "minders" who had carefully watched us during the previous ten days seemed slightly more relaxed now. They were moderately attractive women, obviously expert at guiding tours of foreigners through their country. But leading a group of American journalists was apparently a task that carried more responsibility and tension for them. Just a year earlier Nicholas Daniloff, a reporter for *U.S. News and World Report*, had been arrested by the KGB and held for two weeks on some trumped up charge of illegally accepting documents from a dissident. It wasn't unusual for the Russians to use reporters as pawns in their perennial chess game with Washington. Being "foreign and inquisitive" in the USSR could suddenly land one in the bright lights of an interrogation room.

But the world summit between Mikhail Gorbachev and Ronald Reagan was just a few weeks away. We didn't think our insignificant local TV crew would face the kind of scrutiny that confronted the major news agencies. In our minds, anyway, we traveled under the radar.

One of our female guides was the official Intourist representative, a mandatory requirement on trips through any communist country. The other lady had some odd connection to the Soviet agency that was hosting our visit. We actually weren't sure why she was there. Of the two, the latter paid the closest attention to all we did. Both women spoke excellent English though neither was particularly talkative or forthcoming with any personal information. We did learn that the more attractive of the ladies was married, but each was incredibly skilled at turning aside any and all questions about their personal lives.

For a local television news operation from the American Midwest, this journey into the heart of world communism was unique. We weren't network stiffs; we were just regional affiliates—local yokels from a Colorado cowboy town. Going to another country to write and film a television documentary was heady stuff for us. The dream of traveling abroad on assignment was almost beyond our comprehension. We may as well have been doing an episode about life on Mars, as exotic as this seemed to us. But local TV stations were awash in cash in the 1980s and outrageously expensive news junkets were being approved with some frequency.

Our trip had been stitched together on what seemed like the flimsiest of pretenses. City officials in Denver had set up a sister-city agreement with officials in Tbilisi, Georgia. Our documentary, *"Beyond the Kremlin,"* would explore parallels and contrasts between the lives of people in Colorado and in Soviet Georgia. At least that was the proposal. In truth, none of us had the remotest idea what direction our show would eventually take. We were literally touring Russia because we could.

Author interviews people In Moscow's Red Square

—photo by the author

Those were halcyon days for any American reporter. The U.S. economy had rebounded quickly after the October '87 crash, Reagan was a constant fountain of phenomenal Presidential quotes, national politicians made repeated stops in Colorado to campaign, to make news, to ski, and to shack up with girlfriends. Or boyfriends. Or both at the same time. Even more fascinating was the buzz on the international scene.

## The Glasnost and Perestroika Experiment

These were the days of Soviet glasnost and perestroika, words Americans were hearing for the first time. Mikhail Gorbachev had declared war on government corruption with a strategy of splaying open and exposing ingrained Communist Party secrecy to the world. *Perestroika* referred to Gorbachev's official list of reforms, aggressively opposed of course by hard-line, paranoid communist leaders. *Glasnost* was the new official "openness." Glasnost would supposedly create press freedoms and allow citizens the right of dissent.

Most of the people we met were friendly, talkative, even if slightly cautious. As they spoke to us, they'd keep an eye on our "minders," looking for some hint that glasnost might have its limits. But they generally acted as if they could speak with more candor than in previous years. Talking to foreign journalists was also a novelty for them, a little daring, but more than one citizen was anxious to try out his or her English language skills on us.

Glasnost created some interesting paradoxes. I remember interviewing one couple who operated a small commodities business. They showed me how they were able to keep track of all their purchases and shipping details on a government-issued computer. I tried to show the appropriate amount of curiosity and interest. But I blundered by asking where their printer was. Facing obvious scowls from our Soviet "minders," they responded that they weren't allowed to have one. The government had no problem with people having computers, but printers were rare.

"No printer?" I asked. What good is a computer without a printer?" They simply shrugged and said, "It's not allowed." In essence, their computer was nothing more than an adding machine, incapable of communicating with others either in print or online. The Internet hadn't blossomed yet. Twitter and Facebook were still fifteen years in the future.

## What Is "Izvestia?"

Fax machines were all the rage in the West in the 1980s, and I further aggravated my faux pas by asking if they owned one of those. The reply was, "Oh, no. No one can have fax machines here." One of our "minders" interrupted and said there were plenty of fax machines in the Soviet Union in the offices of government officials. We were quickly maneuvered away from the couple being interviewed.

Later, I tried to ask our "minder" more questions about the private ownership of printers and fax machines. It may have been an unguarded moment for her but she replied, "Giving citizens fax machines would be like giving them a Gutenberg." And another odd comment: "If citizens ever get fax machines and printers, Communism will fail. If people get printers, it would be "izvestia."

I asked the obvious, "What's izvestia?"

She replied, "The spark that started a fire, a conflagration, a revolution."

It was a puzzling conversation, but my mind began playing with a silly equation: printers and fax machines help people communicate. If the common people communicate, then their power grows. If the people have more power, that would threaten the influence of those who tried to suppress printers and fax machines in the first place. Just as the 15th century Gutenberg press sparked the Renaissance, these modern machines were apparently capable of causing disruptive change to the Soviet Union.

Later that year, I remember reading a tiny AP news blurb on a weekend TV newscast that President Gorbachev had decided to make 5,000 fax machines available to rank and file Russian citizens. In the news business those blurbs are called "fillers." They're insignificant stories and not really meant to be broadcast. But "filler stories" keep our own lines of communication open. Still, that brief filler story grabbed my attention because of the earlier "izvestia" comment by our Russian lady.

It was strange, but a mere few months after the announcement of the program to hand out thousands of fax machines and printers, the whole Eastern bloc began falling apart. Coincidence, of course. But I remember thinking at the time, "Ah, our guide must have been right after all." Could the lowly fax machine actually become the 20th Century's Gutenberg?

During our film-making trip we became aware of an intense amount of scrutiny of our personal actions and conversations. Across a thousand miles of the Soviet Union and over ten days, we began recognizing the faces of a dozen or so people who repeatedly crossed our paths in Moscow, Tbilisi, Sochi and back again in Moscow. The coincidences became almost entertaining. At one point we began amusing ourselves by enthusiastically greeting and shaking hands with some of the clumsier of our shadowers.

I was the oldest member of our TV crew, possibly even one of the last of the so-called "duck and cover" generation. As a military brat growing up on Army posts in San Antonio, El Paso, Ft. Meade and Seattle, I was among the many youngsters taught to "duck and cover" if a nuclear missile was ever headed our way. When the school alarm rang, like good Pavlovians, we would all dive under our little wooden desks, crouch down and place both arms over our heads. For some reason never explained, this would protect us from the effects of an atom bomb blast. At that age we didn't ask many questions. We just knew that desktops and arms over our heads would shield us from nuclear annihilation.

Again, these were all odd thoughts to dredge up as our wobbling train slowly screeched over the countryside of this supposedly mortal political enemy. Duck and cover. I wondered if Soviet kids were ever taught that drill.

Our train rumbled on, banging against every joint and spike in the tracks. My back and legs ached. We passed wooden slat fences of peasant farmers. We occasionally persuaded some of them to wave back at us. But once deep into farm country, there wasn't much to see. Soviet greenery didn't look quite as bright as Colorado greenery. Perhaps it was only our imagination. Or just the time of year. But the landscape just seemed to take on some brown tones, beige tones, as we scraped along.

## My Shock Journey into Collectivism!

One memory that comes back quite clearly is passing a vast open space, many hundreds of square miles of apparently empty land. There was little vegetation, just mile after mile of barren, colorless fields that were a little unsettling. At one point, I saw a large building begin to take shape in the distance. It seemed a bit freakish and out of place, a huge field with a single building that seemed to grow taller and taller as we approached. Three stories. Four, five. I don't recall the exact number of stories, but it was odd seeing it standing alone in a big field without a single nearby structure or road.

"What's that?" I asked one of our guides.

"It's a collective," I was told.

My next question raised eyebrows on both ladies' faces. "What's a collective?" For the first time, our two guides must have understood that they were truly hosting a group of bumpkins, unsophisticated unschooled and collectively dumber than a box of rocks.

Collectives, they explained, were groups of farmers, agrarians. The land they worked was all consolidated into one collective farm. Members of this commune tilled together, they sowed together, they harvested together. Each member of the community was exactly equal, no man or woman stood out from another, they lived together in the middle of a flat field in this bleak apartment building. Their possessions, the land, the tools belonged to all equally. The government told them when to plow, what to sow, when to harvest, where to ship, and at some point the people received back some small portion of the harvest. Collectives were essentially communes, the collective life epitomized communism.

It sounded grim, without color or personality. Beige people, beige apartments, beige wives, beige children, beige dinnertime conversations. But what made the conversation especially stand out in my memory was its parallel to the personal adventure I had begun two years earlier on the opposite side of the world.

## My Shock! I Had Become a Collectivist!

In 1986, I had purchased a small piece of property, built my first home, and officially joined my first Homeowners Association. It was in Morrison, Colorado, a mountain suburb southwest of Denver. The agreement to cooperate with neighbors was built right into the real estate papers I had signed. The agreement acknowledged that I was in essence surrendering any claim to my Bill of Rights, giving up my privacy, allowing unannounced property inspections, permitting the assessment of occasional and arbitrary fees and fines. It seemed like an intelligent decision at the time, to be part of a like-minded group of homeowners all anxious to preserve property values.

Such a noble effort, to make sure the wrong kind of people didn't move into our community and corrupt the common good.

"The Willowbrook Homeowners Association," we were repeatedly told, "is a special community. Our covenants ensure that the community atmosphere we've all come to treasure is preserved."

Within the first few months of joining my Colorado commune, I had even received two official letters of admonishment telling me that I had violated certain communal "laws." One letter informed me I had planted the wrong kind of tree in my yard. I had indeed planted a small aspen after noticing that many of my neighbors had aspens. The letter informed me that my choice of vegetation was not at issue. It was, rather, the fact that I hadn't asked advance permission from the architectural control committee. The letter informed me that I would be sued if the aspen tree wasn't removed.

The second letter arrived shortly after I installed several gravel and timber steps near my kitchen door at the back of the house. On this rural property, the steps were flush with the ground and invisible to neighbors. No one could have seen them without a galling act of trespass in an extremely private part of my home. Twice in the first year in my brand new neighborhood, I'd been threatened with lawsuits by my community, by people I hadn't even met.

Now two years later, I was traveling through a foreign country staring at my first communist collective in a barren field where people were politically, economically and racially bound together by contract in a permanent state of "beigeness." On this wobbling, shaking, screeching train I realized with a good bit of embarrassment that on my own side of the world, somehow I had allowed myself to buy into the same philosophy that I had been trained since youth to fear.

Without realizing it, I had willingly signed real estate papers contracting away all my personal rights in favor of the rights of the collective. I had become a communist. It was inadvertent. It was absolutely unintended. But this patriotic, flag-waving, unabashedly Reagan-loving Yankee Army brat had actually become a communist. And across my own country, tens of millions of my white-flight fellow Americans were doing the same. My dim-witted entry into covenant-controlled neighborhood communes would have made Joey Stalin proud. The powers we meekly granted to HOA boards and their attorneys would have intrigued Karl Marx and Mao Tse Tung. We just never saw it coming.

To be sure, there are plenty of people who appreciate life in such communities. They truly believe that property values are better protected in neighborhoods where conformity is high. They don't mind a regimented life where political opinions remain unexpressed and flag flying is reserved for only officially approved holidays. Those people seem to flourish when just certain types of prestige vehicles are allowed inside their golden ghettos.

The paradox, though, is that controlled-life communities across America are actually seething with discontent. Instead of an occasional pair of neighbors-at-war privately and quietly working out their differences, those sparring homeowners are frog-walked into the open before neighborhood meetings where dirty laundry is wrung out and stretched before the crowds. The lawsuits fly and the lawyers feed.

After nearly fifty years of the modern HOA experiment, certain kinds of personality traits are beginning to characterize those who swear by life in gated neighborhood compounds. These traits aren't universal, of course. But they are becoming well enough known that critics are taking note.

Even though life is short and the years temporal, there will always be carrion eaters who feast on the misfortunes of others. They spend their lives obsessed with the hatred of non-conformists. Any personal grief for one is cause for celebration by the other. Any illness or family tragedy for an adversary is, for them, pure joy. They survive by destroying the weak. Their religion demands the annihilation of those who refuse to worship at the altar of neighborhood conformity.

Sadly, this bacterial growth has found a home in the stagnant political and social atmosphere of many beige neighborhoods across America. For many, the "Homeowners Association Experience" hasn't turned out quite the way they expected. Property values have actually lagged as wiser families become increasingly gun-shy of the hatred and hostility that characterize some of the more adversarial compounds. The commune style of life isn't as attractive as it seemed in the beginning.

Occasionally, though, a few people fight back against what they see as political and social decay. Some of those fights even end up benefiting society as a whole. Rebels often sacrifice greatly for their troubles, but once in a while they actually make an impact on racial injustice, creeping socialism and a variety of other political and social inventions designed to eat away at fundamental human rights. It's only through rebellion that some societies have expurgated themselves of fascism, communism, Stalinism, and Nazism. As Thomas Jefferson once observed, "When injustice becomes law, resistance becomes duty."

There will always be schemes and devices created by some to stifle dissent and exert power over others. On the other hand, there will always be a few liberty-minded people who love life and respect the rights of others to live their lives free of government chains. Life wouldn't be worth living without a few here and there who rage against the beige.

If you've kept with me this long, Dear Reader, I thank you. I know the train ride has been unexpectedly bumpy.

I hope it was not too long.

Author Ward Lucas and investigative producer John Fosholt race to catch a train across the old Soviet Union.

# How You Can Help

I hope that after reading my book, you are concerned: concerned enough to get angry and get involved. There are many ways you can help our movement grow:

- When you're finished with this book, share it with a neighbor.
- Mail it to a lawmaker and encourage others to do the same.
- If you share with me the email addresses of six people who might be interested in buying *Neighbors At War*, I will email **at my own expense** a copy of my book to an influential lawmaker somewhere in America. My obvious intent is to bury in books every legislator in the country who has the ability to help change the mindset. Sooner or later, our lawmakers might actually read a copy and start paying attention to their constituents!
- If you hear that tired old statement, "If you don't like your HOA, just move!" Understand that statement only comes from the mouths of the uninformed. Give them a copy of *Neighbors At War*. Every mind we change is another soldier in our army.
- As long as you keep sending me email addresses, I will keep sending out free books and free newsletters with stories on the crazy and often illegal actions of rogue HOAs. I do promise, however, not to spam anyone on my list. I will allow any email recipient to opt out at any time.
- If you have a big enough gathering of interested people in your city, invite me to do a presentation and book-signing.
- Ask book stores in your area to carry *Neighbors At War*.

Finally, keep me posted with stories about outrageous actions by rogue HOAs. If you send me links to news sources, I will continue to share them with others across the country. Contact me at: Ward Lucas, PO Box 27633, Denver, CO 80227.

# Appendix

This Appendix, Dear Reader, contains just four items, each in need of a brief explanation. First, is a proposed Homeowner's Bill of Rights. It is neither inclusive nor thorough and is only a starting point for discussion. Should the courts decree that *de facto* governments must abide by the limits of the U.S. Constitution, then an HOA Bill of Rights would probably be unnecessary.

Second, is a weak attempt at a bibliography. Instead I will just call it a recommended reading list.

Third, is a chapter the author felt was superfluous, but the Book Shepherd insisted should be included somewhere. It isn't a real chapter; it didn't fit anywhere, and finally ended up here as a way of simultaneously stroking two egos, hers and mine.

Fourth, and last, is a marvelous piece I came across while doing my research. At first, I thought it was a great attempt at humor. It was a purported scientific paper describing a mental condition suffered by many victims of HOA abuse. The more I read, the more outrageously hilarious it got. After an hour of laughing, I finally looked up the author of the paper to congratulate him on his humor and ask how he came up with such a marvelous and well-written bit of fiction. He stunned me with his answer, "Oh, it's not fiction. It's a very real mental condition."

Hearing that, I asked if I could republish it. He agreed, so it is included with his kind permission in Appendix D.

# Appendix A
# Proposed Homeowners' Bill of Rights

I. Every Homeowner has the right to be free from the threat of foreclosure by any Homeowner Association, Property Owner Association, or Common Interest Development.

II. Any lien filed against a Homeowner may accrue with interest until matter is resolved or until the sale of said home. However, no lien filed for covenant violation may result in foreclosure of any home.

III. Every Homeowner shall be afforded due process.

IV. Every Homeowner shall be afforded equal and just treatment.

V. Every Homeowner shall have access to zero-cost dispute resolution by an independent body unaffiliated with any Homeowner Association.

VI. Selective enforcement or prosecution of covenant violations are prohibited.

VII. The right of free speech, freedom of religion, and freedom of assembly shall be in accordance with U.S. law.

VIII. The right to own and bear arms shall not be infringed and will be in accordance with state and federal laws.

IX. No Homeowner's privacy of his or her home or automobile shall be violated without a warrant sought from and carried out by proper law enforcement authorities.

X.   No lawsuit shall be filed without a vote by a super-majority of the Homeowners.

XI.  No racial discrimination shall be tolerated.

XII. No discrimination against the handicapped or infirm shall be tolerated.

XIII. No rule shall be enacted forbidding children from playing outside.

XIV. In all collections, reimbursed money must first go to pay down the original debt or fine.

XV.  If a professional debt collector is used, his fees can amount to no more than 20% of the original debt.

XVI. A Homeowner who wins a case against a Homeowner Association in arbitration or court must be awarded 100% of his legal fees. A winning homeowner may not be assessed proportionate legal fees run up by the Homeowner Association.

XVII. ALL official business of the HOA must be transparent and in the open. Every HOA meeting must be videotaped from two different angles showing board members and audience members. These videos MUST BE POSTED on the web within 14 days of the time of the meeting. Absolutely no editing of these videos may be done.

XVIII. Since every member of the HOA can be profoundly impacted by decisions made in secret, there shall be no executive sessions in which any member of the Association may be excluded. Only non-association members may be excluded from executive sessions.

XIX. Any member's attorney may attend any regular session or any executive session of a Homeowners meeting in the place of or accompanied by said Homeowner.

XX. No election ballots may be counted by any member or members of a Homeowner Association or its management company. Only a bonded independent body may count the ballots with up to five Homeowners acting as observers.

XXI. The counting of all ballots shall be videotaped from two angles, with both unedited videos posted to the Internet within 14 days.

# Appendix B
# Recommended Reading

*Mountain Mafia: Organized Crime in the Rockies*, Betty L. Alt & Sandra K. Wells, 2008

*Surviving Homeowner Associations*, Arlene Bandy, 2005

*Little Pink House: A True Story of Defiance and Courage*, Jeff Benedict, 2009

*Homeowner Associations: A Nightmare or a Dream Come True*, Joni Greenwalt, 1998

*Life Without Lawyers*, Philip K. Howard, 2009

*The Death of Common Sense*, Philip K. Howard, 2011

*The Collapse of the Common Good: How America's Lawsuit Culture Undermines Our Freedom*, Philip K. Howard, 2001

*Smaldone: The Untold Story of an American Crime Family*, Dick Kreck, 2009

*Liberty and Tyranny*, Mark Levin, 2009

*The Dirty Dozen: How Twelve Supreme Court Cases Radically Expanded Government and Eroded Freedom*, Robert A. Levy & William Mellor, 2008

*Lucas vs. the Green Machine*, David Lucas, 1995

*Privatopia: Homeowner Associations and the Rise of Residential Private Government*, Evan McKenzie, 1994

*Beyond Privatopia: Re-thinking Residential Private Government*, Evan McKenzie, 2011

*The Best-Laid Plans: How Government Planning Harms Your Quality of Life, Your Pocketbook, and Your Future*, Randal O'Toole, 2007

*Common Sense, Rights of Man, 200ᵗʰ Anniversary Edition*, Thomas Paine, 1969

*African Americans of Denver*, Ronald J. Stephens, La Wanna M. Larson, 2008

*The Federalist Papers*, Hamilton, Madison, Jay

*Villa Appalling: Destroying the Myth of Affordable Community Living*, Donie Vanitzian & Stephen Glassman, 2002

*Declaration of Independence*, and the *Constitution of the United States of America*

# Appendix C
# "Get Out of Jail, Free" Cards

The game of Monopoly is one of the most popular board games in the world. Its roots were squarely in the Great Depression of the 1930s. Eighty-two years later, in the middle of another international fiscal crisis, this author's Book Shepherd, Judith Briles insisted; no, demanded that a two page chapter be added almost ad hoc at the end of my book. Perhaps she had too many margarita fumes wafting over her as she disembarked from her two-week annual vacation cruise. Or perhaps it was her recent nightmarish confrontation with her own Homeowners Association, but she was absolutely immune to any of my anemic last-ditch efforts at dissuasion. She wanted me to produce some sort of "Get Out of Jail Free" card that lists some rules of conduct homeowners could carry in their wallets or pocketbooks at all times to help head off any kind of unexpected meanness from a Homeowners Association.

Certainly, there's enough historical intrigue around the game of Monopoly to merit some sort of study of its perfidious past. Most folks don't know that the British Secret Service once tried to use Monopoly to smuggle certain strategic supplies to prisoners being held by Nazi Germany. Fake charity groups distributed Monopoly sets that contained hidden maps, real money, compasses and any number of items that could ostensibly be used by imprisoned Limeys to conduct "escape and evasion" attempts.

In my business, the Publisher is always right; the Ink-Stained-Wretch is always wrong, so here is a secret document to be hidden inside all future "Get Out of Jail Free" cards distributed to homeowners inside those gated private prisons otherwise known as "planned communities."

The bottom line is that you, as a homeowner, are always wrong. If your dues are several weeks late, you get no grace period. Pay those dues including interest, late fees, collection and attorneys fees, everything. Don't argue. Even if your $300 bill has turned into $10,000, pay it. Like most people, you'll pay $40,000 to win the $10,000 case, but no matter, just get it behind you.

If you have an urge to plant flowers in the springtime, DON'T! Submit an architectural plan containing the exact number of posy seeds, the exact shape of the flower beds, and your future watering plans. Re-submit the same plan each year.

While we're on the subject, if a single board member has been voted in or out, immediately re-submit any and all requests made to previous boards.

Do not put up Christmas lights of any kind.

Don't even think of putting a wading pool in your back yard.

Don't dream of planting a tree in honor of a dead father.

Never, ever think of air conditioners as necessary appliances.

Never have sex in a car within any boundary of an HOA/CID or POA. This restriction includes not just sex, but kissing, hand-holding, snuggling, or any other physical male/female contact that could be misinterpreted by an HOA board member with field glasses.

If you have one too many cats, absolutely do not protest when a board member puts a bowl of anti-freeze on your porch. This is one fight you probably think you can win. You can't.

An outdoor hot tub? Fuggeddaboudit.

If you are assessed a fine because a guest parked his car on the street overnight, do not attempt to argue that it wasn't your guest. If the manager or board member determines the car was close enough that it "could" have been your guest, you're guilty. In fact, in this society, assume you are always guilty. And you become even guiltier each time to try to prove your innocence.

Never say, "I know my rights!"

Never say, "I'm gonna call my lawyer!"

Never say, "I'll see you in court!"

Forget the words, "This isn't fair," and "Everybody else is doing it."

Never ask, "Can't I work out a payment plan?"

As you fold this paper up and clip it to the "Get Out of Jail Free" card in your wallet, please understand that there have been rebels over the years who have won some widely-scattered fights over one or more of these rules with Homeowners Associations. Invariably, those victories have come at enormous and unexpected costs. The one thousand dollar fight you expect to wage in court has a nasty way of turning into several hundred thousand dollars. And rebels die young. They really do.

When you moved into your HOA, you thought you were making a move into Utopia, that gleaming City on a Hill, the Republic envisioned by Socrates, Plato and Aristotle. But the only thing that makes Utopia work is a blandness, a sameness, an agreement of understanding that no member of society will ever make waves. Communism described itself as Utopia. The Third Reich was Utopia. Utopia works because every man has surrendered his loyalty and his soul to a single Central Authority.

Keep this document close to your heart. I promise, and Judith, my Book Shepherd promises, it'll keep you out of trouble.

This three-page chapter is really superfluous, because enough warnings have been scattered throughout *Neighbors at War*. But Book Shepherd Briles is a difficult taskmaster and one does not easily ignore her advice. So here, with apologies to Parker Brothers, is your "Get Out of Jail Free" text with its application for a new era. Keep it in your wallet.

# Appendix D
# HOA Syndome:
# You May Be Entitled to Damages

### A Two-Tailed Psychiatric Disorder

## by Gary Solomon

*History bequeaths a demonstrative message: Some who gain a position of power will inevitably strike down the rights of others, animals and humans, in the name of greed, grandiosity, and evil sadistic gratification. Brief time passes, societies crumble under the weight of rise to power, and without learning prior lessons, the disgorging cycle once again begins.*
—Professor Gary Solomon, A.A., B.A., M.P.H.,
M.S.W., Ph.D., Ph.D.(abd)

Gone are the days when pets, walking their obedient owners, strolled through neighborhoods and waved to fellow neighbors, taking a few moments to stop and chat and get caught up on the latest family news. Void are the invitations from a neighbor to gather and celebrate their child's high school graduation, retirement party, acquisition of a shiny, stealth new car, or a forthcoming marriage. Why? Homeowner's Associations (HOAs) and property management predators have infected entire communities–cities–inducing a pandemic of emotional and physical problems onto bewildered property owners. Welcome my fellow Americans to a new, diagnosable, psychiatric disorder: *HOA Syndrome*.

My name is Gary Solomon, A.A., B.A., MPH., M.S.W., Ph.D., Ph.D.(abd). I am a published author, tenured psychology professor at the College of Southern Nevada, psychotherapist, researcher, expert witness, and human rights advocate. The focus of my ongoing research is the new and ground-breaking field of panspermia, quantum mechanics and nano-technological Darwinism in evolutionary neuropsychology. Right now, however, I am focused on defining a new psychiatric disorder: *HOA Syndrome*.

In 2008 I needed a break. I was overwhelmed with trying to create a scientific answer to identify the origin, cause and ultimately, the cure for psychiatric illness. During my research hiatus I moved to a splendiferous, magnificent Spanish style home nestled on the hillside of a rocky mountain in Henderson, Nevada, a suburb of Las Vegas, Nevada. The name of the community: Calico Ridge.

Overlooking the entire city of Las Vegas I believed I had found nirvana. Nothing shy of a slice of heaven, the seasoned community radiates peace, love and harmony (It would take some digging to learn that my perception was a verisimilitude of a Stephen King-esque novel). I was finally home. In the evening the soft, clear, crepuscular, ambient light radiating from the city of Las Vegas illuminates the labyrinth of streets that lead to the ultimate glitz and flashiness of the Professor Gary Solomon HOA Syndrome Las Vegas Strip. The view's calming effect on my academic research mind and tested nerves is virtually impossible to describe. Summarily, I was at peace with the world. I had arrived. I was finally home... I thought.

Shortly after I moved to Calico Ridge, I began noticing something odd. People appeared to be abnormally anxious, nervous, hypervigilant, worried, irritated, paradoxically unsettled in a well-seasoned community. Being a psychotherapist and researcher, I would not let my own narcissism get in the way of comprehending what was taking place around me, concluding that I was the cause of the problem. "Certainly it was not me. I just got here," I thought to myself. "Yes, I am at the entrance to the subdivision." "Yes, the place could use a little tidying up," I self-acknowledged. "But, I'm a nice, friendly, approachable man. What's going on here?"

It would take me slightly over a year to understand what was happening around me. Ultimately, my awareness would become a spinoff of my current research. I learned that residents, primarily principal homeowners, were living in a war zone, not identifiable by bombs, guns and burning buildings. Rather, a war zone masterfully orchestrated by a few fellow homeowners attempting to control their companion neighbors while making a few bucks on the side and gaining sadistic pleasure from watching their neighbors live in pain.

## What is HOA Syndrome?

*HOA Syndrome* falls into the psychiatric category of Anxiety Disorders. The Syndrome is characterized by a cluster of signs and symptoms–psychophysiological indicators–such as:

- feeling angry much of the time
- tired and fatigued
- anxious
- on-edge or irritable
- unhappy in one's own home
- depressed and sad
- worried
- nihilistic (hopeless)
- over or under eating
- sleeping disorders and/or nightmares
- fear of going to one's own mailbox
- paranoia
- loss of identity
- fear of allowing one's children to play in their own neighborhood
- fear of having one's car ticketed or towed
- stressed out
- body aches and pains
- intestinal problems and/or acid reflux
- memory loss
- obsessive rumination
- temporal mandibular joint problems (TMJ) and/or grinding of teeth
- hypervigilance
- restlessness
- fear of losing one's pet
- sexual dysfunction

## What Causes HOA Syndrome?

At the root of *HOA Syndrome* is intentional, longitudinal and methodical harassment. Shortly after the individual takes possession of their property, the HOA strategically begins to focus on the homeowner's minor, if not non-existent infractions. The purpose for these attacks is to create an income stream. This income stream makes its way into the pockets of the management companies, collection agencies and attorneys, none of whom live within the community that they are harassing. Like ravenous parasites, these organizations feed off of fear-based harassment. The homeowner, now locked into a mortgage, feels powerless over the HOA's relentless hounding for more and more money. In short: the evolution of schoolyard bullying and lunch money stealing has turned into adult comportment known in the legal world as, racketeering, financial exploitation and extortion, and neighborhood money pilfering.

## How Does HOA Syndrome Differ from Post Traumatic Stress Disorder (PTSD)

Post Traumatic Stress Disorder (PTSD) has its root, in most cases, in a single event (an auto accident, a physical fight, a war, a rape, a death, etc.). Sometimes individuals may acquire PTSD over time from such cases as ongoing molestation, living in a violent environment (as seen in our troops returning from Iraq and Afghanistan), extended chaos from fractured, fragmented relationships, or unsafe living conditions. Though both *HOA Syndrome* and PTSD have similar signs and symptoms, *HOA Syndrome* has longitudinal, intermittent, intentional and economical harassment as its primary ongoing characteristics.

## HOA Syndrome: A Two-Tailed Disease

In the case of most psychiatric disorders, the diagnosis is one sided. The diagnostician focuses on an individual's psychopathology to discover if the signs and symptoms meet the criteria (standard) of a specific diagnoses or diagnosis: the Mood Disordered individual; the Sleep Disordered individual, the Schizophrenic Disordered individual, etc. There are a few psychiatric disorders such as Shared Psychotic Disorder and Stockholm Syndrome where individuals and groups are diagnosed (i.e., they, more than one individual, are suffering from presenting psychopathology as a member of the group). I have identified *HOA Syndrome* as having two classifications and refer to it as a two-tailed disorder. The Syndrome may have opposite psychopathological outcomes on each individual from the same source, as a result of the same disease. Simply stated: the origin of the disease can produce diametrically opposing signs and symptoms given the same psychiatric diagnosis, *HOA Syndrome*. The disease manifests itself with different characteristics in the perpetrator—known as the Capo—and the victim. Remarkably, both are homeowners in the same homeowner's association with the association being at the root of *HOA Syndrome*.

## The Predator

The predators, those in a position of authority (Capos) volunteer to be on the board of the HOA. The Capos gain power and an inflated sense of self. Remarkably, they hire outside agencies at enormous cost to themselves and their neighbors to oversee their infliction of fines and penalties. Once in power, they impose more and more punishment on their fellow neighbors. The threat of fines, liens and foreclosure on their neighbors cause these people to lose all touch with reality. Almost as if in a psychotic state or delusion, their actions continue, all the while knowing what they are doing to others. As time passes they become sadists who stand in judgment and control of their fellow human beings. They turn their backs on those in need, especially the elderly who are not in a position to defend or protect themselves, easy prey for the HOA. While this is taking place, private for-profit companies reap the bounty of their free HOA laborers, becoming tantamount to Nazi concentration camp Capos.

This tail of the *HOA Syndrome* seems to spur, for some, the sadistic side of their personality. At the time of the writing of this article I have yet to uncover the origin of their sadism: were they bullied on the school yard? Molested by their neighbors? Traumatized by a death in the family? Is there a neurological anomaly that fosters their cruel behaviors? Or, are they taking the path of their predecessors and going along with the cruelty just to be a part of a group of predators?

## The Victim

Having signed "The Document (the CC&Rs)" these people, the home-owners, unwittingly subordinate their constitutional rights to "The Community." The legal statutes (laws that feed the CC&Rs) is literally the hammer that repeatedly raises and pounds the entire neighborhood into submission: both psychological and physiological ruination. Like something out of Rod Serling's *Twilight Zone,* individuals roam the neighborhoods pointing their fingers at each other searching for the transgressions of their neighbors. "They have a weed!" "Look at the color of their door!" "There, see? They have a brown spot in the lawn!" And on and on and on. As time passes, the individuals residing in communities become stricken, individually and collectively, with *HOA Syndrome.* After a while they begin to go after those neighbors whom they do not like. Each home functions like an island in the middle of a separate country, no longer functioning as a community. Desperate and despondent, the homeowners have acquired so much pathology that the collective hopelessness is visually apparent.

## Terms and Concepts

From a psychiatric point of view, how is *HOA Syndrome* manifested? Because this is a newly identified psychiatric disorder it is important for the reader to capture an understanding of some terminology used in this research article.

Barbed Wire Sickness—
>An overwhelming sense of futility and meaninglessness of existence; involuntary confinement; sadness; depression.

Conspiracy—
>An agreement between two or more parties to deprive a third party–or group–of their legal rights with the goal of deceiving them in order to obtain an illegal objective.

Capo (Kap-O)—
>A position of authority occupied by a fellow homeowner–an HOA board member. Capos–concentration prisoners themselves– who for extra food, better housing and less manual work would carry out and commit horrible atrocities against their fellow inmates at the instructions of their immediate Nazi SS supervisors, also known in German as a Blockführer. They more often than not treated other inmates–homeowners–with extreme harshness, brutality and cruelty.

CC&Rs—
>Covenants, Conditions and Restrictions (CC&Rs) applied to homeowners who live in areas that have a homeowner's association (HOA). CC&Rs set forth particular rules that must be followed by the purchaser. Failure to comply with the CC&Rs can result in warnings, fines and legal action against the homeowner. An agreement to purchase in an HOA community is assessed as an agreement to follow all CC&Rs and give up individual rights.

Ghetto—
>Urban area, in this case, defined as an HOA community because of social, legal or economic pressure exerted on members of the community by the HOA board and management companies.

Elder Abuse—
>A single or repeated act, or lack of appropriate action, occurring within any relationship where there is an expectation of trust which causes harm or distress to an older person(s). Also referred to as: "elder mistreatment,"

"senior abuse," "abuse in later life," "abuse of older adults," "abuse of older women," and "abuse of older men."

Hospice Neighborhood—
Neighborhoods where elderly people reside. As is often the case, one partner dies before the other, leaving them to fend for themselves as they move closer to the end of their life.

Intermittent Episodic Remission—
Moments in time (minutes, hours, days, weeks, etc.), where an individual is free of existing psychophysiological pathology; unpredictable periods where pathology is not evident or recognizable.

Lien—
A legal claim or a "hold" on some type of property, whether personal or real, making it collateral against monies or services owed to another person or entity. Any property that carries a lien can be forced into sale by the lender or HOA, in order to collect what is owed or claimed to be owed. If the borrower decides to sell the property, the lien holder must be paid before the title will be cleared for transfer to a buyer.

Malice Aforethought—
An intention to commit an act (or omission) and a "high degree of probability" that such an act or omission will result in the death or serious injury of another person in the form of money, or physical or emotional harm.

Psychophysiological—
A mind-body illness; any stress-related physical illness.

Racketeering—
An organized conspiracy to commit extortion; an enterprise that has committed any two of 35 crimes–27 federal crimes and 8 state crimes–within a 10 year period.

Tort—
Intentional wrongs against a person: assault, battery, false imprisonment, infliction of emotional distress.

Unjust Enrichment—
Enrichment at the expense of another where an obligation to make restitution arises, regardless of liability or wrongdoing.

## Science and HOA Syndrome

To understand *HOA Syndrome* it is imperative for the observer—the reader—to comprehend at least four previously studied phenomena in human behavior research. The first is the research by Solomon Asch (1955), *Opinions and Social Pressure*. The second, the ground breaking work of Stanley Milgram (1963), *Behavioral Study of Obedience*. The third, the research project created and executed by Phil Zimbardo (1971), *The Stanford Prison Experiment* and *The Lucifer Effect: Understanding How Good People Turn Evil*. Finally, a phenomenological study and investigation by Latane and Darley (1968), *The Bystander Effect*.

## Solomon Asch (1955), *Opinions and Social Pressure*

Asch investigated the concept of conformity in social norms. The experiment he created was simple. In one box he drew three straight perpendicular parallel lines of different lengths. In another box he drew just one straight perpendicular line. The individual line was the same length as one of the three lines in the other box. Eight subjects stood in a room comparing the lengths of the lines. They were instructed to find two lines that were the same length, one line from each of the two boxes. Seven subjects were "insiders" (coincidently, the same name given to people on the HOA board) or "confederates" working in conjunction with the researcher (confederates, HOA board members working in collusion with the management and collection companies). The eighth person, the volunteer participant, did not know what was to take place.

When the subjects were asked to select the lines that were the same length, the seven confederates knowingly identified two lines that were not the same length though they collectively reported that they were correct; that they were the same length. The eighth person, in most cases, sided with the incorrect answer even though that person knew it was the wrong answer. Result: group pressure plays an enormous role in making choices. That is, conformity is a powerful tool in making a choice even if the behavior alters and conflicts with one's attitudes, ethics, morals, and belief systems. Social pressure influences the making of decision.

## Stanley Milgram (1963), *Behavioral Study of Obedience*

After the 2nd World War–the post-Nazi siege and occupation of most of known Europe–many, including myself, asked a fundamental question re garding human behavior: how could one person or a group of people do what they did to another person or group of people? The question specifically re-lates to the inhumane treatment of prisoners of war in Nazi concentration camps such as Auschwitz I, II, and III, Buchenwald, Sobibor, to name a few.

In 1946, during the Trial at Nuremberg, the tortuous, horrific treatment that was inflicted upon millions came to public awareness. Enter a young re-searcher, Stanley Milgram, who decided to implement an experiment asking the question: Are people capable of being inhumane to each other simply be-cause they are instructed to do so by those in positions of authority? Like Asch, the experiment was quite simple. Individuals–the subjects under investiga-tion–were told to induce an electric shock on another fellow subject. The re-cipient of the tortuous shock was a confederate working with the researchers; they were not actually hooked to the electric shocking device. However, when electricity was induced to the other subject–the confederate–a warning light il-luminated in the concealed holding cell. The confederate screamed in agony as if they were actually receiving the shock. The subjects under investigation were told under no uncertain circumstances–in very Nazi-esque terms–to be obedient to the researchers, to do their jobs and to follow instructions no mat-ter the cries and screams that emanated from the holding cell. Much to the surprise of the researcher's, most shocked their fellow subjects to extraordi-nary degrees. Some of the participants induced a lethal electrical shock. The sounds from the holding cell went mute. Result: people will do what they are instructed to do in the name of being obedient.

## Phil Zimbardo (1971), *The Stanford Prison Experiment and The Lucifer Effect: Understanding How Good People Turn Evil*

Housed in the basement at California's Stanford University, Philip Zim-bardo constructed a mock prison. He invited university students–volunteers–to participate in a research experiment. Half of the volunteers became prisoners while the other half became guards. The experiment was intended to last six weeks. In less than six days the experiment was terminated. The student guards, dressed in guard uniforms, brutalized their fellow students–the prisoners–to such a degree that they were causing damage. The student prisoners wanted out. Result: losing their individuality and identity (wearing guard uniforms) and, put in a position of authority and gaining more and more power and control over others, individuals will methodically brutalize subordinates by inducing grave harm and detriment to their fellow human beings. Zimbardo later coined this as, the "Lucifer Effect," noting that good people will turn evil when given the opportunity to have power and control over other humans.

## Latane and Darley (1968), *The Bystander Effect*

Not all experiments are by design. Rather, some are observed after the fact. The 1964 death of Catherine Genovese evolved to be such a post-phenomenological study. The events are as follows:

> Walking home, Kitty as her friends knew her, was attacked and stabbed to death by a man in Kew Gardens, Queens, New York. What was stunning about this murder and follow-up report–there would later be conflicting information–is that there were over 30 witnesses to the attack. No one stepped in to assist Kitty or stop the attack. Some yelled, "What's going on down there?" while others stood or sat and watched the event unfold. The attack took longer than 32 minutes before someone finally called the police. Many, the report indicated, observed the event from the first moments of the attack. The phenomenon identified by the researchers is known today as "diffusion of responsibility" or "the bystander effect." Result: when individuals or groups know that others are observing the same event, individuals become apathetic. They leave it to others to step in and assist the victim (their neighbor).

So let's compile this data from the four research outcomes and move to reasonable conclusions:

1. Regardless of one's attitudes, ethics, morals, and belief systems, people are capable of and will inflict unconscionable cruelty on others, especially when those people are put in a position of power and authority (i.e., HOA board members).
2. Individual and group unconscionability can be fostered when people lose their identity and individuality. Concealing one's identity allows for greater infliction of damage and harm to others (i.e., hiding behind the guise of being an HOA board member).

3. When instructed to obey, individuals will inflict harm, without interruption, in spite of the knowledge and awareness that the events may lead to something as horrific as the death of their fellow human beings (i.e., HOA board members being instructed to harass neighbors with violations and fines by the property management companies).

4. People will stand by and observe harm to individuals or groups especially if they believe that others are also aware of those events (i.e., homeowners who say better my neighbor get the fine than me).

Summarily, HOA board members, management company employees, collection company employees, and their attorneys will knowingly inflict harassment and cruelty on homeowners. Surprised? You think this is not true of you? I postulate that most of you are in denial. Take the following examples.

How many times have you driven by a car stranded on the side of the road without stopping to assist? Have you ever heard the sound of a car, house or building alarm, but done nothing? Walked by some trash on the ground without picking up the trash?: "It's not my job"; "It's not my responsibility". Observed an altercation, but just kept walking? Known that someone was in need, but elected not to assist? Followed through with an action simply because you were told to do that action? One only has to look at some recent history to see what humans do–or don't do–to other humans.

We have seen recent images of the Abu Ghraib Prison torture and abuse. After Hurricane Katrina, we saw armed guards standing at the Greater New Orleans Bridge threatening violence and death to those who would dare seek higher ground. What about watering one's driveway knowing that people are dying of thirst and that the world wide water shortage is getting worse by the hour? Daily events prove that we turn our backs on each other. Furthermore, we intentionally, with malice aforethought, inflict pain and suffering on animals and our fellow human beings. Now, allow me to apply this to the *HOA Syndrome* pandemic.

## The Origin of the HOA

In science we have a group of specialists known as epidemiologists. The job of the epidemiologist is to discover the origin, cause and course of a disease, the etiology of the disease. Once that information is acquired the scientific community works to resolve the problem. Ideally, the end result is to insure that the disease does not have an opportunity to re-engage and propagate: the Asian bird flu, whooping cough, polio, Legionnaire's disease, and many others that have proliferated in the world. But not all diseases are eradicated. AIDS and *HOA Syndrome* are examples of two such diseases.

Like labor unions, HOAs began with good intentions. As early as 1773 labor unions began to emerge with the intent of protecting workers and creating sensible working conditions. By-products of those efforts were child labor laws, safety inspections and reasonable working hours. Over time the unions became massive money making machines. Dues from laborers needed to be paid to the union headquarters and their leaders. More and more dues and fees were levied. A few people at the top became rich and powerful at the expense of those at the bottom of the money chain. HOAs have a similar history.

Communities have existed for thousands of years. History tells us that over time people began living in groups (cities, townships, neighborhoods, blocks, etc.). Concurrent with communal living came fees and charges to occupants of those communities: parts of the kingdom, residence in the countryside, those who hovered around the center of town or the immediate surrounding territory. Most readers have an image in their mind of a scene from a movie where court appointed officers, riding astride armor protected horses storm into town demanding that the locals pay bounty to their king or in the case of my research, the HOA.

Over time, homeowners decided to ban together to make sure that their neighborhoods were safe, clean and inviting; to secure their homes and their investments for the future. To maintain this standing, homeowners agreed to pay dues and fees. In short order fines were put in place to insure that homeowners would stand accountable for the perceived mismanagement of their own property. Management companies sprung up while attorney-owned and operated collection companies masterfully orchestrated more and more strict rules to govern the neighborhoods. More rules, more fines. The enterprises wanted more money—profits to feed the machine. But how could they keep the communities at bay? The natives were getting restless. Something was needed to stay the protests from the growing number of people who were fed up with being harassed. Enter the CC&Rs.

## HOAs and CC&Rs

Some communities in the United States are designed to be managed through a document known as "Covenants, Conditions and Restrictions" (CC&Rs). This document is used to rule the community via management companies who charge the HOA members for their services (some management companies boldly refer to themselves as "The Master" of the community). The Masters use the CC&Rs as the governing sledgehammer or "Bible" to keep individuals and households in line. The actions of the Masters and the HOA Board of Directors leaves one feeling harassed, bullied and raped, emotionally and physically in pain from the fear and powerlessness of the invasion into their privacy, ironically, through the use of their own HOA dues. "What will they steal from me this time?" "I don't own my home...they do."

Once you have purchased property in a subdivision that is ruled by the CC&Rs, you are trapped. The CC&Rs are managed by the HOA, fellow home-owners who in turn are managed and directed by the for-profit Masters, people who more than likely do not live in the community. The HOA works in conjunction with a private management company that issues fines, penalties, liens, and foreclosures for a wide range of infractions: a weed, a trash can, the wrong color paint, a pot in the yard, a bicycle on the property, a vehicle on the street, a misguided act of individuality, and so on. The list is endless and arbitrary. And from here it all gets that much more diabolical.

The members of the board are volunteers who work for free. They receive no financial gain, though as payment for their efforts they may operate under more flexible guidelines than the rest of the subdivision since they enforce themselves. They become their own police. I refer to these individuals as Capos, unpaid servants, those who inflict pain and suffering on others for no other reason than ego and hubris.

Capos drive through their community looking for infractions. They issue notices that produce letters and fines. The individual homeowner is directed to stand before a jury of his peers—Capo Court—to render himself liable for a burned out light, a misplaced rock, a piece of paper lodged in his innocent landscaping. The fine is usually $100.00. If the fine is not paid in a timely manner, the Master quickly escalates the fine into the open arms of a collection company at a rate of four to five times the original amount of the fine. The new fines can result in a lien on the homeowner's property. The lien allows the property to be foreclosed and the owners are out on the street. The end result: attorneys and the management companies have the building blocks of an ever compounding fortune paid out by the victims who have effectively come down with *HOA Syndrome*.

## Hospice Neighbors, Elder Abuse and HOA Syndrome

Many communities are seasoned. And as baby boomers age it is not surprising that the residents of these communities are over the age of 55. For those who elect to live outside of a retirement home it is not unusual for HOA communities to be dominated by individuals in their 60s, 70s, 80s, and 90s. I refer to these housing subdivisions as "Hospice Neighborhoods," the occupants, Hospice neighbors. By definition they are elders and as a result of the deportment of the Capos and the Masters they suffer Elder Abuse.

Like most predators the Capos and the Masters know the profile of the resident in each home making those who are elderly homeowner's targets and easy prey. The Capos begin hounding the elderly with letters and fines. These homeowners usually live on a fixed income. In many cases their spouse has died leaving them to fend for themselves. They may be disoriented and unable to maintain themselves. *HOA Syndrome* exacerbates their health issues. Unable to fend for themselves they are immediate and easy fodder for the roving band of Capos who push for more and more fines to feed their hungry Masters.

## Then and Now

Once upon a time, individuals and families wanted to live in the safe harbinger of a community driven HOA. Like the Berlin Wall, the Wall of China, the dividing wall between the United States and Mexico, the very walls and gates–literally and metaphorically–meant to keep out the unwanted and uninvited, now hold homeowners hostage in infected urban ghettos struck down with barbed wire sickness and *HOA Syndrome*. Compounded by an inimical if not impossible economy HOA homeowners cannot sell their homes. Today people don't want to buy into a HOA neighborhood; people want out.

The footprints left from the past are guide posts for the future. Rome was not built in a day nor did Rome fall in a day. The reality is that it was the people of Rome who built the city and the people of Rome who destroyed the city. People tend to blame organizations as a whole for the collective problems of the world. Rather, blame falls on the shoulders of its parts, the people who make up the whole.

Throughout America violence in HOA meetings is becoming more common place. Some have been killed. Many have been threatened, while other home-owners have been hauled away in the name of being too disruptive–banned from their own HOA meetings. Meetings have shut down. Threats of arrest are rampant. Some homeowners–it is postulated–have committed suicide, a permanent solution to a malignant problem. HOA boards and management companies have hired guards–the brutish looking Gestapo–to keep homeowners in line. But, in the end, it is business as usual and the letters and fines just keep coming.

Association rules and regulations have become irrevocable legal instruments of destruction of the community. Virtually impenetrable, the CC&Rs are designed by the few to control the many. There is rarely recourse for the homeowner. Today, entire communities are collapsing under the weight of their HOA. The economy has slowed construction. The lack of construction puts a halt to new communities. No new communities means no new HOAs. Where are the profits going to emerge? The Masters and collection companies are seeking increased revenue from the pockets of existing homeowners. Fear of legal expenses and confrontation become the homeowners worst enemy.

Now urban ghettoization has cemented the fate of the neighborhood. Should a home owner complain, the Capos move in only to induce more pain and suffering. The end result: the homeowner is psychologically and physically beaten. In desperation, the homeowner decides to pay the fine in the hopes of getting on with their life: induced Intermittent Episodic Remission. The fear of the next violation letter exacerbates the homeowner's *HOA Syndrome* symptomology. Now out of remission, another episode emerges.

## The Solution

We are a population of Hurt People. As Hurt People some, not all, get great sadistic pleasure in paying the hurt forward (Hurt People hurt people). To date there has been no exposed solution to this growing social atrocity that causes *HOA Syndrome*. As roving Capos and Masters pillage the villages for more and more bounty, there has been no respite from the marauders. Know as a health care professional, I offer a solution.

In truth, all of these cases are tantamount to personal injury cases: auto accidents, boating accidents, slip and fall accidents, etc. Summarily, I believe that all HOA homeowners have been and continue to be damaged, victimized by the Capos and the Masters. As a result, I believe that you are entitled to be compensated for those damages. This is no longer a matter of contract law. This is a tort and torts offer relief. Instead of being rear-ended by another driver you have been rear-ended by the HOA and the management companies. Damages, both emotional and physical, are your remedies, awards are due to you. Furthermore, you may be entitled to damages for pain and suffering under the law.

I offer to each of you the following gift: with my permission and release of Copyright, send the following, via Certified Mail to your HOA board, individually and collectively and, to the management company, individually and collectively.

> *If you continue on your current path of pathological persecution, you do so knowing the damage you are causing; you do so with malice aforethought, personally and collectively perpetrating a significant amount of detriment to me and others. As of the date of this letter, you may claim that you did not know what you were doing or the damage it was causing. Now, should you continue, as a post recipient to my letter, I am informing you, collectively and individually, that you do so with knowledge; you do not have the right to claim 'I didn't know.' Your actions are both criminal and civil.*

**Now, you have put them on notice. Now you may take action. Here are your Seven Action Steps:**

1. Acknowledge the problems, both emotional and physical.
2. Keep a record of the problems: document, document, document. Create a log and diary of what you are experiencing in your life as a result of the abuse by the HOA and the management company. Organize and maintain any and all correspondence from the HOA and the management company.
3. Locate a personal injury attorney in your area. The case should be taken on contingency: the attorney is not paid until the case is settled. Remember: this argument is new to the legal community. Don't give up if the first or second attorney that you contact does not take your case. In time you will start hearing advertisements on your local televison inviting you into law offices all over the country.
4. If you are older than 55, seek an attorney that specializes in elder abuse. They will use specific laws that are in place to enforce your rights and help you seek damages. If you are the child or a guardian of an elder person, take action on their behalf.

5. Seek and secure medical attention. Go on record with your doctor regarding your problems and issues. If indicated, request a specialist (your general practitioner should be able to refer you to the indicated specialist). Never minimize or rationalize your emotional or physical problems. Remember: your attorney will assist you in organizing your case file. The types of medical attention you may seek are:

   A. General Medical
   B. Medical Specialist
   C. Pharmaceutical Intervention
   D. Complete Laboratory work-up and analysis
   E. MRI
   F. SPECT
   G. PET Scan
   H. Psychotherapy
   I. Counseling
   J. Chiropractic
   K. Massage

   (Your health care insurance should cover all or most of the cost of your health care including medication. Talk to your attorney about the concept of continuity of treatment.)

6. Seek financial compensation through a jury of your peers. They are on your side. Most jurors, if not all, have had some experiences with HOAs. They know what you are going through and how you feel. They want to have the opportunity to bring the Capos and the Masters to justice.

7. Create HOA support groups. Talk about what is happening to you. Share your stories with others. And, go public whenever possible.

## Professor Solomon's Prediction

"Why didn't someone warn us?" they screech, in a reaction to the news of the day: "...two boys went on a shooting spree as a result of..." "...a man killed his wife and children after..." " ...five are being held hostage because..." "...someone crashed a plane into a building when..." The story is always slightly different, yet the cries are the same: "Why didn't someone warn us?" "Surely someone must have known what was going to happen."

So, now comes Professor Gary Solomon with the following prediction: if we don't put a stop to the actions of the few miscreants, homeowners are going to start "Going HOA." Wait... my prediction has come true: it has already happened.

# End Notes

## Chapter 1. Full Disclosure

[1] *WillowbrookHomeownerAssociation.org*
[2] Stevenson, Robert Lewis, *Alice in Wonderland.*
[3] Ibid.
[4] Ibid.

## Chapter 3. Never Marry "Brown"

[1] *http://www.military.com/Content/MoreContent?file=ML_pinckney_bkp*
[2] Spear, Allan H., *Black Chicago: The Making of a Negro Ghetto, 1890-1920,* University of Chicago Press (1967), p. 11; also cited by Brooks, Richard R. W., *Conventions & Covenants,* Northwestern University School of Law, Research Paper No. 02-8. Brooks' Paper can be downloaded at *http://ssrn.com/abstract_ id=353723.*
[3] *http://caselaw.lp.findlaw.com/cgi-bin/getcase.pl?court=US&vol=334&invol= 1&friend=nytimes*
[4] Rosen, Mark D., *Was Shelley v. Kraemer Incorrectly Decided? Some New Answers,* Cal. L. Rev. (2007), p. 4. *http://www.kentlaw.edu/perritt/blog/2007/06/ was-shelley-v-kraemer-incorrectly.html*
[5] Brooks, Richard R. W., *Conventions & Conventions,* Northwestern University School of Law, Research paper No. 02-8, Sept. 2002, p. 39. *http://ssrn.com/abstract_id=353723*
[6] *http://www.seattleweekly.com/1998-05-06//control-thy-neighbor/*
[7] *http://seattletimes.nwsource.com/html/localnews/2002297312_covenants03m.html*
[8] *http://seattletimes.nwsource.com/html/opinion/2002913362_jamesgregory06.html*
[9] *The Miami Herald,* Donna Gehrke-White, January 9, 2005, *http://www.ccfj. net/HOAFLforeclspiral.html.*
[10] *http://mycropht.wordpress.com/2008/08/04/my-homeowners-association- must-be-stopped/*

[11]"*Best Laid Plans: How Government Planning Harms Your Quality of Life, Your Pocketbook, and Your Future*," Randal O'Toole, Cato Institute (2007), pp. 349-350.

[12]*Sun Sentinel*, Milton D. Carrero Galarza, October 11, 2003.

[13]Ibid.

[14]*http://www.dallasnews.com/sharedcontent/dws/dn/localnews/columnists/jragl and/stories/010308dnmetragland.22f8b4b.html*

[15]*http://www.dallasnews.com/video/?z=y&nvid=203437*

[16]*http://www.dallasnews.com/sharedcontent/dws/dn/localnews/columnists/jragl and/stories/010308dnmetragland.22f8b4b.html*

[17]*http://www.chore.us/050909%20FL%20-%20Majestic%20Oaks%20board %20members%20resign.html*

[18]*http://stoptexashoaforeclosures.com/about.html*

[19]*http://stoptexashoaforeclosures.com*

[20]*http://www.azcentral.com/arizonarepublic/local/articles/2009/06/17/ 20090617condosuit0617.html*

[21]Ibid.

## Chapter 4. The Ultimate Law of the Universe

[1]*Midlake on Big Boulder Lake Condo Assoc v. Cappuccio* (1996).

[2]*The Committee for a Better Twin Rivers v. The Twin Rivers Homeowners Assn.* New Jersey Supreme Court (2007).

[3]*http:/en.wikipedia.org/wiki/FishmanAffidavit*

[4]*http://www.ccfj.net/condofraudarrest.html*

[5]*http://www.ahrc.com/new/index.php/src/business/sub/dir/action/display/id/960*

[6]*http://www.ripoffreport.com/reports/0/234/RipOff0234155.htm*

[7]*http://www.quoted.com/quotes/1467*

[8]*http://www.quotes.ubr.com/quotes-alphabetical/a-quotes/almost-quotes.aspx*

[9]*http://www2.hn.psu.edu/faculty/jmanis/carlyle/heroes.pdf*

[10]Fielding, Henry, Covent Garden Journal (1752).

[11]*http://www.chron.com/disp/story.mpl/metropolitan/casey/2292246.html*

[12]*http://www.hobb.org/content/view/3002/1/*

[13]Ibid.

## Chapter 5. Closer Screwtiny

[1]*http://www.ccfj.net/HOAFLlawnreplace3.html*

[2]*http://pqasb.pqarchiver.com/sptimes/access/329796441.html?FMT=FT&dids= 329796441:329796441&FMTS=ABS:FT&type=current&date=Apr+27%2C+2003&*

*author=MICHAEL+VAN+SICKLER&pub=St.+Petersburg+Times&desc=Give+the
m+an+inch%2C+they'll+take+a+yard%3F*

[3]*http://somerset-hoa.org/modules.php?name=Content&pa=showpage&pid=3*

[4]*http://www.redmountainranch.net/red-october2007.minutes.pdf*

[5]*http://www.househuntnews.com/marketing/consumer/sept05/04.htm*

[6]*http://www.ccfj.net/HOArunawaypower.html*

[7]*http://boortz.com/nuze/200807/07302008.html*

[8]*http://boortz.com/nuze/200807/07302008.html*

[9]*http://seattletimes.nwsource.com/html/localnews/2008231428_reservist
06m.html*

[10]Ibid.

## Chapter 6. "We're Lawyers and You're Stupid"

[1]*http://en.wikipedia.org/wiki/Fifth_Amendment_to_the_United_States_
Constitution*

[2]*http://works.bepress.com/cgi/viewcontent.cgi?article=1006&context=
william_want*

[3]*http://caselaw.lp.findlaw.com/scripts/getcase.pl?navby=CASE&court=
US&vol=505&page=1003*

[4]Lucas, David, *Lucas vs. The Green Machine*. Alexander Books (1995),
p. 251.

[5]*http://www.dartmouth.edu/~wfischel/lucasupdate.html*

[6]Kelo, Suzette. *http://www.conservative.org/pressroom/2006/speech_kelo.asp*

[7]*http://caselaw.lp.findlaw.com/scripts/getcase.pl?court=US&vol=000&invol=
04-108*

[8]Ibid, Justice Thomas dissenting.

[9]*http://caselaw.lp.findlaw.com/data/constitution/amendment05/*

[10]*http://www.youtube.com/watch?v=AyE2XCeqOOE*

[11]*http://www.castlecoalition.org/pdf/publications/survival-guide.pdf*

[12]*Public Power, Public Gain*, April 2003, foreword by Douglas W. Kmiec,
Dean & St. Thomas More Professor of law, Catholic University of America
and senior policy fellow, Pepperdine University.

[13]*http://law.findlaw.com/state-laws/adverse-possession/*

[14]*http://www.freerepublic.com/focus/f-news/1929194/posts*

[15]*http://www.worldnetdaily.com/news/article.asp?ARTICLE_ID=58670*

[16]*http://media.dailycamera.com/bdc/content/static/Salim_Statement_to_
media.pdf*

[17]*http://www.dailycamera.com/news/2008/jun/11/another-land-grab-dispute-in-boulder-fence/*

[18]*http://land-grabber.org/*

## Chapter 7. Bang, Bang, Crash!

[1]*http://www.youtube.com/watch?v=gBut1bdg3TE&feature=related*

[2]*http://www.theledger.com/article/20090628/REPORTER/906245081/1035/ BUSINESS?Title=Legacy-Park-HOA-Files-for-Bankruptcy*

[3]Franklin, Benjamin, *Poor Richard's Almanac,* June 1758.

[4]*HOAwebtv.com*, interview with Marlene Bagarazzi by radio host Austin Hill.

[5]*http://www.eastvalleytribune.com/story/111788,* interview with Clint Goodman by Austin Hill, 2008.

[6]Anderson, J. Craig, *The Arizona Republic,* December 21, 2008.

[7]*http://www.forbes.com/2009/05/11/homes-equity-debt-lifestyle-real-estate-mortgage-underwater.html*

[8]*http://www.responsiblelending.org/mortgage-lending/research-analysis/ soaring-spillover-accelerating-foreclosures-to-cost-neighbors-436-billion-in-2009-alone-73-4-million-homes-lose-5-900-on-average.html*

[9]*http://www.woodstockinst.org/for-the-press/press-releases/new-research-illustrates-devastating-impact-of-foreclosures-on-property-values/*

## Chapter 8. "Nigger Roy" of Russell Gulch

[1]Personal interview with author.

[2]Meadow, James B., "Answering the Howls of Injustice," *Rocky Mountain News,* pp. 5A, February 25, 2001.

[3]*http://www.clickorlando.com/news/18283365/detail.html*

[4]*http://www.autoblog.com/2008/08/18/dallas-hoa-prohibits-parking-f-150-in-driveway-lincoln-mark-lt/*

[5]*http://www.newjerseynewsroom.com/state/howell-homeowners-association-allegedly-discriminating-against-epileptic-with-service-dog*

[6]*http://onlinelunchpail.blogspot.com/2008/06/homeowners-association-harasses-woman.html*

[7]*http://www.kens5.com/news/HOA-and-Stone-Oak-fight-over-gate—96944134.html*

[8]*http://www.theledger.com/apps/pbcs.dll/article?AID=/20101129/NEWS/ 101129505&template=printart*

⁹*http://www.ocala.com/apps/pbcs.dll/article?AID=/20100807/ARTICLES/8071010&template=printart*

¹⁰*http://findarticles.com/p/articles/mi_m0EIN/is_/ai_97825110*

¹¹*http://www.wftv.com/realestate/17949506/detail.html*

¹²*http://www2.tbo.com/content/2009/may/21/na-board-site-discriminated/news-breaking/*

¹³*http://calhomelaw.org/PDF/DFEH%20v%20Lakeshore%202008%20DFEIMG_0001.pdf*

¹⁴*http://www.southernhighlands.com/spa.php*

¹⁵*http://hoawatch.blogspot.com/2005/03/not-so-perfect-life-steven-ferguson.html*

¹⁶Ibid.

¹⁷Ibid.

¹⁸*http://www.realestatejournal.com/buysell/markettrends/20060918-mcmullen.html*

## Chapter 9. Cowboys, Crooks and Bad, Bad Men

¹*http://www.gayoutrage.com*

²*http://www.airportjournals.com/Display.cfm?varID=0305005*

³*http://www.garden-of-eden-lucas-kansas.com/*

⁴*http://www.local6.com/news/4786539/detail.html*

⁵*http://www.snopes.com/photos/risque/ventcover.asp*

⁶*http://cbs2.com/watercooler/Water.Cooler.Stan.2.271539.html*

⁷*http://www.sfgate.com/cgi-bin/object/article?f=/n/a/2008/08/04/national/a125438D48.DTL&o=0*

⁸*http://www.carhenge.com/*

⁹*http://en.wikipedia.org/wiki/2006_Duke_University_lacrosse_case*

¹⁰*http://www.npr.org/templates/story/story.php?storyId=102589818*

¹¹*http://www.google.com/hostednews/ap/article/ALeqM5h88VgykKcn87UozOYaETJS6yufvgD979BIU00*

¹²*http://www.ll.georgetown.edu/federal/judicial/fed/opinions/99opinions/99-1593.pdf p. 9, 2000*

¹³*Life Without Lawyers*, Howard, Philip K, W.W. Norton & Company Inc. (2009) p. 17.

## Chapter 10. Expose Yourself

¹*http://metrocolumnistsblog.dallasnews.com/archives/2009/06/lake-highlands-hoa-retreats-on.html*

[2]*http://www.myfoxdfw.com/dpp/news/Investigation_Homeowners_Hell*
[3]*http://media2.myfoxdfw.com/PDF/HOA/Hoff%20Lawsuit.pdf*
[4]*http://www.hoanewsnetwork.com/media/la_quinta_homeowners_gate_fight_returns_to_court.php*
[5]*http://pages.citebite.com/x1f6o2s3v8mki*
[6]Dutton, W. H. "The Fifth Estate Emerging through the Network of Networks," *Prometheus Press*, Vol. 27, No. 1, March: (2009), pp. 1-15.
[7]*http://www.ahrc.com/old/HOAorg/Media/ma_073097.html*
[8]*http://www.ahrc.se/new/index.php/src/news/sub/pressrel/action/ShowMedia/id/3856*
[9]*http://yourhub.denverpost.com/castlerock/staying-devil/xRU3JafiGYb MhVGDV0ItsO-ugc*
[10]*http://stoptexashoaforeclosures.com/about.html*
[11]*http://www.ccfj.net/*
[12]*http:www.ccfj.net/onewayticket.htm*
[13]*http://pvtgov.org/pvtgov/*
[14]*http://www.thehoaprimer.org/index.htm*
[15]*http://www.latimes.com/classified/realestate/news/la-fi-associations31-2009may31,0,3165389.story*
[16]*http://www.journalism.wisc.edu/~drechsel/j559/readings/sullivan.html*
[17]Ibid.
[18]*http://abclocal.go.com/wtvd/story?section=news/local&id=6752306*
[19]*http://www.apria.com/common/aw_cmp_printNews/1,2762,918028,00.htm*

## Chapter 11. "Cai! Cai! Cai!"

[1]Rathbun, Frank, *CAI VP Communications and Public Relations*, *http://www.caionline.org/info/research/Pages/default.aspx*
[2]*http://www.davis-stirling.com/MainIndex/DavisStirlingAct/tabid/427/Default.aspx*
[3]Villa Milano Homeowners Assn. v. Il Davorge, 84 Cal. App. 4th (2000), p. 819.
[4]Grafton Partners v. Superior Court, 36 Cal. App. 4th (2005), p. 944.
[5]*http://www.calhomelaw.org/doc.asp?id=1300, info@calhomelaw.org*
[6]*http://loan.yahoo.com/m/primer13.html*
[7]Franzese, Paula A., "Privatization and Its Discontents: Common Interest Communities and the Rise of Government for 'the Nice,'" *The Urban Lawyer*, August 2, 2005.

[8]Ibid.

[9]Grumet, Bridget Hall, "Condo Board Says Three's a Crowd," *St. Petersburg Times*, Nov. 18, 2003, p. 1B.

[10]Hannaman, Edward R., *State and Municipal Perspectives—Homeowners Associations*, presented to Rutgers University Center for Government Services, March 19, 2002, p. 231-241.

[11]*Zogby International*, California Legislative Action Committee, 2005.

[12]*Los Angeles Times blogs*: "Pardon Our Dust: Home Improvement Tales with Kathy Price-Robinson," September, 2007.

[13]*http://tinyurl.com/5dz8b9*

[14]*http://www.foxnews.com/story/0,2933,522718,00.html*

[15]*http://www.lasvegassun.com/news/2009/may/16/clinic-plan-meets-prejudice/*

[16]*http://www.wbir.com/news/local/story.aspx?storyid=88385&catid=2*

[17]Frances L. Huff, journalist, "Rebuild," *ORG Finance News*, June 18, 2009, *http://www.rebuild.org/news-article/pay-your-mortage-and-hoa-dues-to-avoid-foreclosure/*.

## Chapter 12. Two Plus Two Equals Four

[1]Rand, Ayn, *Atlas Shrugged*, pp. 404.

[2]CCHAL, "Paying Assessments Electronically? Better Watch Out!" *Online Newsletter*, March 19, 2001.

[3]Abbady, Tal, *Sun Sentinel*, July 22, 2004.

[4]*richard.verrier@latimes.com*, *http://articles.latimes.com/print/20011/mar/05/entertainment/la-ca-los-felizx-estates-20110306*, March 25, 2011.

## Chapter 13. *"De Factos, Ma'am, Just De Factos"*

[1]Madison, James, *Federalist Paper Number 44* (1788).

[2]U.S. Constitution, Article I, Section 9.

[3]U.S. Constitution, Article 1, Section 1.

[4]*http://blog.ng.com/njv_paula_franzese/2007/08/the_costs_of_privatizing_commu.html*

[5]Monica Hatcher, *Miami Herald*, My 29, 2009. *http://www.miamiherald.com/business/story/1070838.html*

[6]*http://www.tcpalm.com/news/2009/may/29/thumbs-down-lawmakers-side-with-delinquents/*

7Catherine Williams Stuart, letter to editor of *TCPalm*, May 23, 2009, *http://www.tcpalm.com/news/2009/may/23/letter-let-crist-know-state-must-address-condo-hoa/?printer=1/*.

8*http://www.forbes.com/2009/05/11/homes-equity-debt-lifestyle-real-estate-mortgage-underwater.html*

9*http://www.responsiblelending.org/mortgage-lending/research-analysis/soaring-spillover-accelerating-foreclosures-to-cost-neighbors-436-billion-in-2009-alone-73-4-million-homes-lose-5-900-on-average.html*

10*http://www.woodstockinst.org/for-the-press/press-releases/new-research-illustrates-devastating-impact-of-foreclosures-on-property-values/*

11*http:www.hoadata.org*

12*http://www.youtube.com/watch?v=5ceIH6UJhnc*

## Chapter 14. Of Guns and Greaseballs

1*http://wwww.ahrc/se/new/index.php/src/sub/news/action/Showrticle/id/1056/print/yes*

2*http://www.ahrc.se/new/contents/media/uploads/249nelms_shooting.pdf*

3*http://www.justnews.com/news/15997287/detail.html*

4Tomsic, Matt, *http://starnewsonline*, September 4, 2010.

5*http://kucinich.us/index.php?option=com_content&task=view&id=2647&Itemid=76*

6*http://www.cnn.com/2008/US/10/03/eviction.suicide.attempt/index.html*

7*http://www.ohio.com/news/addie-polk-akron-face-of-predatory-lending-dies-in-nursing-home-1.146784*

8Regan, Ron, 5 On Your Side Investigation, November 8, 2010. *http://www.newsnet5.com/dpp/news/local_news/investigations/ohio-condo-homeowner-associations-easy-targets-for-theft-embezzlement*

9*http://www.youtube.com/watch?v=5ceIH6UJhnc*

## Chapter 15. The Power to Abuse

1*http://www.youtube.com/watch?v=BcvSNgOHZwk*

2*http://www.ted.com/talks/philip_zimbardo_on_the_psychology_of_evil.html*

3Madison, James, *Letter to Thomas Jefferson*, October 17, 1788.

## Chapter 16. Too Many Snouts, Too Many Stallions

1*http://www.aarp.org/home-garden/housing/info-2006/inb128_homeowner.html*

[2]*http://members.cox.net/concernedhomeowners/PrattBoR.htm*

[3]*http://pvtgov.org/pvtgov/*

[4]*http://www.ccfj.net/HOAbillintro.htm#BILL%20OF%20RIGHTS%20FOR %20HOMEOWNERS*

[5]*http://en.wikipedia.org/wiki/Pogo_(comic_strip)*

[6]Margaret Thatcher, interview with Llew Gardner, *Thames Interview, This Week, Feb 5, 1976 http://www.snopes.com/politics/quotes/thatcher.asp.*

# Index

# About the Author

Ward Lucas has spent 40 years in investigative journalism and has won more than 70 journalism and civic awards for his reporting and writing. From organized crime to wiretapping, to professional arson, Lucas has seen it all. In his new book, *Neighbors At War!,* he presents startling information about how the modern Homeowners Association Movement is impacting Americans.

Ward has a Bachelor of Arts degree in Political Science. He began his broadcasting career at the age of 16 hosting radio talk shows in Seattle, Washington. In 1973 he made the move into television broadcasting, first at *KIRO-TV* in Seattle and then at *KUSA-TV* in Denver Colorado. His investigative reporting has often stirred national controversy and has earned him numerous Emmy Awards, the George Polk Award, and the Responsibility in Journalism Award by the Committee for Scientific Investigation of Claims of the Paranormal (CSICOP).

In 1993, Ward joined ranks with eight nationally known Professors and journalists in the book, *Psychic Sleuths,* (Prometheus Press) which exposed and critiqued the use of psychics by police departments across the country.

**www.NeighborsAtWar.com**

# How to Bring Ward Lucas
# to Your Organization
# and Your Town

**W**ard Lucas is willing to come to your town/organization for an after-dinner talk, book signing, or just general rabble rousing. You can reach him through:

*Ward@NeighborsAtWar.com*
*www.NeighborsAtWar.com*
Twitter: @Ward_Lucas
Facebook: NeighborsAtWar
Blog: NeighborsAtWar.com

Anyone considering buying a home in a Homeowners Association should proceed with extreme caution. If you already live in an HOA you actually could be in grave financial danger. If something in the neighborhood just doesn't "feel right", if you don't like how dues are being spent, protect yourself with a copy of *Neighbors at War!*